Masterclass: Interior Design

Guide to the World's Leading Graduate Schools

Frame Publishers

Contents

Introduction

There are many things to consider when choosing a graduate school and *Masterclass: Interior Design* aims to make this process easier. The focus of a master's degree course can differ greatly from school to school, as can the expectations of the different institutions and the lifestyles that can be enjoyed in the various cities. This book explores what future students can expect from each school and what opportunities await them.

This guide features 30 of the world's leading graduate interior design schools extensively. The articles are fact-filled and follow a similar format for ease of comparison. All the useful school specifications, such as programme description, application details and requirements, lecturers and alumni, student demographics, tuition and scholarship details, and full contact details, can be found herein.

An introduction by the dean or programme leader gives a good insight into the focus of the interior design programme at each school, as well as its specific educational approach. Photos and descriptions of student work and an interview with a successful alumnus provide additional, more personal information along with further insight into the depth of each programme.

Since location plays an important role in the school selection process, Frame gained insight from numerous interviews with current and previous students. How do students experience the city they live in? The various quotes included give an almost personal guide to each city and answers many of the questions future students might have. Each school profile contains information about the school's location regarding housing, transportation and the cultural scene from a student's perspective. A world map indicating the demographic spread of the presented schools is also included.

The featured graduate schools are selected based on a list of criteria including the quality of the student work that Frame has seen over the years. Furthermore, successful players in the interior design field were asked to state which schools they felt best prepare students for their careers. We looked at the list of notable alumni, guest lecturers and current teachers as an indicator of the school's quality. The school's general reputation and other media attention it receives were additional factors. Last but not least, the aim was to create a global overview and thus select schools that offer master's degree courses in interior design from across the world.

A summary table can be found at the end of this guide, which gives a good overview of some important specifications. As part of the selection process, when a shortlist of schools of interest has been made, we encourage all future, potential students to go along and visit as many schools as possible during their open days. Take this guide along and use the notebook section at the end of the book for any findings. Explore the website of each institution, listed on the opening page of every school profile, to learn more about visa requirements for foreign students, how to apply for possible scholarships and the exact application details. Also tuition fees and application dates may have changed since the publication of this book.

All the information offered in this guide results in a very clear impression of what the listed schools have to offer, on every thinkable front that is of relevant to potential students. We are confident this guide can help students find a master's course in the field of interior design that is right for them.

The Aalto Arabia exhibition gallery is bathed in light. Photo Chikako Harada

Aalto University

☎

Aalto University, School of Arts Design and Architecture
Arabia campus
Hämeentie 135 C
00560 Helsinki
Finland

T +358 947 001
eija.salmi@aalto.fi
aalto.fi

The School of Arts, Design and Architecture is based at the Arabia Campus, located in the iconic old Arabia factory building. Photo Chikako Harada

Course
Product and Spatial Design

School
Aalto University

Introduction

'The main focus of our programme is the relationship between spaces and objects'

Pentti Kareoja, head of programme

When was this school established?
The school was established in 1871, as a private vocational craft school. In 1965 it moved into state ownership and in 1973 it acquired university status. In 2010 the School of Art and Design Helsinki merged with the Helsinki Business School and the Helsinki University of Technology to become Aalto University, owned by the Aalto University Foundation. We started offering the master's degree course in architecture in 1995.

What is the mission of the school?
To change the world!

Why should students choose to study here?
It is a unique place, where art, design and architecture education has a long tradition, and we have a solid Scandinavian teaching method. The main focus of our programme is the relationship between spaces and objects. The objective is to add to the students' sensitivity and understanding of the built environment. Ideally the designer can operate as an interpreter between the material world and human aspirations. For us, the atmospheric qualities in spaces and products are even more important than the functional aspects.

What kind of teaching method is found important?
Our teaching is essentially personal face-to-face tutoring and small group work. Our study method is based on experimentation. We work on different scales related to human beings,

starting from the urban scale and ending at the 1:1 scale. Through different case studies we teach (individually and in groups) the practical and theoretical skills of the discipline.

What is expected from the students?
Personality, individuality, talent and hard work. We respect the student's own personal insight and individuality instead of offering them programmatic declarations. We encourage them to find their own voice.

What is the most important thing for students to learn during this course?
To find their own, individual way of designing and to create a better world. In order to understand the built environment fully there is a need to add multisensory skills and artistic capability. It's crucial to learn to read the hidden possibilities of our surroundings and transform them visibly and concretely. The means can include tactile dimensions, use of different materials, colours, lighting and acoustics.

What is the most important skill to master when one wants to become an interior designer?
To have artistic skills in construction and composition, space, forms, materials and colours.

What professional direction do your students usually take?
They go on to work in architects' offices and their own practices.

Programme

The programme educates designers with a distinct design personality. Students will learn to manage design processes and gain knowledge of regulations in construction and materials. They will acquire skills in 3D composition and develop an understanding of the spatiality of people and products. They learn to practice design in the wide environment of product development, business, and culture. In this programme, students learn to interpret their environment and culture.

They also learn to transform both through their personal vision and professional skills. During their studies, students develop an artistic perspective and insight, learn to master their creative process, and deepen their expertise in materials, design tradition, and culture. The programme trains students in personal design expression, ability to master design processes, and ability to understand the discipline's tradition and work from a basis of curiosity and experimentation. Students are also trained to develop technical, aesthetic and research skills to support the design process. They become competent in integrating technologies and in exploring, visualising, creating and demonstrating innovative concepts and experiences using the latest technology.

Students become professionals in design tradition with skills in multi-disciplinary teamwork. The programme enhances students' skills in presentation and visualisation. The students learn skills in creative problem-solving relevant to product and spatial design. The programme provides students with skills needed to continue on to doctoral studies.

Studies are organised in three competence areas that all include several modules ranging in topics and mode of working. The study modules often include a project to take the design inquiry into real world context.

Aalto students designed the school's 2013 show at the Milan Design Week.
Photo Filippo Podestà

Programme
Product and Spatial Design

Leads to
Master of Arts

Structure
The full-time course lasts 2 years in which students should achieve 120 ECTS. Students will participate joint studies of the Department of Design for 20 ECTS. For the MA Product and Spatial Design degree student chooses four courses or projects from the competence area offerings (40 ECTS). And they will produce a thesis project around a design subject (30 ECTS).

Head of programme
Pentti Kareoja

Mentors and lecturers
Jouko Järvisalo, Heikki Määttänen, Martin Relander and Marco Rodriquez.

Notable alumni
Kaj Franck, Simo Heikkilä, Teemu Järvi, Yrjö Kukkapuro, Stefan Lindfors, Samuli Naamanka, Antti Nurmesniemi, Timo Ripatti, Aamu Song, Ilmari Tapiovaara and Yrjö Wiherheimo.

School Facts

Duration of study
2 years

Full time
Yes (40 hours a week)

Part time
No

Female students
65%

Male students
35%

Local students
55%

Students from abroad
45%

Yearly enrolment
14

Tuition fee
Free (mandatory student union membership approx. EUR 100)

Funding/scholarships
No

Minimum requirements for entry
Bachelor's degree

Language
English

Application procedure
The following documents should be submitted:
application form
official transcript of study records
letter of motivation
study plan
portfolio
proof of English proficiency
copy of your passport.
An interview is part of the selection process.

Application details
aalto.fi/en/studies/admissions

Application date
Before 31 January

Graduation rate
80%

Job placement rate
85%

Memberships/affiliations
Cumulus, Erasmus, Cirrus and FIRST + bilateral programmes.

Collaborations with
None

Facilities for students
Each student has a table in the drafting studio. There are workshops in all materials (wood, metal, plastic, glass, ceramics and textiles) available to all students.

Student Work

Arkki (2014)
By Noora Liesimaa

Arkki is a design for a community garden cottage interior (model 1:25). Photo Noora Liesimaa

Torikoju (2012)
By Noora Liesimaa, Tero Kuitunen, Janni Turtiainen, Annaleena Hämäläinen, Tiina Leinonen and Antti Kangas

A furniture design project, Torikoju is a concept for a market square stall. Photos Venla Helenius

Kaisaniemi Shoreline (2012)
By Juha Koskinen, Ilkka Palinperä and Panu Kontakanen

A design concept for floating leisure housing.

Frankfurt Book Fair (2014)
By Nina Kosonen, Natalia Baczyńska Kimberley and Matti Mikkilä

Scheme for Finland's Guest of Honour Pavilion for Frankfurt Book Fair, 2014. Photo Matti Mikkilä

From Töölö Hall to Modern Space (2014)
By Juha Koskinen

Seili (2013)
By Ilkka Palinperä

A study for floating houses. Photos Ilkka Palinperä

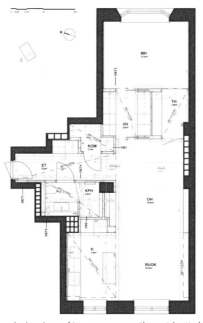

An interior architecture concept. Photos Juha Koskinen

Alumnus

Name Samuli Naamanka
Residence Espoo, Finland
Year of birth 1969
Year of graduation 2000
Current job Owner and founder of Reseptori
Clients Habitek, UPM, Mifuko, City of Helsinki, Concrete Associations of Finland, Il Cantier, Parri, and many more
Website samulinaamanka.com

Why did you choose this school?

The university has a great reputation and history – producing famous Finnish designers including Yrjö Kukkapuro, Ilmari Tapiovaara and Tapio Wirkkala. The school also offers good workshop facilities so you can easily make 1:1 models, which is not possible at many schools.

What was the most important thing you learned here?

Broad-based thinking. We were taught everything from urban planning to the design of small objects. One teaching method was based on excursions, for example to Paris or Amsterdam to study urban structure. On the other hand, the workshops and making models offered a different kind of concreteness.

What was the most interesting project you did?

An interior design project to create an experimental prototype eco house in Paris with Architect Kai Wartiainen, in the Parc de la Villette science park. Wartiainen developed the concept for an upgradeable open technological platform that allows for a gradual transition to non-polluting and energy-generating accommodation. The concept was later developed further with the world's leading technology consultants in several projects. Our course produced scale models of house interior design proposals.

What subject do you wish you paid more attention to?

Technical drawing is important even if it is boring. Students today often have 3D modelling skills but are bad at scale drawing.

Are you still in contact with the school?

Yes, from time to time I lecture there.

What was your graduation project?

Graphic Concrete – a method of creating patterned concrete surfaces. The designed pattern is created on the surface of the concrete slab as a result of the contrast effect between the fair-face and the exposed fine aggregate surface. An image is generated on the concrete surface as a thin relief. The inspiration was to create a real industrial product for large-scale surfaces, a tool with which architects could be more visually creative. Traditional methods were mainly based on handicrafts and represented small pieces of art. Eventually the techniques I developed were patented and the company Graphic Concrete was founded in 2002. The method has been used in several countries in Europe and the first projects have already been launched in the United States and Japan.

What was your favourite place to hang out?

That would have to be the metal and wood workshop!

Was the transformation from graduation to working life a smooth one?

Somehow yes, because I was working all the time during my studies. When I was young I worked in my father's engineering office, and the work is basically similar to design-office work.

Any words of advice for future students?

Work as much as possible during your studies and learn from professionals. Also, networking is the easiest way to find a job for the future.

In his graduation project, Samuli Naamanka devised a method for patterning concrete surfaces, which he called Graphic Concrete and which is now a commercial application.

'Aalto University has the best craft workshops I've seen. When you know how to work with wood, metals, ceramics or glass, you always know what to use in your next project, and whether it will bring added value.'
Anna Krivtsova

'The most valuable experience was working in the metal, plastic and wood workshops – learning by doing.'
Matti Mikkilä

'Helsinki is a great city with a good balance of calm versus exciting urban life. There are a lot of nice bars and galleries in the city, all fairly close to each other, and getting around is easy.'
Erin Turkoglu

Photo Chikako Harada

Photo Chikako Harada

'Together with fellow students, I was able to design Aalto University's exhibitions in Stockholm and in Milan. And at the moment I'm designing Finland's Guest of Honour Pavilion for Frankfurt Book Fair 2014.'
Nina Kosonen

'The most valuable classes were the furniture design ones, because we made the final prototypes on 1:1 scale, from real materials.'
Katja Rouvinen

'What I liked most about the school was the quality of the professional teachers and lecturers and the freedom to try out your own ideas.'
Laura Huhtakangas

City Life

Helsinki is unique among Northern European cities. The lifestyle in the second-most northern capital city in the world is full of contrasts and has been formed by cultural influences from both the East and West. The archipelago that surrounds Helsinki with hundreds of tiny islands creates an idyllic environment.

Over 450 years of history, several architectural layers and the impact of different periods can be clearly seen in Helsinki. Finnish design has also made the country's capital city world famous. The beauty of the surrounding nature blends seamlessly together with high-tech achievements, while old traditions mix with the latest contemporary trends. The city centr has many beautiful parks, and the nearby forests offer an ideal setting for peaceful and quiet walks.

Helsinki's rhythm is laid-back yet at the same time refreshingly vibrant in terms of both the number and quality of restaurants and nightclubs. Everything is nearby – Helsinki is a pocket-sized metropolis that is ideal as a study base.

Finland

Helsinki's Hietalahti harbour, as seen in the winter months. Photo Chikako Harada

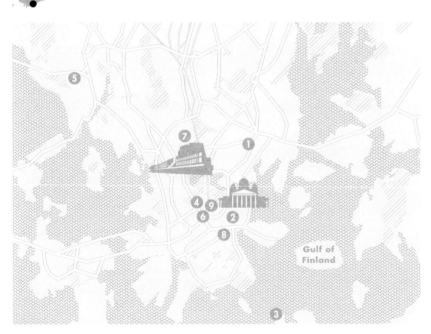

Helsinki

1 Aalto University
2 Senate Square
3 Suomenlinna Island
4 Kiasma
5 The Aalto House
6 Ateneum Art Gallery
7 Olympiastadion
8 Esplanadi Park
9 Train station

Park

Water

Railway

Main road

Course
Product and Spatial Design

School
Aalto University

City Facts

nate Square ❷
The beautiful neoclassical Senat Square is reminiscent of Saint Petersburg – not surprisingly, as it had the same architect: Carl Ludvig Engel.

omenlinna Island ❸
Begun in 1748, this massively impressive island fortress complex is now a UNESCO World Heritage monument hosting a variety of events. It's an enjoyable 15-minute ferry ride from Helsinki proper.
suomenlinna.fi

asma ❹
A dramatic Steven Holl building houses Helsinki's museum of contemporary art. Light, airy galleries make viewing the exhibitions a pleasure.
kiasma.fi

Helsinki Design
Bringing together the international design community and local practitioners, after 10 years Helsinki Design Week is Northern Europe's biggest design event.
helsinkidesignweek.com

The Aalto House ❺
A visit to the home and studio of the great Finnish architect and designer Alvar Aalto is essential for an understanding of his life and work.
alvaraalto.fi

Ateneum Art Gallery ❻
All the landmarks of Finnish art are here – recent exhibitions have included one devoted to Moomin artist Tove Jansson.
ateneum.fi

Olympiastadion ❼
Built in 1938 by Yrjö Lindegren, the functionalist stadium missed out on the Olympic Games of 1940 due to World War II (it hosted the 1952 games eventually). The tower boasts one of Helsinki's best views.
stadion.fi

EMMA
The Espoo Museum Of Modern Art (EMMA) is the largest art museum in Finland. Housed in a unique building designed by modernist architect Aarno Ruusuvuori in 1965, it presents design, modern and contemporary art in an impressive space.
emma.museum

Esplanadi Park ❽
The green heart of Helsinki, Esplanadi Park is the perfect place for a picnic lunch.

Viikki Nature Reserve
Helsinki's most important nature conservation area, Viikki is close to the centre yet offers a taste of unspoilt wilderness.
gardenia-helsinki.fi/viikkinature/index.htm

w to get around
Around 200 international flights a day arrive at Helsinki-Vantaa Airport, which is situated 19 km from the centre of Helsinki and can be reached by car in approx. 25 minutes. It is also possible to take a taxi, the Finnair airport bus or bus 615 to the Central railway station ❾. A taxi to city centre costs approx. EUR 30. There are excellent train connections from Helsinki to all major towns in Finland as well as to Lapland. There is also a daily train service to St. Petersburg and Moscow. The Central railway station is a landmark itself in Helsinki. Buses from all around Finland arrive to the Central bus station, from the largest cites almost every hour. There are daily ferry services to Helsinki from Estonia, Sweden and Germany. All the ferry companies offer also possibility to take a car with you. The main building of the School of Arts, Design and Architecture is located in Arabianranta, the oldest part of Helsinki.

Arranging housing
Average

Housing support by school
No

Cost of room in the city
Between EUR 500 and EUR 600

Cost of campus housing
n/a

City
Helsinki

Country
Finland

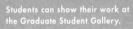
Students can show their work at
the Graduate Student Gallery.

Art Center College of Design

**Art Center College
of Design (ACCD)**
1700 Lida Street
Pasadena, CA 91103
United States

T +1 (0)626 396 2495
admissions@artcenter.edu
artcenter.edu

Art Center's South Campus – a former aviation wind tunnel – opened in 20

Course
Environmental Design

School
Art Center College of Design

'Our alumni need to be game changers, not followers'

David Mocarski, chair of the programme Environmental Design

Has your school changed much over the years?
Now 85 years old, Art Center is one of the most nimble educational institutions when it comes to curricular content and change. We pride ourselves on being industry-driven with an eye on the future. As we all know, the world is changing faster than ever, so why wouldn't the way we teach change to address the needs of our evolving culture. Our alumni need to be game changers, not followers. They need to understand what currently drives the industry and be able to start to envision where it is going in the immediate future.

What is studying Art Center all about?
Our programme concentrates on extensive conceptual rigor crossed with business practices, a focus on conceptual and theoretical rigor, technical innovation, manufacturing, fabrication and project execution. We are a crit, presentation and build-based culture. We value the depth of ideas, extensive research, conclusion-based designed strategies and a rich understanding of making and manufacturing.

What is the strength of the school?
Our balance between creative expression, concept/context and industry standards. We think it, imagine it and build it. Our plan is to build on an understanding of the impact of scenography, the staging of spaces. We shape total environmental experiences from the inside out through a holistic design filter.

What is expected of the students?
Year one tests our student's knowledge and skill base. We look for students who want to push beyond their current limits. Year two addresses a thesis project, which will be self-defining and set a career direction.

When did you start offering this master's degree course?
We are a young graduate programme; we launched our two tracks in 2012, a Spatial Experience track and Furniture & Fixtures track.

What is the most important thing for students to learn during the course?
Simply put, they will learn who they are as creatives and how to place their individual creative passions into industry driven careers. It is our goal to create opportunity seekers, designers who question where, when and why and continue to push beyond their own and industry boundaries.

What kind of jobs do your former students mostly end up doing?
Because of our multi-scale, content-driven and conceptual focus, our students pursue careers in a number of fields, including hospitality design, brand driven retail, exhibition and trade design, residential design, brand strategy, colour and materials forecasting and residential design.

Programme

Environmental Design is a human-centred discipline that focuses on the total spatial experience – from the first moment of encounter to the last moment of interaction. ACCD approaches spatial design from the inside out and we view projects as sensorial experiences. Students look beyond the single object, moment or place to see how collectively they can make an impact in projects ranging from branded retail, theme-driven dining, new hospitality, to exhibition and residential design – delivering effective, inclusive environments using responsible material choices and manufacturing practices. Our programme investigates spatial experience design through the filter of scenography, 'the staging of spaces'. Becaus of an emphasis on spatial experience, Art Center graduates are leaders in the design of furniture, lighting, and interior/exterior livin components. They pursue a global sense of industry-driven design that investigates ever aspect of where and how people live, work and play. Our students gain a global awareness through transdisciplinary studios, international study abroad and sponsored projects with industry leading companies, corporations and organisations as well as Designmatters sponsored projects on behalf humanitarian organisations globally.

Students here admit to spending a lot of time in their studios due to the intense pace of activity.

Programme
Environmental Design

Leads to
Master of Science in Environmental Design

Structure
Art Center's two-track grad programme is built on a strong conceptual and critical thinking base. It is comprised of 5 semesters of study. Students are required to take a rigorous and defined course of study during year one to insure conceptual and technical excellence; year two is focused on individually self-defining of one's next steps. Identifying one's personal voice and setting strategies for career paths inform their thesis content and project focus. The Spatic Experience Design track addresses th relationships between the body, materials, space and motion, while th Furniture & Fixtures Design track investigates the relationships betwee space, place, function and applicatic

Head of programme
David Mocarski

Mentors and lecturers
Rob Ball, James Meraz, Yo Oshima, David Mocarski and Kenneth Cameron.

Notable alumni
Chris Adamick, Chris Alvarado, Cory Grosser, Jason Pilarski and Michael Neumayr.

School Facts

Duration of study
2 or 3 years

Full time
Yes (25 hours a week)

Part time
No

Female students
49.5%

Male students
50.5%

Local students
74%

Students from abroad
26%

Yearly enrolment
20

Tuition fee
USD 19,726 (approx. EUR 14,500)
per semester

Funding/scholarships
Federal and state financial aid;
merit-based scholarships.

Minimum requirements for entry
Bachelor's degree in design or related
field. Proven knowledge of the English
language.

Language
English

Application procedure
The following documents must be
submitted in order to complete the
application:
a completed application form
official transcripts from all colleges
attended
your portfolio
an essay outlining why you have
chosen this particular course
your English TOEFL or IELTS
proficiency test (if appropriate)
a receipt of payment of the non-
refundable application fee of USD 50
(approx. EUR 37) for US citizens
and USD 70 (approx. EUR 51) for
non-US citizens.
The faculty and chair of the specialty
area make the evaluation and final
admissions decision regarding each
candidate.

Application details
artcenter.edu/accd/admissions.jsp

Application date
Before 1 February

Graduation rate
70%

Job placement rate
80%

Memberships/affiliations
AIA, IIDA, ISDA

Collaborations with
ATU International and Bernhardt
Design.

Facilities for students
Dedicated computer labs and
personal studios.

City
Pasadena

Country
United States

Student Work

Re-envisioning the Neighbourhood (2014)
By William Shin

This project proposes a holistic world of green technologies, sustainable environmental values embedded in a lifestyle re-imagined as a vertical farming village. This new neighbourhood is envisioned as a self-sustaining high-rise building in downtown Los Angeles that encompasses the traditional altruistic elements a real neighbourhood – creating a sense of place, combined with state of the art high-efficiency construction technologies.

Amy Love Seat and Lounge (2014)
By Hines Fischer

This project explores shell construction as a method to design a comfortable and visually lightweight love seat and lounge. The upholstered shell, on a simple wood base, provides a strong embrace through its confident angled arms and gently curved seat.

Course
Environmental Design

School
Art Center College of Design

xhale (2014)
y Jae Lim

hale is a mixed media installation space located between
ice buildings that encourages workers to better connect
th each other on their break and after work. By creating
rious seating combinations, configurations and positions,
n believes that Exhale has the ability to transform any
ice plaza into a temporary oasis that can ease stress and
roduce workers to a new kind of office break culture.

Pinporium (2014)
By Shuning Li

This project translates the virtual world of Pinterest into a
physical retail experience where buyers determine exactly
what is sold. This new paradigm highlights a constantly
changing, dynamic inventory that combines both digital and
physical worlds. The act of pinning becomes a powerful
marketing statement. Pinporium will be tailored to consumer's
personal shopping preferences by tracking a user's database to
determine the most popular items online.

Hotel Aurora (2014)
By Angela Chang

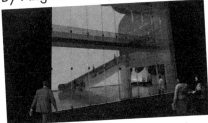

Hotel trends today suggest highly stylised but home like spaces while promoting well-being for their guests.
However, recent integration of dynamic art and new technologies have given designers the capability to create
even more interactive spaces with higher sensorial experiences. Chang's project, Aurora, looks at the next
generation of hospitality design that uses sensorial triggers to adjust the mood of its guests. Physiological and
psychological integration of colour, light and sound are 'mixed' by each guest to create their desired experience
depending on their mood.

Alumnus

Name Hines Fischer
Residence New York City, United States
Year of birth 1990
Year of graduation 2014
Current job Furniture designer at Yabu Pushelberg
Websites hinesfischer.com, yabupushelberg.com

Why did you choose this school?

I did not choose Art Center lightly – I researched every major furniture programme in the world. In the end I only applied to Art Center. I have long since concluded that no one will ever believe me when I tell them how hard I worked at Art Center – no one except fellow graduates. I worked 16 to 18 hour days, 7 days a week, for months. But it changed my life.

What was the most important thing you learned?

Human interaction is what makes furniture design eternally relevant.

What was the most interesting project you did?

I designed a desk for the home office in my second term. I began with a simple question. So much effort is put into making the most comfortable and comforting chairs, beds, sofas, but what if we made a table, desk, or counter comforting? It's a ludicrous and lovely idea, but what I created was an upholstered desk. I named the desk Hug after the way the upholstered panels wrap around you. The upholstery allowed me to invisibly run USB ports to all the pockets and drawers.

What was your graduation project about?

As technology is becoming more integrated, the purpose of office furniture and the office environment is changing. The office community typically comes together in meeting rooms. While meeting rooms may take many forms, they are almost always centred on a giant table. In the home, the family room is, in many ways, what the meeting room is to the office. It is ideally a comforting space that encourages interaction, community, and mental peace. Who if we took the productive benefits of the office environment and the comforting aspects of the home environment and brought them together?

Any words of advice for future students?

It's worth it. There is no better school to study applied design. The teachers manage to both push you to the edge of your breaking point, and care for you as an individual. Deciding to go to Art Center College of Design is the best decision I've made in my life.

Are you still in contact with the school?

I still text or email the instructors all the time for advice or just their opinion on a new design. I found lifelong mentors and friends in Art Center's instructors.

Was the transformation from graduation to working life a smooth one?

I'm not sure smooth is the right word. I got job interviews before I even started looking. Quite to my surprise I found a job at Yabu Pushelberg in Manhattan very quickly. The job gives me so much creative freedom and the chance to work with some of the greatest designers in the world. I signed up right away, and within a month of graduating I was in New York.

Hines Fischer's graduation project explored merging the conventions of the office meeting room with those of the family room in the home.

Course
Environmental Design

School
Art Center College of Design

Current Students

'I hope the course has helped me to become a well-rounded and diverse designer who can think within the entire design vernacular to achieve a successful design solution for any spatial problem.'
Therese Swanepoel

'I don't think it's accurate to call this an interior design programme. Here at Art Center we call our specialised area of study environmental design and I think this is more accurate because we're being prepared most broadly to be multidisciplinary creatives and makers.'
Marc Scimé

'The best place to hang out? The complex cultural area called Old Town Pasadena near the school in Pasadena City. It's filled with many exciting places like theatres, restaurants where you can enjoy the food of various countries, galleries, museums, cafe, sports and shopping centres.'
William Shin

'I would say to future students, be ready to work hard because this programme is going to push you to your limit and make you sprint another extra 100 miles, so that by the time you graduate, you'll literally be the best.'
Julia Ok

City Life

Pasadena, only 20 km from Los Angeles, is a vibrant city of about 150,000. Known as the City of Learning, it has the second highest concentration of art, in the United States. There is a rich architectural and design history in Pasadena, including works by Frank Lloyd Wright, the Greene brothers, Wallace Neff and other artisans of the Arroyo Craftsman Style. It also hosts an impressive collect of cultural institutions including The Norton Simon Museum and The Huntington Library, art collection and botanical gardens, as well as The Armory Center for the Arts and the Pacific Asia Museum. Pasadena has long been a centre for scientific and aerospace innovation, and is home to both California Institute of Technology and NASA's Jet Propulsion Laboratory. Many students and alumni choose to live nearby and set up their own entrepreneurial businesses and studios. The freedom to experiment with new ideas doesn't stop at the ACCD as the Los Angeles region is one of the most innovative and entrepreneurial environments in the world. The creative industries alone generate nearly one million jobs in the region.

United States

A view of downtown Pasadena with the spectacular backdrop of the San Gabri mountain range.

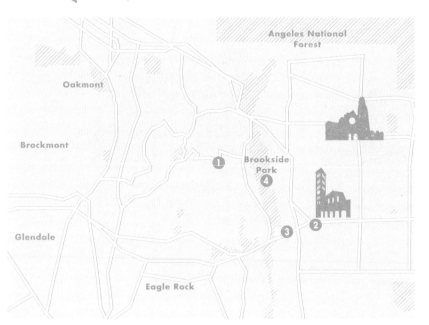

Pasadena

1 ACCD
2 Armory Center for the Arts
3 Norton Simon Museum of Art
4 Rose Bowl Stadium

Park

Main road

Course
Environmental Design

School
Art Center College of Design

City Facts

rmory Center for the Arts ②
The Armory builds on the power of art to transform lives and communities through creating, teaching and presenting the arts. Special art classes for children, teenagers, adults and families are available in the summer.
armoryarts.org

orton Simon Museum of Art ③
Over a period of 30 years, the 20th-century industrialist Norton Simon (1907–1993) amassed an astonishing collection of European art from the Renaissance to the 20th century and a stellar collection of South and Southeast Asian art spanning 2000 years.
nortonsimon.org

ose Bowl Stadium ④
The stadium is the home of the tournament of Roses Football Game, UCLA Bruin Football, Americafest 4th of July celebration, concerts, religious services, filmings and the world's largest flea market.
rosebowlstadium.com

Pacific Design Center
A 110,000 m² multi-use facility for the design community in West Hollywood. It hosts many screenings, events, lectures and exhibitions.
pacificdesigncenter.com

Petersen Automotive Museum
One of the world's largest automotive museums, with 150 vehicles on display in its main gallery.
petersen.org

Walt Disney Concert Hall
The stunning stainless steel-clad fourth hall of the Los Angeles Music Center was designed by Frank Gehry and is home to the Los Angeles Philharmonic orchestra and the Los Angeles Master Chorale.
disney.losangelesboxoffice.com

J. Paul Getty Museum
As well as the Getty Center collection of Western art from the Middle Ages, the museum also features a re-creation of the Villa of the Papyri at Herculaneum.
getty.edu/museum

Griffith Observatory
The famous Mount Hollywood observatory has an extensive array of space and science-related displays.
griffithobs.org

The Hollywood Bowl
This elegant 1920s amphitheatre in Hollywood is used primarily for music performances.
hollywoodbowl.com

Universal Studio's Hollywood
Universal Studios lets you ride the movies and go behind the scenes of a real working movie studio. There are also many dining and shopping opportunities.
universalstudioshollywood.com

Angeles National Forest
The Angeles National Forest provides 1500 km² of open space and a variety of recreation opportunities year-around.
fs.usda.gov/angeles

ow to get around
ACCD has two campuses: Hillside and South. In order to get to Pasadena by plane you can pick one of the three nearest airports: Bob Hope Airport (27 km), Los Angeles International Airport (45 km) and Los Angeles/Ontario International Airport (64 km). Three state highways enter the city of Pasadena, and four freeways run through Pasadena. Pasadena is a control city for all of them. Pasadena is the northern terminus of the Los Angeles Metro Gold Line light rail, which originates at the Atlantic station in East Los Angeles. Public transportation to ACCD is available through the Los Angeles County Metro Transit Authority bus and rail system and the Pasadena Area Rapid Transit System (ARTS) bus. The Fillmore station along the Metro Gold Line is located one block north of South Campus. The route 51/52 ARTS bus provides weekday service throughout Old Pasadena, with stops at both campuses. For private transportation, students may choose to rent or purchase a car.

Arranging housing
Average

Housing support by school
No campus housing, but students can seek assistance through the office of Student Experience.

Cost of room in the city
Between USD 900 and USD 1200 per month (approx. EUR 650 to EUR 875)

Cost of campus housing
n/a

ArtEZ Institute of the Arts

ArtEZ Institute of the Arts
Rhijnvis Feithlaan 50
8021 AM Zwolle
The Netherlands

T +31 (0)38 427 0500
interieurarchitectuur.zwolle@
artez.nl
artez.nl/architectuur

Students of the ArtEZ MA in Interior Architecture spend the majority of their time at this Zwolle location.

Course
Interior Architecture

School
ArtEZ Institute of the Arts

'The main focus of our course is based on research into the relationship between the body and space'

Ingrid van Zanten, head of programme

When was this course introduced?
The MA course Interior Architecture was launched 3 years ago. The course is part of the Faculty of Architecture and Interior, of which the BA course has existed for more than 35 years and the MA in architecture 60 years.

Has the course changed since then?
Ever since we started the MA in Interior Architecture, we have been continuously changing the details of the programme. The experiences of our students, guest lecturers and tutors keep us alert to new developments in the field of interior architecture. At the same time, the main focus of our course remains based on research into the relationship between the body and space – a theme that we translate as 'Corpo Reality'.

What is studying at this school all about?
Our mission is to work with students on issues that are related to the body, and the way in which people relate to space. We challenge students to contribute to the international discourse in the field of interior architecture through the research that they conduct here – both into theory and into practice. The main theme of the MA Interior Architecture, 'Corpo Reality', refers to the students' responsibility when designing spaces where people will live and work. This philosophy has been developed in three dimensions: the bodily, the social and the reflective.

Why should students choose this particular school?
ArtEZ provides training for more than 3000 students in the fine arts, fashion, design, architecture, interior architecture, music, dance and drama in three locations: Arnhem, Enschede and Zwolle. The quality of its courses is reflected by the level of recognition that they have achieved throughout the professional field, not only nationally but also internationally.

What kind of teaching method is applied here?
We ask students to draw up an individual study plan in which they describe their goals in the working field for the future. This, together with an analysis of their skills and competences, leads to a unique route for determining their individual goals during the programme. Every 3 weeks, students and tutor/coach meet together for a status report, in which attention is focused on these individual issues.

What do your students tend to do after completing this course?
They mostly go on to start their own businesses.

City
Arnhem/Zwolle

Country
The Netherlands

27

Programme

Our philosophy has been developed in three dimensions: the bodily, the social and the reflective. The focus of this course lies mainly on the area of research. The programme seeks to cross and connect the borders between the different scales, inside/outside, and small/large. It also applies a strong focus to social sustainability and responsibility towards society.

Bodily: in the five design studios, students work individually on various projects where much attention is devoted to lighting, construction techniques and the use of sustainable materials. Technical skills – such as being familiar with regulations, building physics and installation techniques – are covered by combining design studios with guest lectures and workshops. In this way, the course prepares them for today's increasingly complex design assignments.

Social: in the case study, students collaborate together on an actual assignment for instance involving collective clients, the interior of school buildings or the future in working spaces for intellectual disabled. Other disciplines are represented here by, for example, an environmental psychologist, a visual artist, an anthropologist or a social demographer.

Reflective: students attend theory classes that emphasise the relationship between recent developments in interior architecture and its history. They start their research on a topic of their own choice. Students formulate their research question in consultatio with tutors, resulting in a written thesis. The theory of this thesis is explored in projec which they work on in the studios during the second year.

Considering 'Space in Motion': one of the many themes that ArtEZ students are required to address.

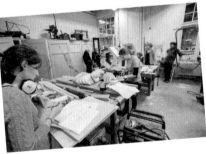

Next to theory, studen spend time in worksho which develop more practical skills.

Programme
Interior Architecture

Leads to
Master of Arts

Structure
The course is based on 4 semesters of 14 weeks plus two project periods in January (between the autumn and spring semesters).

Head of programme
Ingrid van Zanten

Mentors and lecturers
Ynte Alkema, Henk Döll, Rob Hendriks, Harry Kurzhals, Eric de Leeuw, Helen de Leur, Ton Matton, Irene Müller, Marc Proosten, Ana Rocha, Marie-Leen Ryckaert, Roeland Tweelinckx, Aat Vos, Ingrid van Zanten and Margriet de Zwart.

School Facts

Duration of study
2 years

Full time
Yes (40 hours a week)

Part time
No

Female students
75%

Male students
25%

Local students
90%

Students from abroad
10%

Yearly enrolment
20

Tuition fee
- EUR 1906 for EU citizens
- EUR 9120 for non-EU citizens

Funding/scholarships
Yes, ArtEZ annually provides a limited number of scholarships.

Minimum requirements for entry
Bachelor's degree in related field (other degrees considered in the admission procedure). Proficency in Dutch.

Language
Dutch

Application procedure
Apply by registering through Studielink and sending the following documents:
your curriculum vitae
your portfolio
a letter of motivation in which you describe yourself as an interior designer, your plans and expectations of the course
a copy of passport or identity card
a copy of qualifying degree.
After receiving your documents you will be invited for an admissions interview with the selection committee. This will take place in May or June.

Application details
artez.nl/english/Applying

Application date
Before 1 May

Graduation rate
90%

Job placement rate
n/a

Memberships/affiliations
The MA Interior Architecture course is part of the Faculty of Architecture and Interior and works together with the other courses in interior design and architecture. In addition, the course is embedded in an environment of bachelor's and master's programme in art and design.

Collaborations with
Multinationals including DSM, local government including the Province of Groningen, festivals including OEROL, organisations including Biennale Interieur Kortrijk, and 's Heeren Loo.

Facilities for students
ArtEZ MediaLab, libraries and workshops for audio-visual productions, computers, photography, graphics, wood, ceramics, plastics and metal.

Student Work

Re-Use (2013)
By Marleen Garstenveld

A new product – composite boards built from wood and piles of recycled paper. The material shows a wide variation in structure, colour and brightness, with many possibilities for furniture and interiors.

Case-Study 2.0 (2013)
By Annet Braakman, Jorien van Glabbeek, Rike van der Grift, Frederique Hanlo and Sahar Jaber

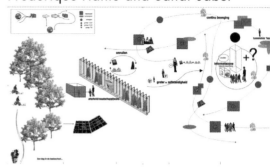

This visual essay represents the rituals of a child's school day. Arriving at school, saying goodbye to its parents, greeting the teacher, exchanging knowledge and building its school environment. The research in this case-study was performed for 'Scholenbouwmeester', an organisation that promotes the design of excellent school buildings in the northern parts of the Netherlands. The atlas for school buildings that the students developed contains many innovating designs for the primary schools of the future.

Re-Connect (2013)
By Jorien van Glabbeek

A visualisation of research into rituals. Boundaries between living spaces are not necessarily physical. For example, the transition from living room to bedroom is defined by different parts of the bed ritual.

Re-Connect (2013)
By Sahar Jaber

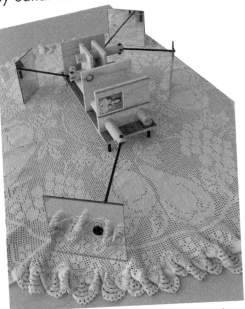

Designs for elderly people are based on research into the way their living space changes as they age. Studies showed that old people experience time differently, and make different use of space during the day. This installation offers the elderly a wider view of space within their homes.

Re-Stay (2013)
By Jip Zewald

Designing the connection between the digital and the physical world for visitors to a fast food restaurant, this concept sees the robust physical surroundings as a counterpart to the elusive virtuality of social media.

-Stay (2013)
Marleen Garstenveld

eloping new forms of 'digitecture', this is an innovative cept for fast food restaurants which uses holograms onnect people in both the virtual and the physical world.

Re-Use (2013)
By Stephanie Klein Holkenborg

A curtain of wood chips was straightened and connected by ironing them piece by piece. The curtain shows an interesting diversity in the way that it filters sunlight.

Alumnus

For a case study during his master's Middendorp developed an installation called 'Capsa Sensibus', the box of senses.

Name Robert van Middendorp
Residence Zwolle, the Netherlands
Year of birth 1987
Year of graduation 2013
Current job Several jobs while developing own studio
Website ateliervanmiddendorp.com

Why did you choose this school?
I chose ArtEZ because of the size of the academy and the personal approach.
Time for personal development is important. They don't push you in one direction, they guide you with every step you take.

What was the most interesting or fun project you did?
As far as I'm concerned, the most interesting projects are the ones where we could enjoy the most freedom. I realised I am a maker, so during the course I did a few internships with five masters in crafts. Next to the literary research and the internships, I also was making 3D pieces. With these I could apply the techniques that I picked up at my internships.

Photo Jenne Bleijenburg

What was your graduation project?
I looked at the Netherlands' problem of repurposing our empty churches. First I did hundreds of interviews in the neighbourhood of the church I chose to work with. I let the people in the area think about the role of the church, formerly as an institution but now mainly as a building. I discovered that the people missed the social gathering, so I decided to open up the church for them to meet each other 24 hours a day. By adding a garden complex around the church, I also connected the neighbouring school and nursing home. By making students, the elderly and other residents responsible for the cultivation of vegetables, I wanted to restore or build a connection between the different people. In a communal kitchen, they can cook with the vegetables they grow, serving meals the former church. By making a couple of small interventions in the church, a meeting place emerged. To complete the story, I designed a special bowl for passing around and a kind of cookie that they could share. I am still involve in this project.

Any words of advice for future students?
Realise what an important task you have as a designer. Go your own way and make beautiful things.

Are you still in contact with the school?
I have a problem with sitting still, so during my studies you could always find me in the wood and metal shop. I am still a regular as workshop has everything I need. I recently started as a teacher too. I'm afraid that they won't get rid of me any time soon!

Course
Interior Architecture

School
ArtEZ Institute of the Arts

'The most important part about this course is to find out who you are as a designer and what makes you unique.'
Jip Zewald

'The course is great for finding a deeper layer of design, with a lot of research.'
Annet Braakman

'ArtEZ is a large institution, but because of the different locations, the academies are small and homely. This atmosphere really appeals to me. The programme has this too – everyone knows each other, and you can ask anyone for help.'
Jorien van Glabbeek

'If you don't like to do research before you start to design, if you are more a doer than a thinker, and if you give up easily – consider another course!'
Rike van de Grift

'I don't think there is just one "most valuable" workshop, for me what was great was the combination of all the workshops together.'
Marleen Garstenveld

City Life

The MA Interior Architecture course is taught at two locations: Arnhem and Zwolle. Students spend most of their time in Zwolle, a lively provincial capital with almost 120,000 residents which offers plenty of possibilities in terms of art and culture. Zwolle's quaint old town is filled with bars, cafe terraces and other leisure spots, such as the Spiegel Odeon theatres, the film house, cinemas and Het Vliegend Paard student cafe. Having a music college in the city naturally means that there are lots of concerts and related activities.

There's also plenty of art to be found at, for instance, Museum De Fundatie, the Stedelijk Museum Zwolle and the city's many small galleries. The R10 cultural workplace supports young artists, theatre people, designers and musicians for a period of 4 years as they launch their own creative enterprises.

In nearby Arnhem, students can take advantage of a rich cultural climate, especially in fashion and design. The city hosts the Arnhem Mode Biënnale and has a number of good fashion and design labels and shops. The city offers plenty of nightlife, theatre, music and eating options. Alternatively you can simply relax in the rolling green expanses of the lush Sonsbeekpark.

Paleis a/d Blijmarkt is one of Zwolle's lively cultural institutions.

The Netherlands

Zwolle

1 ArtEZ Institute of the Art
2 Museum De Fundatie
3 Stedelijk Museum Zwolle
4 Cultuurwerkplaats R10
5 Stadsfestival Zwolle
6 Bevrijdingsfestival
7 The Glass Angel
8 De Sassenpoort

Park

Water

Railway

Main road

Course
Interior Architecture

School
ArtEZ Institute of the Arts

City Facts

Museum De Fundatie ②
Works by Piet Mondrian, Marc Chagall and Franz Marc feature in the collection of the Museum de Fundatie, which also stages temporary exhibitions in two stunning venues: the Paleis a/d Blijmarkt and Kasteel Het Nijenhuis.
museumdefundatie.nl

Stedelijk Museum Zwolle ③
An attractive museum in two parts: a 16th-century historic home devoted to local history, and a modern addition housing temporary exhibitions.
stedelijkmuseumzwolle.nl

Cultuurwerkplaats R10 ④
R10 provides young creative entrepreneurs a place to start with affordable facilities, advice, workshops, projects and a network. Entrepreneurs can enjoy 4 years of support here before heading out into the big bad world.
R10.nl

Stadsfestival Zwolle ⑤
Zwolle's city festivea takes place every September, with music and theatre lighting up the city's Hanseatic-era canals.
stadsfestival.nl

Bevrijdingsfestival ⑥
On May 5 every year, the province of Overijssel celebrates the Liberation in Zwolle, with a festival featuring several stages, dozens of performances, hundreds of volunteers, a maximum of 145,000 visitors and many satellite events.
bevrijdingsfestivaloverijssel.nl

The Glass Angel ⑦
Every visitor to Zwolle takes a selfie next to this statue of archangel Michael, the city's patron saint. He's made from 350 layers of glass, each one 1 cm thick.

De Sassenpoort ⑧
This fairytale looking structure is a gate in the city walls which was built in the late 14th and early 15th century as part of the city defenses. Today, it's a UNESCO monument.
sassenpoortzwolle.nl

How to get around
Cycling is easy and fun in Zwolle and Arnhem as elsewhere in the Netherlands, but the public transport system is easy to use as well. Most students have a bike, but in bad weather or for longer journeys the bus is a useful back up. Travellers use a smart card called the OV chip card.

Arranging housing
Average

Housing support by school
ArtEZ doesn't have any housing provision for students but it does provide advice, eg a list of websites to consult.

Cost of room in the city
Between EUR 300 and EUR 350 per month

Cost of campus housing
n/a

City
Arnhem/Zwolle

Country
The Netherlands

At nighttime, the Arts University Bournemouth presents a brightly illuminated spectacle. Photo Phil Jones

Arts University Bournemouth

Summer at the Arts University Bournemouth, looking across the courtyard to University House. Photo Phil Jones

Arts University Bournemouth (AUB)
Wallisdown Campus
Fern Barrow
Poole BH12 5HH
United Kingdom

T +44 (0)120 2363 088
rgagg@aub.ac.uk
aub.ac.uk

Course
Architecture: Spatial Practices

School
Arts University Bournemouth

'We offer an environment which allows and encourages experimentation and risk-taking'

Russell Gagg, course leader

What is this school all about?

Arts University Bournemouth (AUB) dates back to 1885. It has grown considerably in recent years, and currently has over 3000 students. Today, we offer a wide portfolio of undergraduate and postgraduate courses including those related to architecture, spatial practices, fashion, film, acting, animation, illustration, photography, fine art and graphic design. These are all located on one campus comprising purpose-built studios and extensive modern workshops to offer an environment which allows and encourages experimentation and risk-taking.

Why should students choose this university?

We employ a rigorous approach to help students to develop their practice through establishing a theoretical and contextual framework relevant to their chosen specialism. We offer the students the opportunity to learn through experimentation and encourage them to apply their practice in unfamiliar situations that help to foster an understanding, and the potential for, risk.

What kind of teaching method is applied here?

A wide range, including tutorials, lectures, seminars, critiques and workshops. One important aspect of delivery is the understanding that subject knowledge and learning in different courses is often complementary and this has informed teaching at the university in a number of ways. Students

on the MA Architecture: Spatial Practices course explore design thinking as well as research methodologies and methods alongside students from other MA courses like photography and graphic design.

What is expected from the students?

The students are asked to analyse and reflect on their practice and to use this as a starting point in the development of a study proposal for their master's project that approaches and challenges the forefront of their discipline.

What is the most important thing for students to learn during this course?

The opportunity to engage with 'design thinking', and with spatial thinking: the complexity of contexts that this encourages and demands, and the recognition of these as key factors in driving innovation and economic development through the understanding of complexity in processes and the needs of a global society.

What kind of careers do former students tend to gravitate towards?

The MA Architecture: Spatial Practices encourages the student, through the structure of the course, to engage with different, but complementary, themes to their studies, such as entrepreneurship, editing and curatorial and academic enquiry.

Programme

The course engages with the potential and complexities of space and spatial design in a global context. It supports and encourages students to investigate their individual practice within a framework of complementary disciplines whilst developing a critical theoretical context for their work. Students have the opportunity to engage with spatial and architectural thinking and modes of production as located within cultural, social, political and economic contexts. They develop as professionals who consider their creative practice holistically and globally.

Thinking as a designer, 'design thinking', is now recognised the world over as a key factor in driving innovation and economic development through the understanding of complexity in processes and the needs of society.

The course asks students to engage with contemporary conditions and pressing issues with which space is always entangled, including but not exclusively: the ubiquity of the global in the everyday, and the needs of the local in a globalised world; the life-changing effects of the mixing of the virtual and the 'real'; the consequences of an overwhelmingly consumerist society (and questions of scarcity); the regeneration of our cities and communities; and the precarious state of our ecology.

Students look at what people and society do; as designers they are encouraged to respond to, and inform, the impact of the actions that people take, whether this be on an international, regional or local context. As designers we are part of a global community and our decisions, however small, impact on this community.

A view across the courtyard from the refectory to the AUB's Enterprise Pavilion.
Photo Phil Jones

Programme
Architecture: Spatial Practices

Leads to
Master of Arts

Structure
The full-time course lasts 1 year of which 45 weeks are taught (three blocks of 15 weeks). MA combined sessions are compulsory for all Postgraduate Network students to attend, and MA specialist sessions are particular to individual MA courses. Master's Projects 1 and 2 involve periods of study that determine your major body of practical work. Master's Project 1 will require you to formalise your intentions in a Study Plan, and in Master's Project 2 you will carry through your plan of action identified in the Study Plan and establish ways of presenting and disseminating the outcomes of your project in ways that communicate to both specialist and non-specialist audiences.

Head of programme
Russell Gagg

Mentors and lecturers
Michael Cavagin, Ronnie Inglis, Or Lieberman, Sonia Nicolson and Edward Ward.

Notable alumni
Andree van Zyl

School Facts

Duration of study
1 year (45 weeks)

Full time
Yes (40 hours a week)

Part time
Yes (2 years)

Female students
66%

Male students
34%

Local students
34%

Students from abroad
66%

Yearly enrolment
3–10

Tuition fee
- GBP 4950 per year (GBP 2475 part time) for UK and EU citizens (approx. EUR 6134, or EUR 3067 part time)
- GBP 13,500 per year for non-UK and non-EU citizens (approx. EUR 16,728)

Funding/scholarships
Yes, scholarships of up GBP 3000 (approx. EUR 3717) by AUB and a number of external scholarships. Tuition fee discounts related to early payment of fees are available for international students on all full-time courses. American students are eligible to apply to the Family Federal Education Loan Program (FFELP).

Minimum requirements for entry
Bachelor degree with honours in Arts, Design, Media or Performance and a relevant English language qualification.

Language
English

Application procedure
Your online application should contain:
the completed application form
your portfolio
personal statement in which you describe why choosing this course
a copy of your passport or identity card
a copy of your qualifying degree
a copy of your language certificate
references.
After receiving your documents you will be invited for an admissions interview with the selection committee.

Application details
aub.ac.uk/apply/apply-now

Application date
None for applications but before 31 July for a bursary.

Graduation rate
100%

Job placement rate
High

Memberships/affiliations
None

Collaborations with
MA Fine Art, MA Photography, MA Graphic Design, MA Illustration and MA Arch (Masters of Architecture).

Facilities for students
Studios, workshops, digital manufacture hub, Art Sway (external studio spaces), a library and cafeteria.

City
Bournemouth

Country
United Kingdom

Student Work

Final Major Project (2013)
By Katie Thomas

The design and construction of a sound installation for the Grassmarket Project, Edinburgh, to allow people to create and control their own personal soundscape.

Strategies for Practice (2013)
By Andree van Zyl

This project explored the use of indigenous timber to visually represent the diversity of indigenous language in the landscape of South Africa.

Strategies for Practice (2013)
By Rory Johnson

Looking at the journey of an alien object as a vehicle for the exploration of the chines (a local word for ravines or valleys) around Bournemouth coastline.

trategies for Practice (2013)
y Emily Manns

e urban fabric of Boscombe town is considered as the vessel
r memories of its Victorian glory. Photo Russell Gagg

Final Major Project (2013)
By Nattakan Bayliss

The redesign of New Milton railway station to provide a
gateway to the New Forest in Hampshire, United Kingdom.

The Monochromium (2013)
By Leoni Bullcock

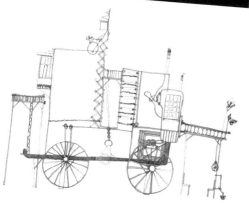

e design and construction of The Monochromium, a travelling
cus and performance theatre.

Final Major Project (2013)
By Natalia Maslanka

Design and construction of performance and set for
The Ink Mountain, by the artists Hazel Evans at the Shelley
Theatre, Boscombe.

Alumna

Name Andree van Zyl
Residence Cape Town, South Africa
Year of birth 1989
Year of graduation 2013
Current job Freelance
Website behance.net/andree_vanzyl

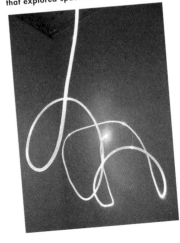

For her graduation project, Andree van Zyl created a multifacetted installation that explored space through light.

Why did you choose this school?

I was looking for something that would combine fine art and architecture. This course allows students from almost any discipline to engage in architectural thinking and apply it to their field of interest. It is also an art school with a realistic outlook based on being commercially viable.

What was the most important thing you learned here?

The immense benefit of intercultural peer learning. The master's programme at the AUB is internationally orientated and represents students from across the globe. I found that this broadened my academic enquiry as well as my personal experiences. Academic knowledge can be taught, but culture has to be experienced. It is important to embrace this wherever you choose to study – it is not always about seeing eye-to-eye, but rather about seeing through the eyes of others.

Were there any classes you found particularly difficult or easy?

The master's programme at the AUB is designed so that you share most of your theory classes with the other MA courses. This can be quite challenging, because your field of study is so vast, but at the same time it is very interesting, because you learn so much about other disciplines as well as your own.

What was your graduation project?

I ended up making three different works of art that communicated with each other to form an overarching theme. Sketches, entitled *Tekeninge*, are drawings of imaginary spaces. I chose to exhibit them as 3D objects by mounting them in blocks of acrylic on custom-built plinths. The nature of the acrylic acts as a lens that distorts the image from different viewpoints. A light sculpture, V*asgevang in Vastestof*, explored time-based space. I used fibre optic cable as a drawing tool. The cable is a solid acrylic tube giving the illusion of glass carrying light. The 'light drawing' was illuminated by a pulsating light source, set to the rhythm of very slow breathing. The biggest work was an immersive light installation made up of 200m illuminated fibre optic sparkle cable. The work, *Refraksie*, echoed architectural forms and explored the space within the gallery through the use of light.

Any words of advice for future students?

Harvest what you can! I was not proactive enough in using the facilities at the school. The AUB has a fantastic workshop area with laser cutters, a 3D printer, a textile printer, wood and metalwork equipment, photography and printmaking studios and technical staff for support. And get a bicycle, it is much nicer than using public transport and you get to know the area better that way as well.

'Bournemouth has a surprising amount of nightspots considering its size. There are many promoters bringing real quality names in club culture in nearly every week. I would hang-out at Sixty Million Postcards and would go out to venues like the 02 Academy, The Winchester or Orange Rooms/Old Firestation. The town caters for a lot of tastes and cultures.'
Rory Johnson

'My advice for future students? Welcome the opportunities with open arms, be creative with your work, think outside the box and push boundaries to the limits!'
Michaela Balzan

choose the school primarily ecause of the course, but so for the fantastic facilities ch as the workshop d printmaking room. The cation helped too!'
Emily Manns

'Get to know the area well when you move to Bournemouth, as there are lots of shortcuts and areas of the town that many people do not know about. It is a great place to explore – full of unexpected gems, perfect for adventures!'
Katie Thomas

'I was particularly impressed with the vibrant atmosphere of Bournemouth town, which really suited my creative style, and I found the beaches in Dorset to be a unique source of inspiration.'
Hannah Coombe

City Life

Bournemouth and the neighbouring town of Poole are home to two universities. In addition there are language schools and other educational institutions dotted around the town. Consequently there is a youthful population here that brings an exciting mix of cultural events of every description. There are large venues such as The Lighthouse in Poole and the Bournemouth International Centre, and more intimate student friendly spaces such as Sixty Million Postcards. Bournemouth is only 1.5 hours from London by fast train and yet is surrounded by countryside. The New Forest, a National Park, is on its doorstep and there are beautiful beaches and coastal walks in and around the town.

The campus is situated a short bus journey or cycle ride from the centre of town, and a short walk from the area of Winton, where many students choose to live. The whole area provides a rich tapestry of contrasts. There is the city, the countryside, and the sea and some of the most expensive real estate in the world only a few miles from younger and more alternative cultural enclaves along the coast. This diversity has been a source of study for a number of students who have considered the local geography and context as the basis for innovative, collaborative projects.

United Kingdom

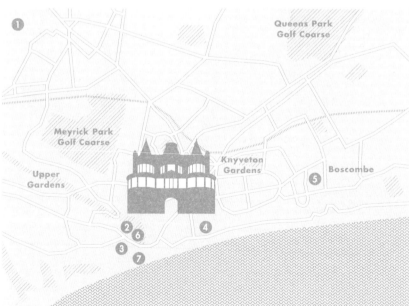

View across Bournemouth Square in the city centre.

Bournemouth

1 AUB
2 Sixty Million Postcards
3 International Centre
4 Russell-Cotes Art Gallery and Museum
5 O2 Academy
6 Bar So
7 West Beach

Park

Water

Railway

Main road

Course
Architecture: Spatial Practices

School
Arts University Bournemouth

...ixty Million Postcards ②
A hard-to-pigeonhole venue combining a bar, food, live music, workshops and disco nights. It also claims to have 'the best quiz in town or possibly the world'.
sixtymillionpostcards.com

...ournemouth International Centre ③
This is a major venue in the city for conferences and exhibitions, as well as entertainment events including music concerts, opera, ballet and comedy performances.
bic.co.uk

...ssell-Cotes Art Gallery and Museum ④
A well-preserved Art Nouveau building built by Sir Merton and Lady Russell-Cotes, beautifully furnished with a period mix of painting, sculpture and artefacts. The museum-house also features contemporary art through the Art House Gallery at the Russell-Cotes and boasts a great cafe.
russell-cotes.bournemouth.gov.uk

O2 Academy ⑤

A music venue situated in an old music hall, which still has many period features including a proscenium arch with royal boxes and booths.
The university sometimes uses it as a location for its Graduation Ball.
o2academybournemouth.co.uk

Bar So ⑥
Stylish bar and nightclub in the heart of Bournemouth serving food and drinks through the day and transforming into a destination for clubbers at night.
bar-so.com

WestBeach ⑦
A restaurant with amazing views of Bournemouth beach. In addition to providing fine food WestBeach also sponsors AUB's The Gallery and collaborates with exhibitions held there.
west-beach.co.uk

Littledown Centre
A sports centre where you can swim, use the gym, play football or racquet sports, or take to the high ropes in Littledown Park.
littledowncentre.co.uk

The Lighthouse Poole
The Lighthouse Poole hosts a variety of cultural events with theatre, opera, music, stand-up comedy, film and visual arts. The university stages theatrical productions here, and MA students have exhibited in the gallery.
lighthousepoole.co.uk

Bournemouth Beaches
Miles and miles of sand with something for everyone – from the nature reserve at Hengistbury Head, through family beaches, piers and waterside restaurants to sports including surfing, windsurfing, kite-boarding, sailing, kayaking and just plain swimming.
bournemouth.co.uk

Pop-up Galleries
The Arts University Bournemouth has been responsible for several pop-up galleries which show student work. Though by their very nature a temporary phenomenon, they inject a cultural pulse into different parts of the town.

...w to get around
Bournemouth is only 1.5 hours from London by fast train. The airport is only 10.5 km from the school and 7 km from the city centre. There are direct flights to more than 35 international destinations in 19 countries. National Express coaches serve Bournemouth Travel Interchange and Bournemouth University and this connects to numerous cities and towns in the United Kingdom, as well as Eurolines coaches to mainland Europe. There are more buses that serve the campus including Unilinx bus service. There are also a number of cycle paths that link the campus to the city. Many students live close to the university in Winton, which is within walking distance. Students who live further afield often use one of the bus services that stop regularly at the university campus. Other students cycle. The campus is served by a number of cycle lanes that connect the campus to the town and there are a variety of places where you can secure your bicycle on campus.

Arranging housing
Never a problem

Housing support by school
Yes

Cost of room in the city
GBP 350 per month
(approx. EUR 440)

Cost of campus housing
GBP 420 per month
(approx. EUR 530)

Staff and students at the Department of Design are now gathered in Kong Oscars gate in the city centre. Photo Kjetil Helland

Bergen Academy of Art and Design

Bergen Academy of Art and Design (KHiB)
Kong Oscars gate 62
5015 Bergen
Norway

T +47 5558 7300
khib@khib.no
khib.no

Despite the traditional-looking exterior, Bergen Academy of Art and Design prides itself on its experimental approach. This is one of the six locations used by KHiB. Photo Peter Klasson

'Students are encouraged to be critical, independent and experimental'

Mona Larsen, dean of Department of Design

What is studying at this school all about?
Key words to describe Bergen Academy of Art and Design (KHiB) are: stimulating, experimental, vibrant and grounded. Our vision is to be a sustainable and experimental learning and working environment for creative activity. We educate artists and designers who set the agenda in their fields. The Academy provides conditions that foster comprehensive understanding, critical reflection and conceptual thinking. It builds on the relationship between artistic research and education. It ensures that the education it offers is relevant, and promotes the importance of art and design in society. We offer optimal opportunities for working across media and subject areas and emphasises communication and dialogue with relevant artistic and professional environments. We also offer a learning environment in which students are encouraged to be critical, independent and experimental. The Academy has a national and international profile that is reflected in the composition of its staff and students. It offers artistically relevant, flexible and stable lifelong learning that is closely connected to its core activities.

What kind of teaching method is important here?
Studies at KHiB are experimental.

Why should students choose this particular school?
Students at Bergen Academy of Art and Design are creative, motivated and thinking people wanting to develop their personal skills in the area of art and design. Bergen is internationally renowned for good design, creative artists and a thriving music and club scene. The academy is situated in the midst of this milieu, drawing energy from it as much as boosting it. We have an international staff and students, who collaborate closely with each other. The student community is active and takes responsibility for its own learning. We tutor and lecture in both Norwegian and English, and with our small student groups we focus on social engagement.

What is expected from the students?
Design students at KHiB should develop social and functional design solutions for a rapidly changing environment. They need to develop their skills to think comprehensively and address complex problems based on a broad and thorough understanding of design as method.

What is the most important thing for students to learn during this course?
To find the underlying, actual challenge behind the assignment and to compassionately put themselves in the situation of the user.

What kind of jobs do students mostly go on to do?
They get good positions in design or architecture companies nationally. Some of them establish their own design studios with other interior architects or designers.

Programme

The goal of the programme is to educate cutting-edge designers who develop functional and strong design solutions for a changing world with boldness, empathy and insight. The programme is interdisciplinary and gives the students the practical, methodological and theoretical skills required to work in design at a high level – aesthetically, ethically and functionally. The core of the programme is the individual student's master's project, which is a large, independent and experimental design work. Through their master's projects, students contribute to fresh thinking and development of the subject area, often across established professional boundaries. The students will learn to present their own projects in writing, orally and through exhibitions.

Relevant theory helps the students to refle critically on their work. To be able to meet th needs and challenges of the future, it is important to understand the role design can play in a changing society.

An essential part of the programme is learning through participation in conversations and discussions about design - between the students and in meetings with tutors. The programme as a whole emphasis the dynamic relationship between individual and collective work and therefore includes several mandatory collaborative elements throughout the course of the study.

The programme is based on critical reflection and on developing professional integrity through open and experimental approaches to design processes. The education offered is based on artistic resear and development. The programme follows a progressive model that initially focuses on methods, then expands to include in-depth study and further expands to include a focus on rhetoric and preparations for a professional career.

Students at the design workshop. Photo Kjetil Helland

Programme
Furniture and Spatial Design / Interior Architecture

Leads to
Master of Arts

Structure
The initial focus of the curriculum emphasises methodology, progresses with focus on the students' own MA projects and concludes with courses in rhetoric and the transition to professional life. All students share the same theoretical foundation, independent of their specialisation. Theory includes three main segments: communication, the market and cultural skills, and methodology. The independent master's project requires an individual course of stu Any exchange periods or practical training periods, plus courses, projects and workshops, are chosen on the basis of their relevance to the individual master's project.

Head of programme
Eli-Kirstin Eide

Mentors and lecturers
Torbjørn Anderssen, Petter Bergerue Steinar Hindenes, Bente Irminger an Dave Vikøren.

Notable alumni
Torbjørn Anderssen, Olav Eldøy, Andreas Engesvik, Steinar Hindene Peter Opsvik, Lars Tornøe and Dave Vikøren.

School Facts

Duration of study
2 years

Full time
Yes

Part time
No

Female students
65%

Male students
35%

Local students
79%

Students from abroad
21%

Yearly enrolment
40

Tuition fee
Free

Funding/scholarships
International students provide their own funding to cover living expenses and material. Through the national Quota Scheme, KHiB can offer a small financial support to a very limited number of MA students from specific countries. Norwegian citizens may have financial support from the Norwegian State Educational Loan Fund.

Minimum requirements for entry
Bachelor's degree in design or other relevant study programme corresponding to 180 credits.

Language
English and Norwegian

Application procedure
The following documents must be submitted in order to complete the application:
a completed online application form
a copy of your latest certificate of qualification
your portfolio
a written project description including motivation.
Shortlisted applicants will be invited for an interview. Admission will be determined by an overall assessment of the applicant's qualifications, the quality of previous artistic work demonstrated by submitted documentation, the statement of motivation and the interview.

Application details
khib.no/english/studies/information-for-applicants/how-to-apply-to-ma-in-design/

Application date
Before 1 April

Graduation rate
100%

Job placement rate
100%

Memberships/affiliations
Norwegian Organisation for Interior Architects and Furniture Designers (NIL), European Council of Interior Architects (ECIA), ELIA and Cumulus.

Collaborations with
The furniture industry in Norway, Federation of Norwegian Industries, Norwegian Design Council, Design Region Bergen, Norwegian Ministry of Foreign Affairs, Oslo National Academy of the Arts, Innovation Norway, Hordaland County Administration and Bergen Municipal Council.

Facilities for students
Individual workplaces, wood workshop, metal workshop, library, canteen, showrooms, project rooms and parking.

Student Work

Distraction As Treatment – Treatment Centre For Eating Disorders (2013)
By Kine Hetland

Can design and architecture support treatment methods currently offered to those suffering from eating disorders? The general concept of this project is about using distraction, based on shapes and forms found in nature, as a tool.

Among Islands and Skerries (2013)
By Daniel Ness Turco

How can I inspire families with young children to make use of nature, where the local natural surroundings and spaces for the backdrop to and a platform for creativity, expression and play? This project sets out is to develop the bathing area on Geiteskjær and the island as a recreational space, interpreting the relationship between nature, place and people.

Course
Furniture and Spatial Design / Interior Architecture

School
Bergen Academy of Art and Design

An Intoxicating Space (2012)
By Karoline Grepperud

ow can the physical environment contribute to dignity and safety for substance abusers? This shelter is inspired by the comfortable simplicity
f life in a primitive cottage and aims to cover the clients' basic needs and offer a safer, dignified environment for them.

uitful (2013)
y Hanne Kari Ravndal

w can the teaching of food technology in schools become a social arena that inspires exploration, expression and
rning? This project aims to familiarise young people with the kitchen and encourage them to explore the joys of
king by rethinking the shape and functionality of the school kitchens used for lessons.

Alumnus

For his graduation project, Morten Skjærpe Knarrum did a project on design for correctional facilities.

Name Morten Skjærpe Knarrum
Residence Bergen, Norway
Year of birth 1980
Year of graduation 2011
Current job Furniture and interior architect MNIL at Morten&Jonas and designer in the Norwegian correctional services/ Bjørgvin prison
Clients Northern Lighting
Website morten-jonas.no

Why did you choose this school?
For its location in Bergen on the west coast of Norway, and because it is a well-known Academy. I grew up at the west coast, south of Stavanger, and thought Bergen was a beautiful city. Also, I had heard that the student environment was very good.

What was the most interesting project you did?
My master's project was one of them. It was great to have the luxury of working on one project for a whole year. Also, I was given a scholarship by The Federation of Norwegian Industries, which lasted for 3 months. We travelled around Norway and visited several furniture producers and suppliers. As part of the scholarship I attended as a trainee for 4 weeks with a Norwegian furniture company. It was a great opportunity to learn about this industry and meet the people involved.

Was there any class you found particularly difficult or easy?
Each course had its challenges in different ways. And most of the time things became easier after some practice. Like working in the workshops. I had never done anything like

wood carpeting or metalwork before, but after a while I got the hang of it.

What was your graduation project about?
I did a project on design and the Norwegian correctional services. I set out to answer the question: How can design interact with the future correctional services in Norway, and in what way? I'm currently working on that subje as a designer in the correctional services.

Any words of advice for future students?
Being a student is a privilege that should not b wasted. It is a fantastic time in life where you work hard – exploring, learning, growing but also making friends for life and building important networks for your future career.

Are you still in contact with the school?
Yes. Now I am a guest teacher at the Department of Design.

Are you still in contact with your fellow students?
I'm currently working together with one of them, Jonas Nordheim. Some of my other fellow students have become friends for life.

Was the transformation from graduation to working life a smooth one?
Transformations do often include some kind o challenge, and mine did as well. Going from safe and carefree school environment to a mo brutal business world has been a challenge. B we are learning something new every day, an that is a privilege.

'Future students can expect a great variety of subjects and courses both theoretical and practical, engaged teachers with a lot of knowledge and insight, and a creative and open student environment. You will be well trained for a future career.'
Elisabeth Våpenstad Holm

'During the 2 years you learn how to develop a project and do the right research. You are also taught to express and explain the project professionally through a written description, which makes you more aware of the choices you make.'
Pernille Akselsen

'My favourite class was design theory. Many of the principles taught in that course were directly applicable to the master's project that I am working on.'
Marte Straalberg

'Even though Bergen is a city, it has more of a small town feel to it. I fell in love with the place when I visited it for the interview. The centre is so open and beautiful, especially in the summer when everything is in bloom.'
Anna Birna Björnsdóttir

City Life

The city of Bergen, located on the western coast of Norway, is the second largest city in Norway, although with 250,000 inhabitants, it is small by international standards. On the shores of the Atlantic Ocean, Bergen has seen its history and development closely linked to trade routes at sea and a constant interaction with the outside world. The city centre – which includes a UNESCO-listed Hanseatic-era harbour – is naturally framed by mountains as well as the sea. This has resulted in a compactness that ensures that most things are within easy walking distance and provides a feeling that everything is close at hand.

The surrounding nature is a huge plus, with Bergen also the gateway to Norway's spectacular fjord landscapes which are within easy reach.

With considerable personality and charm, Bergen has a lively cultural character that belies its small size. Festivals are held throughout the year, peaking during the spring when the city becomes green, sunny and full of life, and adding to the unique atmosphere. As a Norwegian poet once declared: 'Bergen is not a place, but a condition in my soul.'

Bergen's old harbour is a UNESCO monument and a relic of the city's rich maritime history.
Photo Peter Klasson

Norway

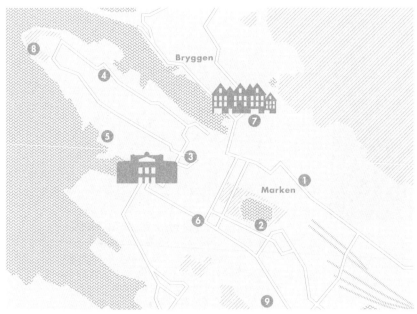

Bryggen

Marken

Bergen

1 KHiB – Kong Oscars gat
2 Grieghallen Concert Ha
3 The National Venue of Theatre (DNS)
4 BIT Teatergarasjen
5 Carte Blanche
6 Bergen Filmklubb
7 Fløibanen Funicular
8 Nordnes Sjøbad
9 Nygårdsparken

Park

Water

Railway

Main road

Course
Furniture and Spatial Design / Interior Architecture

School
Bergen Academy of Art and Desig

City Facts

Bergen internasjonale filmfestival
The international film festival's main venue is Bergen Cinema's Magnus Barefoot Cinema Centre, with additional screenings taking place at the local art film theatre at Georgernes Verft and at the student cinema at Kvarteret.
biff.no

Grieghallen Concert Hall 2
Named after Bergen's famous composer Edvard Grieg, Grieghallen Concert Hall is the home of Bergen Philharmonic Orchestra. There are student discounts on Thursdays.
harmonien.no

The National Venue of Theatre (DNS) 3
Bergen hosts Norway's oldest permanent theatre. Today, it houses three stages and presents approximately 20 productions each year, including international and national classics, musicals and contemporary drama. Most productions offer a student discount.
dns.no

BIT Teatergarasjen 4
An international theatre which produces, co-produces and presents international and Norwegian contemporary theatre and dance.
bit-teatergarasjen.no

Carte Blanche 5
The national contemporary dance company Carte Blanche is also located in Bergen. The company produces a minimum of three new choreographic works a year and performs an average of four to six productions a year.
carteblanche.no

Bergen Filmklubb 6
Founded in 1961, Bergen Filmklubb screens movies every Wednesday and Sunday at Det Akademiske Kvarter.
bergen-filmklubb.no

Fløibanen Funicular 7
Take the fløibanen (funicular train) up to the top of Mount Floyen for beautiful views of the city, plus hiking trails.
floibanen.com

Nordnes Sjøbad 8
This outdoor heated pool (27 °C) at the cold water's edge of Nordnes park is very popular amongst students in Bergen.

Nygårdsparken 9
A very nicely landscaped park laid out in the late 1800s in the style of a typical English park. The park is a popular picnic place for families, and a perfect barbeque spot for students.
bergen.kommune.no

How to get around
Bergen airport (18 km from the city) has direct flights from around 30 European destinations. An airport shuttle bus departs every 15 minutes (every 30 minutes during weekends). Bergen has good train links to the rest of the country and Scandinavia: the line between Bergen and Oslo is considered one of the world's most scenically spectacular. In the city itself, distances are fairly compact making walking an attractive option. Buses and the light-rail are another easy way to get around town. A 1-month student bus card for students aged under 32 costs NOK 400 (approx. EUR 45); for students over 32 it is NOK 660 (approx. EUR 80).

Arranging housing
Average

Housing support by school
Yes

Cost of room in the city
NOK 2995 per month (approx. EUR 400)

Cost of campus housing
n/a

Domus Academy

The modern academy building is located in Milan's vibrant and historic Navigli quarter.
Photo Sette Secondi Circa

Domus Academy
Via C. Darwin 20
20143 Milan
Italy

T +39 02 4241 4001
info@domusacademy.it
domusacademy.com

The Domus Academy first opened its doors in 1982 as Italy's first postgraduate design school, and has been educating creatives to a high level ever since.

Course
Interior and Living Design

School
Domus Academy

'Our mission is to help students become protagonists in the highly competitive world of fashion and design'

Francesca Vargiu, course leader of the Master in Interior and Living Design

When was the school founded?
Domus Academy was co-founded in 1982 by Maria Grazia Mazzocchi along with remarkable figures in the art and design world including Pierre Restany, Alessandro Mendini, Valerio Castelli, Alessandro Guerriero and Andrea Branzi.

Has it changed much over the years?
It all started with the Master in Design, but programmes have been added to enhance and match the academic offer with the growing needs of contemporary society and new research areas, including design, fashion, business design and interior design, as well as architectural design. In December 2009, Domus Academy joined the Laureate International Universities, a leading international network of almost 75 innovative institutions of higher education.

What is studying at this school all about?
Our mission is to help students become protagonists in the highly competitive world of fashion and design. We embrace a multidisciplinary and practical approach to the design profession in which students solve real-life design problems with the help of world-class faculty members who are opinion leaders in their fields.

What kind of teaching method does Domus Academy use?
We follow a carefully synthesised approach that reflects the double nature of academy and

laboratory. It is based on a 'learning by designing' methodology, in which students learn by actively carrying out their projects under the mentorship of experienced, professional designers. It's a system which puts processes at its core, maintaining the human being as the focal point of any project.

Why should students choose this particular school?
For the chance to receive an internationally recognised degree, to learn from our industry-leading faculty and professionals, to work on actual design projects with top Italian and international companies, and to intern with a leading design brand, gaining valuable tools and connections. Students have the opportunity to intern at a prestigious design company, where they can gain valuable tools and connections. Moreover, EU and non-EU students are eligible to participate in the internships and can extend their permit of stay to work in Italy for up to 1 year after degree completion.

What is the most important thing for students to learn during this course?
The programme is designed to widen our graduates' perspective, providing them with a cultural knowledge that is half way between the design domain and socio-cultural disciplines. Graduates will learn a combination of skills, and be encouraged to develop a synergetic approach that will constantly challenge both the material as well as the socio-cultural and environmental components of a project.

Programme

The course aims to enable students to reflect on changes and transformations of inhabited space, promoting innovative solutions in the interior and living design field. The master's programme takes an ideas-based, conceptual and future-orientated approach: it combines space and services applications, encouraging students to utilise technical competences and expertise, with anthropological factors, cultural dimensions and strategic thinking in order to identify and envision new and forthcoming scenarios. Students face actual, complex design challenges relating to a variety of contexts and issues concerning model living scenarios. The programme is designed to widen graduates' perspective, providing them with a cultural knowledge that is half way between the design domain and socio-cultural disciplines. Patricia Urquiola, the internationally renowned designer, is mentor of the programme and actively leading workshops with the students in collaboration with companies such as Moroso, Flos, B&B and Kvadrat.

Students benefit from the expertise of a star-studded faculty when it comes to fine-tuning and polishing their projects. Photo Max Zambelli for Mutina

The inside story: Domus Academy prides itself on its creative approach – displayed here in the school entrance. Photo Paolo Pellion, Illustration Olimpia Zagnoli

Programme
Interior and Living Design

Leads to
Master in Interior and Living Design

Structure
Students follow courses (History of Design, Design Culture); attend a technical-methodological lab (Visual Presentation Skills); and participate in four workshops (Interior Design Lifestyle, Social/Personal Spaces, Design for Business and Retail Spaces and Design for Public Spaces). They also complete an internship and their final master project.

Head of programme
Francesca Vargiu

Mentors and lecturers
Patricia Urquiola, Michael Anastassiades, Andrea Branzi, Francesco Franchi, Paolo Giachi, Joseph Grima, Francesco Librizzi, Marco Rainò and Jan Christoph Zoels.

Notable alumni
Raffaele Correale, Deniz Galip, Andrya Kohlmann, David Perri, Adriano Ferraro and Emeline Paik.

School Facts

Duration of study
1 year

Full time
Yes (40 hours a week)

Part time
No

Female students
85%

Male students
15%

Local students
5%

Students from abroad
95%

Yearly enrolment
58 (intake divided between 33 in September and 25 in February)

Tuition fee
- EUR 16,990 per year for EU citizens
- EUR 24,990 per year for non-EU citizens

Funding/scholarships
A partial reduction in tuition fees can be granted to deserving students with financial constraints. Financial aid applicants must fill in and submit the relevant required form, with official documents proving their financial situation. Every year, Domus Academy launches international competitions granting a scholarship (worth up to 70% of fees).

Minimum requirements for entry
Applicants should be young graduates or professionals in the design field. Students with different degrees or diplomas may also be considered, if the applicant is motivated by a research interest towards the programme topics. Students should be proficient in English.

Language
English

Application procedure
The following documents must be submitted:
your curriculum vitae
your portfolio of projects
a motivation letter
an academic transcript of previous studies, translated into English, listing subjects and exams with corresponding number of hours/credits and short description of each subject's programme
a copy of degree/diploma (translated into English)
documentation regarding further courses or seminars attended (if available)
an English language certificate (if applicable)

- a copy of your passport
- a receipt of the application fee. The evaluation commission, led by the course leader, will evaluate each candidate.

Application details
admissions@domusacademy.it

Application date
- Before 1 December for the winter semester
- Before 1 August for the autumn semester

Graduation rate
90%

Job placement rate
100%

Memberships/affiliations
Laureate International Universities network

Collaborations with
B&B, Boffi, Flos, Kvadrat, Moroso, Mutina, Pitti, Park Hyatt, 10 CorsoComo, Club Med, K-Way, Lago, Moleskine, Mondadori, Tucano and Triennale di Milano.

Facilities for students
The academy has a library, containing approximately 9000 books, 50 periodicals, about 200 DVDs, 800 VHS tapes and over 2000 theses, plus a laboratory with model-making, metal, wood, plastic and 3D sections. There is also a fashion laboratory equipped with sewing machines, mannequins, irons, a sewing table and additional tools. Computers are located in several dedicated areas.

City
Milan

Country
Italy

Student Work

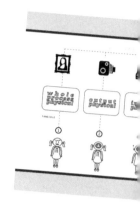

Plast-It (2013)
By Camila Paulon Sautchuk, Alreem Aldoseri, Tina Abou Jaoude and Katherine Antaki

"ONE MAN'S TRASH IS ANOTHER'S TREASURE."

Estroverso (2013)
By Claudia Lira Grajales and Camila Paulon Sautchuk

ONLY 10% OF PLASTIC IS RECYCLED
PLASTIC

Plast-it reprocesses type 2 plastic into a piece of Moroso furniture, giving value to old rubbish. Using open source technology, a machine is created which shreds, cleans, melts, and reshapes the plastic. Members of the public take their plastic to the Moroso bins located around the city, receive a ticket for it and later attend Plast-it events in Milan during Design Week. Here they receive a 'revalued' plastic piece from Moroso. Using the web and the city as tools of exposure, the machine highlights the recycling process.

Representing the extrovert trapped in each and every individual, Estroverso challenges the idea of finding comfort in privacy. A second textile skin is applied to the Koloro desk, a workspace in the sha of a box, that allows for privacy in public spaces. Externalising the functions of the box, elements we added to the space, such as a carpet, speakers and shelves. The designers draw on their own expressionist cultures: those of Brazil and Mexico.

Course
Interior and Living Design

School
Domus Academy

Memento (2013)
By Vanja Bovan, Claudia Lira Grajales, Michela Matrisciano and Sandra Montaño Gómez-Farías

MEMENTO
COLLECTION
IN COLLABORATION
WITH MOROSO

In the digital age, when modern life is saturated by technology, the way memories are stored and are retained has evolved. With the alarming lack of individual privacy, do people still even own their personal memories? Memento is a collection of objects that depict the different stages of experience, from analogue to digital.

Samovar (2013)
By Binny Aryuniputri, Ayda Jabbari, Joanna Smolinski and Roanne Beth So

The primary focus of the project was to revisit the origins of tea culture by redesigning aspects from various cultures that hold tea central to their traditions. Exploring tea ware – the 'samovar' – led to a collection resembling a traditional tea set with a pot, creamer, sugar bowl, saucer, spoon and glasses. Samovar celebrates the more collective approach in experiencing tea through pop-up spaces. Modular, minimalist features vary in height and brass gold-plated finishes appear, enhancing the comfort of the upholstered, silver tray-filled space one imagines with tea.

x

City
Milan

Country
Italy

61

Alumnus

Name Esteban Marquez Vasquez
Residence Milan, Italy
Year of birth 1988
Year of graduation 2013
Current job Entrepreneur Design Studio
Clients Alessi, Venice Design Week, Italcementi
Website emvarchitecture.com

Why did you choose this school?
Domus Academy is and has always been a leader in terms of design. It is an open laboratory, a school where you work rather than study. It sums up 'Made in Italy'. Even more importantly, Milan is the hometown of design. It's a city with an exotic beauty, a metropolis with the patina of a bygone era, with great hidden corners to discover, a city that pushes your own sensibility and creativity.

What was the most important thing you learned here?
That creativity is not invention, but just a sensible interpretation. Good design knows this, which is why it is simple and straightforward. Realising this brings joy and opportunities, it creates your mood and inevitably boosts your activities.

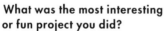

What was the most interesting or fun project you did?
Actually all of them were interesting. You always work in collaboration with a company. You do everything, from industrial to product to urban design, of course all based around interiors. But if I had to choose one, I would say that my favourite was a workshop I did with Tucano. This was a retail design project where the purpose was to rethink the branded store as an urban element.

What subject do you wish you paid more attention to?
Exhibition design. In the end, I think our proje was kind of weak, because we needed to engage with the target market more. We ende up creating more of a window display than a real story.

Was there any class you found particularly difficult?
That question does not apply to Domus Academ There are no classes. Learning comes from yo classmates, the projects you do and a constan interaction with professionals in the sector.

What was your graduation project?
Core Collector, a co-working space for LAGO Company. It is an open laboratory with temporary living spaces – a sort of mix between a co-working space and a hostel, or friend's house.

Any words of advice for future students?
Don't focus 100% on your own master's degre leave at least 20% for the other master's degree It's an open space. And knowledge gained fro other subjects can boost your own projects.

What was your favourite place to hang out?
An excellent bar at Naviglio Grande called Mc

Are you still in contact with the school and other students?
Yes – in fact, I took some extra courses! You create strong relationships with your contemporaries at Domus Academy, and you always have the opportunity to collaborate in certain projects. So some of the other student have become good friends.

Was the transformation from graduation to working life a smooth one?
Being an entrepreneur is always difficult.

If you were to do the course again, what would you do differently?
Plan my time better, and take some more time to think about the next step.

'Colonne San Lorenzo is my favourite place to hang out in Milan. Students, artists, designers and grandparents all meet up there amid the beautiful ancient architecture, exchanging a few laughs over a bite to eat.'
Alreem Aldoseri

'Our projects ranged from designing spaces to installations, videos, micro environments and garments, so there's a real fusion of disciplines.'
Vanja Bovan

...e DIY workshop was the ...st valuable for me. We had ... simulate a real company ...d project, from research and ...velopment to sales and ...tribution – surely the best way ...sum up all the knowledge ...t we had accumulated during ... course.'
Camila Paulon Sautchuk

'I would like to tell future students to always keep a positive attitude. Also, never forget why you came, and always focus on your dream and vision.'
Katherine Antaki

'In all our workshops we had the opportunity to work with top Italian design companies. What I enjoyed the most was that at the end of each workshop we discussed our ideas with the leaders of these companies – while having Patricia Urquiola by our side as a mentor.'
Sandra Montaño Gómez-Farías

City Life

The Duomo, Milan's cathedral, is an early example of the city's inimitable approach to all things style-related. Photo by Andrea Raffir

There is no better place to pursue a design education than Milan, the city where a passion for design is part of the fabric of daily life. Studying in Milan means being immersed in a stimulating creative culture and in the thriving commercial design industry. Domus Academy is in a specialised art and design education campus in the Navigli area, one of the liveliest places in Milan with lots of interesting shops, restaurants and markets.

The city is of course the world capital of fashion and design and you can always find innovative and creative people, emerging labels and chic concept stores here. Milan's centre is full of all the most important design and fashion flagship stores, including Cappellini, Driade, Kartell and Versace, as well as Armani and Valentino. Milan is the engine of the Italian economy too, but what really sets the city apart is the work of the world's leading designers. Here, you have access to the finest artisans and the production and fabrication facilities responsible for Made in Italy craftsmanship.

Italy

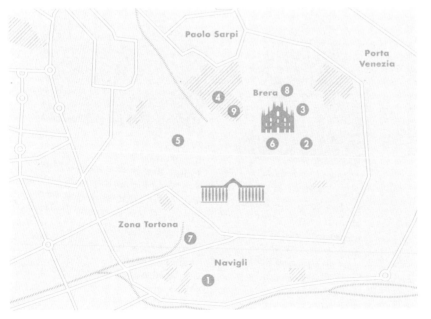

Milan

1 Domus Academy
2 Duomo
3 Teatro La Scala
4 Triennale Design Museu
5 Santa Maria Delle Graz
6 Museo Del Novecento
7 Navigli Area
8 Brera Area
9 Castello Sforzesco

Park

Railway

Main road

Course
Interior and Living Design

School
Domus Academy

City Facts

e more Milan City Facts on p.166 and p.256

omo (2)
Milan's cathedral is a late-Gothic
wonder featuring a forest of spires,
pinnacles and pillars, all woven
together with a web of flying
buttresses.
duomomilano.it

atro La Scala (3)
La Scala, Milan's famous and
fabulous opera house, first raised its
curtain in 1778. Practically destroyed
during WWII, it was rebuilt and
reopened in 1946 under the baton of
Arturo Toscanini.
teatroallascala.org

ennale Design Museum (4)
Lushly located in Parco Sempione, the
museum hosts exhibitions and events
which highlight contemporary Italian
design, urban planning, architecture,
music, and media arts. Also has a
good permanent collection.
triennaledesignmuseum.it

Santa Maria Delle Grazie (5)
The big draw here is *The Last Supper*
by Leonardo da Vinci, which is in the
refectory of this medieval convent.
grazieop.it

Museo Del Novecento (6)
This museum dedicated to the 20th
century has sections devoted to
Futurism, Spatialism and Arte Povera,
and works by Modigliani, De Chirico,
Pellizza Da Volpedo, Boccioni, Balla,
Carrà, Fontana, Morandi, Sironi and
many international artists.
museodelnovecento.org

Navigli Area (7)
The history of Milan is closely
connected with the system of canals
which pass through the whole city –
nowhere more picturesquely than in
the lovely Navigli area.
navigli.milano.it

Brera Area (8)
The Brera neighbourhood is
considered the 'artistic' area of
Milan, with restaurants and bars
clustering around the Accademia di
Brera with its wonderful fine art
collection.

Salone del Mobile (Milan Design Week)
The largest trade fair of its kind in the
world, Salone del Mobile showcases
the latest in furniture and design from
countries around the world.
cosmit.it

Milan Fashion Week
Twice a year, the city is the global
capital of fashion, thanks to Milan
Fashion Week, established in 1958
and one of the Big Four (with Paris,
London and New York).
milanfashionweek.com

Castello Sforzesco (9)
Originally a military fortress, the
Castello Sforzesco was completely
remodelled by the more comfort-
minded Francesco Sforza. The new
and improved defences were
designed by uber-engineer Leonardo
da Vinci.
milanocastello.it

w to get around
In Milan, buses, trams, metro
(underground) and trains are run by
the same company, ATM (Azienda
Trasporti Milanese). With more than
50 urban bus routes, the bus system
sometimes offers a more direct route
than the underground. The fare costs
EUR 1.50 and you can get on and off
as many times as you want for 90
minutes. The metro system consists of
three lines: M1 (red), M2 (green), M3
(yellow). There is also a blue line, the
passante ferroviario, which is a
railway but can be used with the same
ticket as the urban tracks.

Arranging housing
Quite easy

Housing support by school
Yes, full support

Cost of room in the city
Between EUR 300 and
EUR 600 per month

Cost of campus housing
Between EUR 300 and
EUR 600 per month

City
Milan

Country
Italy

The new main entrance facade and the old buildings – with the Pantheon at the far end of the street – in the very heart of the Latin District. Photo EnsAD/Laurence Sudre

École nationale supérieure des Arts Décoratifs

École nationale
supérieure des Arts
Décoratifs (EnsAD)
31 rue d'Ulm
75240 Paris
France

T +33 (0)1 4234 9700
ensad.fr

The courtyard during the open day with a transparent struc
Photo EnsAD/Didier Plowy

Course
Interior Architecture

School
École nationale supérieure des Arts Décora

'Our students develop their creative, inventive, and aesthetic abilities, and also their knowledge of the principles of use, ergonomics, and functionality'

Sylvestre Monnier, head of programme

Photo EnsAD/Jean-François Fourmond

When was the school founded?
The origins of the École des Arts Décoratifs date back to the École Royale Gratuite de Dessin, founded in 1766 by Jean-Jacques Bachelier. The école's mission was to develop craftmanship in the arts and thus improve the quality of the products in the field.

What is studying at this school all about?
The interior design course, which covers disciplines ranging from experimental research to design techniques, is a laboratory for ideas, which never loses sight of the human and social dimensions.

What teaching methods are applied?
The approach is holistic, unitary, and transdisciplinary, in accordance with the schools pedagogical approach. Interior Architecture includes industrial design, set design, and colour design. The training also includes courses in the history of the arts and humanities. The students are assisted by a team of lecturers composed of qualified professionals who are all actively involved in the field of design. Internships introduce the students to real projects and the practical side of the work. On-site visits allow them to compare the project with its realisation, and see how the project is developing.

Why should students choose EnsAD?
The experimental projects and internships are complemented by courses in project management and artistic management, which acquaint the students with regulatory requirements.

What is expected from the students?
The students learn to develop their creative, inventive, and aesthetic abilities, and also their knowledge of the principles of use, ergonomics, and functionality. They have to have good communication skills to follow a particular project, develop it and promote it to the project managers; they also need these skills to manage a team and organise collective projects that involve all sorts of different crafts.

What is the most important thing for students to learn during this course?
Independent thought and creativity, by adopting a holistic approach to the process.

What is the most important skill that an aspiring interior designer needs to master?
Technical mastery and aesthetic innovation.

Where do your former students mostly end up?
They become designers and creators of living spaces, which are either renovated or designed to meet societal and environmental needs. The organisation of interior spaces extends into urban planning.

City
Paris

Country
France

Programme

This all-inclusive discipline imagines new living spaces at the interface of the visual, symbolic, and technical arts, for which it provides space and social context. The 2-year course, which includes businesses internships in design and production, has been devised to gradually professionalise students. The aim is to develop their creative potential as well as their aesthetic, technical, and social relevance as they finalise their experimental projects.

The project workshops – led by teacher practitioners – act as the educational backbone. They are opportunities for critical analysis, research, experimentation, and synthesis that cover the most important areas of creation related to inhabited space (design, spatial composition, anticipation of the future, spatial art, stage design, decoration) and that address essential social needs (habitat, activities, urban art, public and private cultural equipment).

The specialised courses in interior architecture provide most of the aesthetic and technical knowledge that contributes to the design and production of interior spaces and their exteriors, as well as to good communication about it (simulation and expressive sketches): light, colour, volume, construction, relationships, materials and equipment, ergonomics, form, function and symbol, history of modern arts and trends, computer graphics, sociology, project management and prospective, etc.

Finally, visits to analyse 'built situations' (successes or failures) enable students to test whether their design expectations meet the achievement experienced.

The student band in one of the Art section studio's. Photo Didier Plowy

Programme
Interior Architecture

Leads to
Master of Arts

Structure
The Interior Architecture programme is a 2-year full-time course. Each year consists of 2 semesters where students can earn 30 credits per semester. Each semester is 15 weeks of which the students are taught 5 days a week.

Head of programme
Sylvestre Monnier

Mentors and lecturers
Fabrice Dusapin, Marc Iseppi, Charlotte Lardinois and Denis Mont

Notable alumni
François Champsaur, Christian Germanaz, Christian Liaigre and Pascal Mourgues.

Course
Interior Architecture

School
École nationale supérieure des Arts Décora

School Facts

Duration of study
2 years

Full time
Yes (25 hours a week)

Part time
No

Female students
60%

Male students
40%

Local students
90%

Students from abroad
10%

Yearly enrolment
15

Tuition fee
EUR 637 per year

Funding/scholarships
Yes, through the school and foundations.

Minimum requirements for entry
Bachelor's degree or 5 years of experience in this field; all candidates for the master's programme must pass a competitive entrance examination. Proficiency in French.

Language
French

Application procedure
Apply for submitting the following by normal post:
a completed application form
a copy of your passport
a copy of tour qualifying degree
for foreign residents, a copy of the authorisation of stay
a EUR 51 cheque for the registration fee (EUR 26 for grant holders)
a copy of your DALF or TCF language certificate (if appropriate).
Appropriate candidates will receive an invitation for a test by mail.
Candidates must send in their portfolio, their motivation letter and CV. They will also have an interview with the jury. Candidates will be informed about their admission before the end of June.

Application details
Ensad.fr/admissions

Application date
Before 31 January

Graduation rate
100%

Job placement rate
High

Memberships/affiliations
CFAI (Conseil français des Architectes d'intérieur)

Collaborations with
Musée d'art et d'histoire du judaisme, Paris, and Festival international des jardins, Chaumont-sur-Loire.

Facilities for students
Printers, silkscreen workshop, motion studio, wood atelier, personal workstations with individual iMacs, metal and plastic workshops, 3D printers, library, cafeteria and workshops facilities.

Student Work

Daytime and Night-time Station (2013)
By Goulven Jaffrès

In Paris, the Bassin de l'Arsenal, which is already overgrown, and a disused metro station, form an ensemble arranged for daytime strolls and festive events at night.

Cold Storage Facilities: Open-Air Workshops (2013)
By Laura Cambon

For the last 30 years, old cold-storage facilities have been used as studios by artists and artisans. This alternative area in an industrial suburb will be transformed into a major cultural centre in an area that is undergoing complete renovation.

SenseAble Party (2012)
By Lauranne Schmitt

An attempt to provide a (real) poetic alternative to (virtual) dating sites which takes the form of artistic installations presented during parties held around the pool on the outdoor terrace of the Palais de Tokyo museum complex.

Free Wheels (2012)
By Philippe Bonan

The project involves the construction of a training centre for physically challenged adults in Vietnam, after an on-site visit to ascertain local cultural and architectural specificities.

Course
Interior Architecture

School
École nationale supérieure des Arts Décora

A European Poetic Space (2013)
By Guillaume Babin

The project involves the transformation of certain old border checkpoints, which have been abandoned since the Schengen Agreement in 1995, into spaces for cultural and recreational activities.

Urban Games (2012)
By Martin Gasc

The project aims to develop an area where people can (re)discover and play games. Aimed at everyone, the project intends to meet the real needs of city dwellers.

The Arts House (2012)
By Julia Schults

n the outskirts of Beijing, this project involves the establishment of a community centre dedicated to art and culture, where urban modernity d traditional ways of life come together.

Alumna

Name Anne Geistdoerfer
Residence Paris, France
Year of birth 1972
Year of graduation 1997
Current job Interior designer
Website doubleg.fr

Why did you choose this school?
It's difficult to get in because of the entrance test but it's one of the best schools for interior design.

What subject do you wish you paid more attention to?
All of them! I realised only later that this school gives you opportunities to try out almost all of the techniques in the world of art, and to meet so many professionals.

Was there any class you found particularly difficult or easy?
I had to draw much better then I was used to. The level was really high. None of the work was really easy, but it becomes fun to do.

What was your graduation project?
Actually I did three different projects; a dream house, a museum built around an artist and a mémoire. My dream house was a sea house on a cliff which was strong where it touched the rock and more and more fragile as it rose above the cliff. The museum was built around the artist Ian Pei Ming who creates enormous portraits. For him I made a huge space where you can climb on a well-designed scaffolding structure so as to be able to have a view of the paintings from far.

Any words of advice for future students?
Don't be too proud – you will have a lot to learn after school. Also work as much as you can, find out what you like and you'll be able to find your way.

Are you still in contact with the school?
I am part of the 'anciens des arts deco' – the association of former students which was established in 1911. I go back to visit whenever I can in order to see what the school is doing.

Are you still in contact with your fellow students?
Yes, almost all my friends are from the school. We keep in touch and we also work together sometimes. In the first year you are together with all the other design disciplines, so now I know a lot of professionals in many fields.

Was the transformation from graduation to working life a smooth one?
More or less. I found a job very quickly – I met a designer who had just started her own studio and although I was young she let me do everything. I stayed there for 7 years in order to learn more on the job. Very quickly I became responsible for big projects in quite a few countries. I worked hard and long hours but it was very interesting and I learned a lot.

Course
Interior Architecture

School
École nationale supérieure des Arts Décorat

'EnsAD has very well equipped workshop studios with technicians always ready to give you good advice. This is a really useful feature for students, and I regret not having spent more time there!'
Guillaume Babin

'For me, whether I like a project or not, the most important thing is overall consistency: the concept and the design have to be coherent. This is also the way teachers think at EnsAD – they don't focus on good or bad taste, but insist that you take time to think about your projects.'
Clara Rea

'I really love the Abbesses area. It's like a little village at the beginning of Montmartre and there are lots of little boutiques for design and vintage goods. I even found a bar where they revamp and sell furniture, so you go in for a drink and leave with a chair.'
Lauranne Schmitt

'Paris is a really attractive city, and that makes for a rich experience: it's worth taking the time to discover things every day. Sometimes, cycling is a good option, but the traffic can make it uncomfortable. If you have a meeting on the other side of the city, there's no other option but the metro.'
Lucie Calise

'The school is like a tool: if you can handle it in right way, you can make fabulous projects!'
Goulven Jaffrès

'I chose this school because even if you are studying interior design, there is a close relationship with the other school sectors, such as graphic design, scenography and textile design.'
Lucile Dugal

City Life

With an estimated population of over 2.2 million inhabitants, Paris is the capital and largest city of France. The river Seine divides the city in two parts.

Paris is today one of the world's leading business and cultural centres, and its influences on politics, education, entertainment, media, fashion, science and the arts all contribute to its status as one of the world's major global cities. It hosts the headquarters of many international organisations, such as UNESCO, OECD, the International Chamber of Commerce and the European Space Agency. Paris is considered to be one of the greenest and most liveable cities in Europe. It is also one of the most expensive. Three of the most famous Parisian landmarks are the 12th-century cathedral Notre Dame de Paris on the Île de la Cité, the Napoleonic Arc de Triomphe and the 19th-century Eiffel Tower.

Ever since the beginning of the 20th century Paris has been famous for its cultural and artistic communities and its nightlife. Many historical figures located to the city of light in search of inspiration, including Russian composer Stravinsky, American writer Hemingway and Spanish painters Picasso and Dalí.

View of Paris from the top of the Centre Pompidou with the Eiffel Tower a prominent landmark on the city skyline.
Photo Archibald Ballantine

France

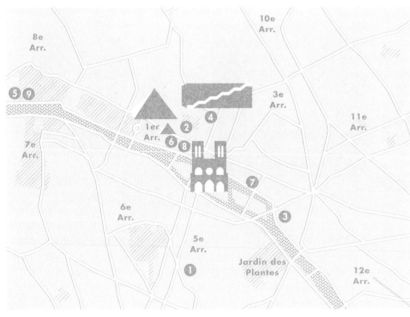

Paris

1 EnsAD
2 Bibliothèque du Musée des Arts Décoratifs
3 Bibliothèque Forney
4 CCI
5 Cité de l'architecture et du patrimoine
6 Librairie Galignani
7 Maison Européenne de la Photographie
8 Musée des Arts Décoratifs
9 Palais de Tokyo

Park

Water

Railway

Main road

City Facts

**ibliothèque du Musée
s Arts Décoratifs** 2
  The library's catalogue contains an
  outstanding collection of works –
  printed volumes, periodicals,
  exhibition catalogues, salon
  catalogues, and sales catalogues – on
  the decorative arts, graphic arts,
  design, architecture, costume and
  fashion, and the history of art.
  lesartsdecoratifs.fr

ibliothèque Forney 3
  The library has a large collection of
  works on art and architecture, with an
  extensive collection of books,
  brochures, posters, catalogues, and
  periodicals on the graphic arts,
  printing, and typography.
  equipement.paris.fr/bibliotheque-forney-18

I 4
  The Centre de Création Industrielle
  (Center for Industrial Design) in the
  Centre Pompidou adopts a
  functionalist and multidisciplinary
  approach: it focuses on new aspects
  of industrial design in industrial
  societies by taking into account
  graphic design, architecture, urban
  planning, industrial design, and
  visual communications.
  centrepompidou.fr

Cité de l'architecture et du patrimoine 5
  The aims of the institution are:
  providing French Architecture with an
  international showcase, promoting the
  knowledge and appreciation of the
  French Heritage, training varied
  public in architecture, providing
  resources to professionals, historians
  and researchers, promoting
  contemporary architectural creation,
  and forming close ties with companies.
  It houses three departments
  (Architecture, Heritage, Training), an
  Archive Center and a library.
  citechaillot.fr

Librairie Galignani 6
  The bookshop stocks Anglo-American
  and French fine art books and has a
  wide selection of architecture and
  decorative arts.
  gakignani.com

Maison Européenne de la Photographie 7
  Its collection includes international
  photographic creations from the
  1950s to contemporary works. It
  presents photography in all its forms:
  reports, fashion photography,
  contemporary documentary practices,
  and works that combine photography
  and the plastic arts.
  mep-fr.org

Musée des Arts Décoratifs 8
  The museum has a large collection of
  textiles that comprises silks,
  embroidery, printed cotton, liturgical
  clothing, lace, and tapestries. These
  collections (costumes, fashion
  accessories, and pieces of textile)
  retrace the history of clothes, the
  development of innovations in textiles,
  and the history of Parisian couturiers.
  lesartsdecoratifs.fr

Palais de Tokyo 9
  The Palais de Tokyo opened in 2002
  and is one of Europe's largest
  contemporary art centres. It promotes
  contemporary creativity – in art,
  design, fashion, video, film, literature
  and dance – and its exhibition
  program focuses on emerging and
  internationally recognised artists.
  palaisdetokyo.com

w to get around
  Roissy-Charles-de-Gaulle airport
  takes the majority of international
  flights to and from Paris, and Orly is
  a host to mostly domestic and
  European airline companies. The
  former airfields of Issy-les-
  Moulineaux have become a heliport
  annex of Paris, and Le Bourget an
  airfield reserved for smaller aircrafts.
  As far as national and European
  destinations are concerned, rail
  transport is beginning to outdistance
  air travel in both travel time and
  efficiency. Amsterdam, London,
  Brussels and Cologne can be
  reached within hours using the

French high-speed TGV rail network
which offers services more than 10
times a day.
A combination of traffic jams and the
lack of parking spaces means that
driving a car in the capital of France
is not a very attractive prospect.
Besides 14 metro lines, 58 bus lines,
5 railway lines, some tramlines and
one funicular (in Montmartre), Paris
offers 20,000 bikes for rent.
In order to reach ENSAD, you can
take metro lines 7 or 10, RER B or bus
lines 21, 27, 47 and 38.

Arranging housing
  Difficult

Housing support by school
  No

Cost of room in the city
  EUR 600 per month

Cost of campus housing
  n/a

Founded in 1961, ELISAVA was the first design school in Spain.

ELISAVA School of Design and Engineering

**ELISAVA Barcelona School
of Design and Engineering**
La Rambla 30-32
08002 Barcelona
Spain

T +34 (0)93 317 4715
elisava@elisava.net
elisava.net

Students can enjoy a vibrant campus in a vibrant city.

Course
Retail Space: Retail Design

School
ELISAVA School of Design and Engineering

'We focus on all necessary skills, ranging from the creative process to the technicalities of project development'

Ramon Benedito Graells, dean

When was the school founded?
Founded in 1961, ELISAVA was the first design school to be established in Spain. Because of this, it has played a decisive role in shaping design culture in Catalonia and in Spain.

What is studying at ELISAVA all about?
Innovation, creativity and technology. For over half a century, these have been the guiding principles for ELISAVA in its domestic and international development, as well as in its relationship with companies and institutions.

What is the strength of this school?
It is a cosmopolitan environment that fosters debate and networking. We cater to new professional profiles where design work is seen as multidisciplinary and cross-functional, anticipating the demands of society and adapting to different environments and projects.

What is the most important aspect of the course for students?
The school develops the course in direct contact with companies and institutions, resulting in more than 100 real-life projects developed annually both domestically and abroad. All programmes are taught by highly qualified working professionals and include in-house internships in companies that facilitate job placement.

What kind of teaching method is important?
Promoting research and innovation is a pivotal element of how we manage our student's talent. True to its roots as a pioneer in teaching design and engineering, ELISAVA's educators focus on all necessary skills, ranging from the creative process to the technical details of project development.

What is expected from the students?
More than 2000 students from around the world come together each year at ELISAVA, people who want to develop their ideas and transform them into reality. They are all committed to our methodology which stresses the importance of interaction between creativity, communication, science, technology, economics, research and social science.

Programme

The MA in Retail Space: Retail Design offers a specialised programme that explores the possibilities of designing for retail interiors.

The course is created for professionals who wish to acquire the specific knowledge required to excel in designing retail spaces – from small boutiques to spaces for huge multinational brands. With a constant emphasis on professionalism, lecturers endeavour to educate students on the broad spectrum of disciplines involved in retail.

Emphasis is placed on the analysis and study of trends and innovation in the market and society, in order to get a close-up view of the elements involved in designing a retail space.

All subjects – including communications, virtual aspects and sensory perceptions – are dealt with in theory and in practice. Students work with renowned companies such as IKEA, Sony and Vinçon on projects worldwide and also participate in international competitions such as the student's competition run by New York Retail Design Institute.

Today, the school has over 2000 students and a faculty of over 700.

Internationally minded: ELISAVA prides itself on its cosmopolitan attitude.

Programme
Retail Space: Retail Design

Leads to
Master of Arts

Structure
The 1-year full-time course is divided into two programmes: 'Design and Space' (shopping) and 'From Concept to Design' (brands). It is a 60-credit course with 30 credits allocated to each programme. The goal is to study and apply – in a practical way – the key elements of design needed for the development of retail. Students present a final project at the end of the year.

Head of programme
Carmen Malvar

Mentors and lecturers
Agustín Cámara, Amaia Celaya, Elisabeth de Morentin, Jordi Ballest Pablo Soto, Tito Perez, Jordi Cano, Enric Jaulent, María Callís, Rut Martín, Iñigo Lanz, Ramón Malvar, Javier Creus, Benjamin Vill Kirsten Van Dam, Jorge Rodríguez and Luki Huber.

Notable alumni
Mariana Recinos, Deyanira Palacio Gisella Stiglich, Cynthia Ratkevicius and Giuseppe Casuccio.

Course
Retail Space: Retail Design

School
ELISAVA School of Design and Engineering

School Facts

Duration of study
1 year

Full time
Yes

Part time
No

Female students
90%

Male students
10%

Local students
20%

Students from abroad
80%

Yearly enrolment
25

Tuition fee
- EUR 10,000 per year for students undertaking the English-taught programme
- EUR 9200 per year for students undertaking the Spanish-taught programme

Funding/scholarships
Yes, financial aid is available.

Minimum requirements for entry
Bachelor's degree or professional experience in a related field including design, fine art, communication, architecture and/or proven professional experience in these subject areas.

Language
English or Spanish

Application procedure
The following documents must be submitted in order to complete the application:
a completed online application form
your portfolio
your curriculum vitae
proof of payment of the EUR 400 application fee.
Successful candidates will be informed by email.

Application details
elisava.net

Application date
Before 8 February for the February edition
Before 2 September for the September edition

Graduation rate
95%

Job placement rate
80%

Memberships/affiliations
None

Collaborations with
IKEA, Vinçon, REC Experimental Stores, Biosca&Botey, Arenas C.C., Gastón y Daniela, Sony, Beiñ, Kiehl's and Retail Design Institute.

Facilities for students
Workshop, library, exhibition room, photography studio and black-and-white darkrooms.

City
Barcelona

Country
Spain

Student Work

All Animals are Equal, but Some Animals are More Equal than Others (2014)
By Ali Mahmoud, Isabelle Whiteley, Tatiana Smotrova and Xiang Li

Using the line from George Orwell's *Animal Farm* as a starting point, the students created a window display for Vinçon encompassing four figures – pigs standing on their hind legs – brandishing knives at a ham. The lighting and simple use of props brings the fable to life, captures the imagination of passers-by and showcases Vinçon's products. Photos courtesy of ELISAVA

The MotorCIRCLE in the City (20
By Vanya Suleva, Patricia Bernardino, Vicky Ballesteros and Nuria Martínez

With interactivity becoming ever-popular in the display of goods, students created one such installation for Biosca&Botey to exhibit 16 motorcycles. The innovative solution is inspired by optical illusion games encouragi visitors to engage with the space. Photo Hector H

All Kinds of Crazy (2014)
By Laura Aguilar Carvajal, Isabel Garnier, Lara Kardas and Adrian López

Taking inspiration from Vinçon's motto 'Crazy sin 1941', students created a window display that plays with dark humour. By subtly presenting the emotions associated with mental illnesses, the display encourages viewers to create their own story from the concept presented before them. Photo courtesy of ELISAVA

Course
Retail Space: Retail Design

School
ELISAVA School of Design and Engineering

360º Arenas Food Experience (2013)
By Margarita Delgado, Sebastian Pardo, Andres Cabrera and José Manuel Matallana

The pop-up installation created for Arenas uses food, not only to tantalise the taste buds but also to present a strong visual element. The installation was aimed at making the restaurant's customers more aware of the food-making process. Photo courtesy of ELISAVA

Sweet Spring (2014)
By María Camila Casas, Juliana Maretzki Haagensen, Sonia Oliva, Ana Cristina Serrano and Jessica Teló

Tasked with creating a window display for Sony, students came up with a candy-inspired theme to celebrate the spring season. Sony products sit on the stick of a giant lollypop – created by local outfit Papabubble – providing a focal point for the entire display. Reflecting the brand's links to technology, the students invited viewers to take photos and share online via a dedicated hashtag. Photo courtesy of ELISAVA

Beiñ Pop-Up Store (2013)
By Tali Oren, Francisco Ramón, Jessica Teló and Rut Martin

Spanish tailoring and craftsmanship formed the basis for the display featured in Beiñ's pop-up store at the corner of the Roger Smith Hotel in New York. Students promoted Spanish brands and designers through a thread installation that focused on deconstructing fabrics. Photo Tatiana Marín

City
Barcelona

Country
Spain

Alumna

Name Laura Aguilar Carvajal
Residence San Jose, Costa Rica
Year of birth 1987
Year of graduation 2014
Current job Freelancer
Website milibretazen.blogspot.com

Why did you choose this school?
I previously studied fashion design and worked as a visual merchandiser, so I wanted an MA that would support and strengthen my work experience. I focused on schools in Europe, but very few specialised in the field I wanted to explore. I chose ELISAVA after it was highly recommended to me by an established designer. Another deciding factor was the fact that the programme is so well considered and covers many key areas for me.

What was the most important thing you learned here?
The importance of teamwork. In the real world, it is rare that people work entirely alone. The professional world is very competitive and learning to work as part of a team is vital.

What was the most interesting project you did?
There were several, but one of the most fun and interesting for me was one developed for Sony. We had to design a campaign based on three fundamental elements: window display, customer experience and social networking. In addition to these, we proposed a performance in the public space following the campaign, in order to create more of a hype around the brand. It was interesting and fun because our team experimented with new techniques to capture the idea we wanted to portray.

We went beyond what the client requested but more importantly, enjoyed every sleepless night!

Was there any class you found particularly interesting?
Travel retail. These classes were very specific and, therefore, very interesting because it wa a completely new market for me, and now I understand the potential of a business model such as this.

Was the transformation from graduation to working life a smooth one?
I think there are different phases. I consider th working life much more demanding as it involves more responsibility, however, it's very exciting when concepts become reality.

Any words of advice for future students?
Always go further than required by the customer.

Invisible Heartbeat was a group project that Carvajal worked for a pop-up store in Barcelona during her time at ELISAVA.

Course
Retail Space: Retail Design

School
ELISAVA School of Design and Engineering

'Every day I discover new places in Barcelona. I like to walk in El Barrio Gotico, El Raval or El Born. Each area has a variety of restaurants, bars and unique shops.'
María Camila Casas

fter graduating, I know I will ave a rich understanding retail design and be epared to work in the best d most demanding mpanies in the market.'
Carla León Tarrillo

'Students get a good understanding of retail spaces and strategies which allows them to use design to provoke and stimulate buying decisions.'
Ali Mahmoud

'It's a major plus to learn about retail in a city as well known for its architecture and design as Barcelona.'
Lara Kardas

'I get around the city by motorbike, but public transport and bicycles are also a good option. Barcelona has a good balance, it's neither too big nor too small.'
Yasmina Moukhmalji Garcia

City Life

Barcelona is a cosmopolitan and open city offering its residents a high quality of life. This is one of the most attractive European cities to live in with excellent educational, cultural and leisure facilities its safety, efficient transport and health services, beautiful climate and natural attractions inviting people to enjoy the sea and mountain year-round. Barcelona is also known as a city that lives and breathes design. Design permeates the entire urban fabric, which is dotted with museums, art galleries, exhibition halls and showrooms, as well as restaurants, bookstores and establishments of all kinds which express their unique identity through their own furniture, lighting, commercial signs, etc. It is a real magnet for creative and designers from around the world. They are attracted by the city's display of latest trends and they know that the ecosystem surrounding them is also conduciv to nurturing their creativity. All this makes Barcelona one of the best European destinations for design students. In fact, twelve percent of college students in the city come from abroad to this Mediterranean spo Barcelona leads the quality of life ranking in Spain and is close to the top overall Europea ranking. The city blends together the artistic legacy of over two millennia with avant-gare architecture. Nowadays, Barcelon is a landmark in the world of fashion, art, design and new technologies.

Spain

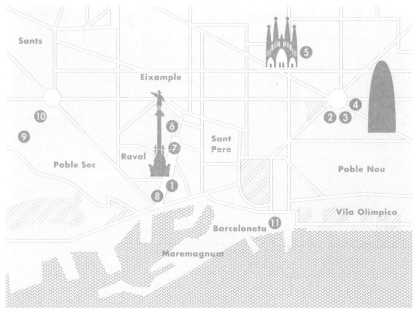

Barcelona is a cosmopolitan and open city offering its residents a high quality of life.
Photo Turisme de Barcelona / Espai d'imatge

Barcelona

1 ELISAVA
2 DHUB Barcelona
3 Barcelona Design Week
4 Agbar Tower
5 La Sagrada Família
6 CCCB
7 La Rambla
8 Arts Santa Mònica
9 Sónar Festival
10 Mies van der Rohe Pavil
11 Barcelona Beaches

Park

Water

Main road

Course
Retail Space: Retail Design

School
ELISAVA School of Design and Engineering

HUB Barcelona ②
The Disseny Hub Barcelona will be the reference space for design in Barcelona and the future site of the city's main design institutions. The DHUB includes collections of historical and contemporary decorative arts, ceramics, industrial design, textiles, clothing and graphic arts.
dhub-bcn.cat/en

rcelona Design Week ③
This international event focuses on design, innovation and business addressed to those companies and professionals in any industry or productive services that use knowledge and creativity as a driver of its business activity.
barcelonadesignweek.com

bar Tower ④
Jean Nouvel's majestic Agbar Tower has stood in the Plaça de les Glòries since 2003. Its modern, louvered facade contrasts with the old flour mill, the Farinera del Clot, and the Mercat de Bellcaire, the city's flea market.
torreagbar.com

La Sagrada Família ⑤
The expiatory church is in the centre of Barcelona and over the years it has become one of the most universal signs of identity of the city and the country.
sagradafamilia.cat

Centre de Cultura Contemporània de Barcelona ⑥
The CCCB organises and produces exhibitions, debates, festivals and concerts, programmes film cycles, courses and lectures, and encourages creation using new technologies.
cccb.org

La Rambla ⑦
Barcelona wouldn't be Barcelona without La Rambla. As you walk along, you'll see landmark buildings, such as the greatest theatre of Barcelona's opera, the Gran Teatre del Liceu, the Palau de la Virreina and the spectacular Boqueria Market.
laramblabcn.com

Arts Santa Mònica ⑧
Arts Santa Mònica generates ideas, projects, research and materials that stimulate the dialogue between the local, and all it has to offer, and the global dimension of current society.
artssantamonica.cat

Sónar Festival ⑨
Sónar is the International Festival of Advanced Music and New Media Art taking place in Barcelona for 3 days every June.
sonar.es/ca

Mies van der Rohe Pavilion ⑩
Built from glass, steel and different kinds of marble, the pavilion was conceived to accommodate the official reception presided over by King Alphonso XIII of Spain along with the German authorities.
miesbcn.com

Barcelona Beaches ⑪
All Barcelonan beaches are well communicated, maintained and equipped with all the services. By proximity, the most popular ones are those of Barceloneta, Sant Miquel and Sant Sebastià.
barcelonaturisme.com

w to get around
Barcelona and its metropolitan area have many options of public transport that allow reaching every spot in the city in an easy and comfortable way. Six lines of underground with a running frequency of between 2 and 3 minutes, an urban network of trains, a modern tram, more than a 1000 buses and a simple, practical and sustainable urban transport system based on the shared use of the bicycle, the Bicing.

Barcelona airport gets direct flights from the most important Spanish, European and world cities. Barcelona is also connected with Madrid by means of the AVE (high-speed train), apart from having other long-distance trains that connect it with other important cities of the country.

Arranging housing
Never a problem

Housing support by school
Yes

Cost of room in the city
Between EUR 300 and EUR 475 per month

Cost of campus housing
n/a

City
Barcelona

Country
Spain

The good weather in Porto allows for events and receptions to be held the school grounds.

Escola Superior de Artes e Design

Escola Superior de Artes e Design
Av. Calouste Gulbenkian
4460-268 Senhora da Hora
Matosinhos
Portugal

T +351 229 578 750
info@esad.pt
esad.pt

The school hall with student work on show during the ESAD Interiors Week ev

Course
Interior Design

School
Escola Superior de Artes e Design

'One of the main aims of the course is to support a strong practice that takes into consideration the demands of the user'

Maria Millano, head of programme

What is studying at this school all about?
ESAD was founded in 1989. The interior design course started in 2006, and in 2009, with the implementation of the Bologna system, it expanded and gained international reputation.
One of the main aims of the course is to support a strong practice that takes into consideration the demands of the user. It focuses on a critical interpretation of the brief, considering both functionality and poetry and expression with reflecting on the relationship between individual and space. The student is encouraged to understand space as a place for activating a progressive process of identification.

What kind of teaching method is applied?
Projects are developed through a gradual process of construction. Thus, student projects emerge as whole with a coherent relation between form and structure. Throughout the year students engage in project discussions, within an open class environment, where they meet with guest lecturers and renowned national and international professionals.

Why should students choose ESAD?
The course constantly stimulates a critical perspective which is grounded in pragmatism. This approach enhances creativity and experimentation within the process of developing a technical and constructive consciousness

of the brief. The partnerships with businesses ensure traineeships and allow the students to enter the marketplace with a privileged position. Interior design has specificities that are necessary for different situations from commercial spaces, to stands, exhibitions, workplaces, accommodation and furniture.

What is expected from the students?
We expect our students to be enthusiastic and dedicated, and be aware that projecting is a self-nurturing process that is progressively built. We expect them to be able to think critically, but also to make, searching for maximum reintegration, in the project process, between hand and mind.

What is the most important skill to master when one wants to become an interior designer?
Interior design is a multidisciplinary course. For a student to be an exceptional professional he or she needs to be receptive to stimuli outside the project that can emerge from art and other forms of culture, contemporary society, and other sources.

Where or in what kind of jobs do your former interior design students mostly end up?
Most graduates create their own practices, however some are employed in furniture and interior project stores while others are integrated in architecture studios and in multidisciplinary project teams.

Programme

Interior design is a multidisciplinary field that uses skills from architecture, design, communication and art. The MA course integrates these skills in a set of projects and experiments engaging the students in the rehabilitation of existing buildings and interiors and furniture projects. The teaching philosophy stimulates the students to respect pre-existence. Within project development, it is necessary to understand the past as a resource, instead of as an obstacle to the actualisation of the functions of contemporary living. The project of the pre-existing is a project of coexistence, integration and overlays, which creates a habitat filled with meaning, looking for a personal and critical strategy of intervention and project, developed from the analysis of its spatial,

structural and public/private dimensions. A unique characteristic of the course is solid project training – history and technical and construction based – and a close relationship between lecturers and students which results in a programme adjusted to an individual group of students each year. Partnerships with businesses assure traineeships to the top students every year.

The school lobby during ESAD's Interiors Week, featuring an exhibition of student work in interior

ESAD and Câmara Municipal de Matosinhos invited the architects Rintala e Eggertsson, Mestriner and Spadoni to participate in the Viewport workshop, a project to create a sustainable wine bar and lounge area.

Programme
Interior Design

Leads to
Master of Arts

Structure
The 2-year full-time course is divided into modules. The first year features an interior project, laboratory of interior design, interior construction techniques, advanced virtual models and contextual studies. In the second year, students develop their major project proposal in the form of either an internship report, a written dissertation, or a practical project. The course timetable allows students to work and study independently outside of class hours. In the first year, there are 20 contact hours per week and in the second year, there are 12 contact hours in first semeste

Head of programme
Joana Santos

Mentors and lecturers
Maria Milano, João Gomes, Marta Cruz, and Rui Canela. Guest professors are Paolo Deganello, Jos António Teixeira, José Gigante, Arquitetos Anónimos among others.

Notable alumni
Mónica Couto, Filipa Freitas, Raquel Machado, Leonor Magalhãe and Francesca Vita.

Course
Interior Design

School
Escola Superior de Artes e Design

School Facts

Duration of study
2 years

Full time
Yes

Part time
No

Female students
85%

Male students
15%

Local students
90%

Students from abroad
10%

Yearly enrolment
24

Tuition fee
EUR 3795 per year plus
EUR 700 administration fees

Funding/scholarships
Yes, one school-awarded grant of
50% of costs for each year based on
best portfolio and qualifications.

Minimum requirements for entry
Bachelor (honours) degree

Language
Portuguese and English

Application procedure
Apply online with the following:
completed application form
a copy of your passport
a copy of your certificates of
academic qualification
your curriculum vitae
a digital portfolio with examples
of recent work.
There is an application fee of
EUR 170.

Application details
me.esad.pt/en/candidaturas

Application date
Before 28 August

Graduation rate
90%

Job placement rate
85%

Memberships/affiliations
Cumulus, RARimobiliária and
Câmara Municipal Matosinho.

Collaborations with
Many educational collaborations
including 37 art and design colleges
in 27 countries.

Facilities for students
Auditorium, canteen, audiovisual
studio, library, materials shop,
screen-printing studio, 3D workshop,
life-drawing studio, jewelry
workshop and exhibition gallery.

Student Work

Designer Residence (2013)
By Joana Rosa

Farmville (2013)
By Teresa Cabral

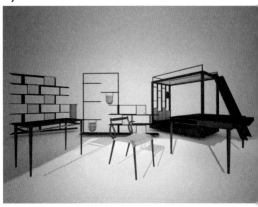

The project Farmville was based on the concept of an artistic and creative living space for designers – an idea which started with the making of a chair using the concept of origami and light and clean straight lines. The objective was to create a space with the furniture. The final result was an apartment with a comfortable and relaxed space that stimulates the creativity of the user.

A playful but functional space for artists, designed according the needs of the user, comprising workspace, dining and recreation areas and bedroom. The furniture design uses the concept of mes that is shaped by the body and objects to create a comfortable environment promoting creativity.

Duets: an Idea for The World in a Chair (2012)
By Mónica Couto

Part of an international event (Art on Chairs), this exhibition included eleven chairs which were the result of 'duets' between a designer and an internationally renowned individual. The installation attempted to communicate a poetic narrative in the 3D space, with the purpose of transmitting emotions and values.

Course
Interior Design

School
Escola Superior de Artes e Design

fanor (2013)
y Sílvia Rolla

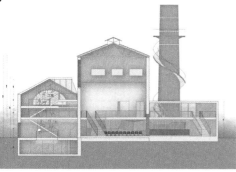

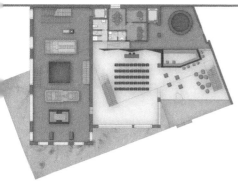

old textile factory is converted into a museum and a space
temporary exhibitions. A new building is added to the old
e and rotated to create connections between old and new
ace. The new plan cuts the interior space in two and creates
w observations points.

pider Chair (2013)
y Catarina Ramada

The Spider Chair is an upgrading project born from an old armchair.
The main problem to be solved was the instability of the base and a
broken hydraulic system. The base was upgraded, keeping the seat.
The result reveals the organic forms of an arachnid.

Viral Architecture as a Rehabilitation Method of the City (2013)
By Ana Rita Ramos

Eight abandoned houses are repurposed in an unconventional
way. They are cut, filled and crafted, and volumes and paths
inserted and shaped as (internal and external) parasites, pasting
new material layers and enhancing the temporal contrasts, in
order to reformulate the houses for a new functional programme.

Path as Sensorial Experience (2013)
By Alexandrine Costa

This project deals with the rehabilitation and conversion of an
old industrial slaughterhouse in Porto into a cultural and
performance complex. A narrative path was devised to lead
the user through the space. The creation of an element of
distribution and connection — with paths on higher and ground
levels — allows a rich sensory experience.

Alumna

Name Francesca Vita
Residence Bologna, Italy
Year of birth 1988
Year of graduation 2013
Current job Trainee interior designer at Poligono, Lisbon

Why did you choose this school?
After my first degree at the Politecnico of Milano, I was looking for a place to regenerate myself, to restore my energies, to refresh my mind, to look at design and its potential from a different perspective – and I found all that in Portugal and ESAD.

What was the most important thing you learned here?
I improved my skills in technical drawing, I could follow entire projects from their conceptualisation to their execution, and I really felt part of an architectural culture. But ESAD gave me much more than academic knowledge. It gave me a place where I felt safe to express myself and to experiment with unconventional ways of designing.

What was the most fun project you did?
I really enjoyed working on my first year project, which dealt with the renovation of a typical city centre Porto building. We were supposed to make a renovation project combining living and working spaces concerning a hypothetical customer. The project started with a visit of this very old and dusty house, which was amazing! We did a metric survey and passed the results to Autocad. Then every student had to choose a hypothetical client – I chose a group of four Amish friends who had to spend some years in Porto. This project gave me the opportunity to work with recycled materials, and when I completed the bathroom floor using traditional Portuguese tiles I realised that second-hand materials have great qualities that need to be rediscovered.

Were there any classes you found particularly difficult?
The most difficult class was Constructive Technique for Interior Design. In Milan we didn't do a lot of technical drawings, while in ESAD we did plenty on the 1:20 to 1:5 scale.

What was your graduation project?
At the end of the first year, I realised that my knowledge of Portuguese architectural history was still poor. So I decided to deal with the language and with the history of architecture. I developed a Portuguese-written theoretical dissertation about the need for a relationship between architecture, interior design and scenography. It started from a case study of Joõ Mendes Ribeiro, a Portuguese contemporary architect and scenographer. His interior renovation projects are a great example of thinking of interiors in a flexible and temporary way; he looks at how people experience a space instead only at the space itself.

Any words of advice for future students?
Always be excited by everything – because if someone sees your passion this leads to more exciting things.

Francesca Vita's 4Years House project looked at reusing a space and materials for a fictional client. It featured a bathroom floor of recycled Portuguese tiles.

Course
Interior Design

School
Escola Superior de Artes e Design

'I was pleasantly surprised at how many workshops the school offers. I particularly enjoyed the one on furniture design, tutored by Paolo Deganello, the famous Italian architect.'
Angie Krebs

t the moment, I'm finishing my esis and I'm already missing the ace and the work of the last months – 's addictive! The more we work, 1e more we can see the results and ratch ourselves blossoming as lesigners.'
Ana Rita Ramos

'I think that the Project Class was the most valuable one, because it didn't allow us to work alone – it forced us to brainstorm, to show others what we were doing and vice versa.'
Joana Xavier

'The location of ESAD is incredible! Matosinhos is just 15 minutes from beautiful Porto. It has the ocean, the beach, lots of esplanades and a design gallery associated with ESAD. In Porto, I love the area of Rua Miguel Bombarda – the artistic neighbourhood.'
Alexandrine Costa

'Public transport is excellent here in Porto. It is really comfortable and fast, and delays are unusual, so it's easy to get around.'
Raquel Fonseca

City Life

Porto is the second largest city in Portugal. Located along the Douro river estuary in the north of the country, it was recognised as a World Heritage Site by UNESCO in 1996. But Porto is not just full of historical buildings. The Porto school of architecture is world famous and the city boasts some of the most-visited examples of contemporary European architecture – among others by three Pritzker prize winners: Álvaro Siza Vieira, Eduardo Souto de Moura and Rem Koolhaas.

Porto offers a variety of green spaces, from the Crystal Palace high over the Douro river and the nearby Botanic gardens, to the Serralves Museum of Contemporary Art park and gardens. The city park, covering an area of 205 acres and the largest urban park in Portugal, deserves a special mention.

If it's beaches you want, then Porto and adjoining districts have plenty to offer, even more so if you want to join the vibrant local surfing community.

Portugal

Porto is stunningly located along the Douro river estuary in the north of Portugal and is one of Europe's oldest cities.

Porto

1 ESAD
2 Serralves Museum of Contemporary Art
3 Lello bookshop
4 Casa da Música
5 Mercado do Bolhão

Park

Water

Railway

Main road

Course
Interior Design

School
Escola Superior de Artes e Design

rralves Museum of ntemporary Art ②

Serralves Museum opened in 1999 in order to endow Porto with a space dedicated to contemporary art. The museum's core objectives are the constitution of a representative collection of Portuguese and international contemporary art.
serralves.pt

lo Bookshop ③

Along with Bertrand in Lisbon, this is one of the oldest bookstores in Portugal. In 2011, Lello was classified as the third best bookstore in the world.

sa da Música ④

This major concert hall space, in which houses the cultural institution of the same name with its three orchestras, was built as part of Porto's project for European Culture Capital in 2001.
casadamusica.com

rcado do Bolhão ⑤

Just east of Aliados lies the 19th century, wrought-iron Mercado do Bolhão, where earthy vendors sell fresh produce, including cheeses, olives, smoked meats, fresh flowers and more.

Fantasporto Film Festival

Giving screen space to fantasy/ science fiction/horror-oriented commercial feature films, auteur films and experimental projects from all over the world, Fantasporto has created enthusiastic audiences, ranging from cinephiles to more popular spectators.
fantasporto.pt

Sé

From Praça da Ribeira rises a tangle of medieval alleys and stairways that eventually reach the hulking, hilltop fortress of the Sé. Inside, a rose window and a 14th century Gothic cloister remain from its early days.

Cc Bombarda

Inside this shopping gallery, you'll find stores selling locally designed urban wear, bonsai trees, stylish home knick-knacks, Portuguese indie rock and other hipster-pleasing delights. There's a shop (Frida) where you can order a doll made to your own likeness and a cafe (Pimenta Rosa) serving light fare on an inner courtyard.

Gardens of the Crystal Palace

Sitting atop bluffs just west of Porto's old centre, the leafy Jardim do Palácio de Cristal is home to a domed sports pavilion, the hi-tech Biblioteca Municipal Almeida Garrett and pleasant tree-lined footpaths with fantastic river views.
goporto.com

Vila Nova de Gaia

Vila Nova de Gaia is a coastal town and municipality in the Portuguese district of Porto. The city is located opposite Porto, on the south bank of the Douro, and is the centre of all Port wines.

Ponte de Dom Luís I

Completed in 1886 by a student of Gustave Eiffel, the double-decker bridge's top deck is reserved for pedestrians, the lower deck bears regular traffic. Both afford wonderful views.

w to get around

Porto is served by Francisco Sá Carneiro Airport which is located in Pedras Rubras, Moreira civil parish of neighbouring Municipality of Maia, approximately 15 km to the north-west of the city centre. Porto's main railway station is situated in Campanhã, located in the eastern part of the city. From here, both light rail and suburban rail services connect to the city centre. The main central station is São Bento Station, which is itself a notable landmark located in the centre of

Porto. A tram network, of which only four lines remain, one of them being a tourist line on the shores of the Douro, saw its construction begin in September 1895, and was therefore the first in the Iberian Peninsula. The lines in operation today all use vintage tramcars, so the service has become a heritage tramway. The easiest way from the city centre to ESAD is by underground, using the blue line (A) with the direction Senhor de Matosinhos, to the stop Estádio do Mar.

Arranging housing

Never a problem

Housing support by school

No

Cost of room in the city

Between EUR 150 and EUR 200 per month

Cost of campus housing

n/a

Charles Rennie Mackintosh's 1909
Glasgow School of Art facade,
left, is in striking contrast to
Steven Holl's new Reid Building,
with its greenish glass facade.

Glasgow
School of Art

A 'Circuit of Connection' runs throughout the new Reid Building and encourages the 'creat
abrasion' across and between departments that is central to the workings of the school.

Glasgow School of Art (GSA)
167 Renfrew Street
Glasgow G3 6RQ
United Kingdom

T +44 (0)141 353 4500
info@gsa.ac.uk
gsa.ac.uk

Course
Interior Design

School
Glasgow School of Art

'Our students learn how to advocate for the central role of interior design in the consideration of urban development'

Patrick Macklin, head of department

What is studying at this school all about?

Glasgow School of Art fosters the conditions for creativity in order to promote critical thinking, experimentation, discovery and innovation. Proudly independent and outward-looking, we continuously extend the boundaries of our knowledge, geographic reach and impact through collaboration and partnership locally, nationally and internationally. We are socially and environmentally responsible in our organisational culture and academic provision. We seek to be exceptional but not exclusive, aspirational but accessible.

What kind of teaching method is applied here?

Our distinctive pedagogy and research promote studio culture as the basis for creative communities, the meeting ground for diversity of opinion, independence of thought, and learning from each other.

Why should students choose this particular school?

GSA has an intimate campus set in a compact university city. This is of great value, enabling inter-departmental, cross-school and trans-institutional conversation. The physical proximity of its faculty buildings provides direct opportunities for collaboration, widened intellectual stimulation and critical reflection across a diversity of creative practices.

What is expected from the students?

Students are expected to reappraise their relationship to the discipline of interior design with a view to extending their practice. From this fresh perspective they are challenged to be critical, creative and constructive in their approaches to placemaking.

When did you start offering this course?

Academic year 2011/12.

What is the most important thing for students to learn during this course?

Students learn how to advocate for the central role of interior design in the consideration of urban development. From this subject-centred position, they may embark on the journey to becoming advanced practitioners who can confidently bridge the chasm between current expectations, into nascent and uncharted areas for this particular field of design.

What is the most important skill to master for an interior designer?

How to promote more diverse approaches to the way we think about using space, and how to turn those approaches into reality.

What kind of jobs do your former interior design students mostly go on to do?

Of the two cohorts who have completed the programme, most are working in interior design, or in academia. Some have remained in the UK, others are working further afield including in India, China the USA and the Middle East.

City
Glasgow

Country
United Kingdom

Programme

The programme aims to explore both the existing territory and the hinterland of the discipline. It ventures to ask why interiors are produced, rather than how. It encourages reflective and analytical approaches to subject-centred themes grouped around the core areas of context and speculation, and draws from diverse fields of enquiry and practice. From this position, the programme's main areas of focus have been on matters such as the future of the High Street; place and memory, archaeologies of the recent past; materials of persuasion; augmented shopping and tele-presence; technologies, dislocation and utopias; the psychology of enclosure; hard and soft/analogue and digital representations of constructed space. Future excursions will be made into areas such as four dimensional design-interiors, cinema, theatre; and bricks and pixels: materiality and the representation of the unseen.

The school was established in the city during its most intense period of industrialisation and rapid expansion – followed by its subsequent economic and social convulsions. Glasgow contains examples of both visionary creations and failed utopias. It is the major UK retail centre outside London, with significant residual undeveloped building stock, and specific types of housing and healthcare challenges

As a post-industrial city, it has an educationally stimulating type of urban layering exhibiting traces of the medieval, an abundance of the Victorian and fragments of the modernist, sometimes simultaneously. These factors combine to feed course content providing a live laboratory for investigation and testing new ideas and observing the consequences of older ones.

The light-filled interior design studio in the Reid Building.

Programme
Interior Design

Leads to
Master of Design in Interior Design

Structure
The 1-year course is structured into three stages. Stage 1 leads towards a Postgraduate Certificate (60 credits). Stage 2 leads towards a Postgraduate Diploma (120 credits). These two stages are project-based and primarily explore site contingency and the importance of place. The third stage leads towards the Master of Design (180 credits) and is a self-directed research project.

Head of programme
Patrick Macklin

Mentors and lecturers
Pamela Flanagan

Course
Interior Design

School
Glasgow School of Art

School Facts

Duration of study
1 year

Full time
Yes

Part time
Yes (hours per week negotiated within credit guidelines)

Female students
90%

Male students
10%

Local students
5%

Students from abroad
95%

Yearly enrolment
18–20

Tuition fee
- GBP 5580 per year for EU students (approx. EUR 6991)
- GBP 13,140 per year for non-EU students (approx. EUR 16,464)

Funding/scholarships
Yes

Minimum requirements for entry
Bachelor (honours) degree in a relevant subject area or professional experience and proficiency in English.

Language
English

Application procedure
The following documents must be submitted in order to complete the application:
completed application form
statement of intent
evidence of academic qualifications (certified photocopies/transcripts)
academic references (two)
evidence of English language proficiency e.g. IELTS (if appropriate)
copy of passport
portfolio (submitted electronically).

Application details
gsa.ac.uk/study/graduate-degrees/how-to-apply

Application date
Before 31 July for Visa purposes

Graduation rate
100%

Job placement rate
High

Memberships/affiliations
The Department of Interior Design at GSA is one of the founder members of Interior Educators (IE)

Collaborations with
Visit idgsa.co.uk for details

Facilities for students
3D Making Workshops (incl. wood, metal, casting and plastics workshops, 3D printing and laser cutting), Media Studio (digital audio, film, photography and image processing as well as more experimental sensor-based work), facilities in Fashion & Textiles, Printmaking, Photography (analogue and digital including photography studio) and Digital Media.

Student Work

Changing Habits, Changing Boundaries (2012)
By Katerina Antonopoulou

Boundaries are strongly linked with habits, since we learn how to identify and behave around them from an early age. In order to change a habit you have to change the routine but keep the old cue and the old reward, likewise in order to change a boundary you have to reverse its previous use or position but the reward and the cue will remain the same. Throughout the research, collages and photomontages illustrate specific elements; a phrase or a statement is translated into an image and together they develop an idea, a statement or a thought or a memory.

A Bizarre World (2013)
By Marianna Kapsimali

Temporary accommodation that aims to create the conditions of a small 'oasis' in a controlled and tedious future city. Unpredictable situations, inside the rotunda, will remind inhabitants of scenes from home or holidays, creating an intimate, lazy, relaxing and unexpected space.

Visualisation of New Spaces (2011)
By Eleanna Koumarianou

This work is based on visualisation and creation of new spaces – giving new life to spaces that are neglected, unknown, unused, or places of no meaning.

Independent Building (2013)
By Claire Sheffield

Through the analysis of the site, the user and various design theories, this accommodation explores the concept of layers and of interior spaces originating from somewhere between the body and clothing.

Course
Interior Design

School
Glasgow School of Art

emporary Accommodation (2013)
y Konstantina Tsirogianni

Seating with Curtain (2012)
By Eva Grochová

e building is explored as a space for a temporary
perience and accommodation for global nomads. Within the
ace, projected images and visuals imitate the materials of
e skinless surfaces. The surfaces themselves take on the
aracteristics of the images, while light becomes the means of
rceiving this fluctuating environment.

Seating with translucent curtains was proposed for the central
courtyard of a Victorian, A-listed, former fish market located
in Glasgow. Its monumental volume with a glazed roof is
subject to rapid temperature variations. In acknowledgement
of this, each seating area has independent climate control.

Rehearsal Space (2013)
By Andriana Themeli

e cylindrical form of a 1890s building shapes a rehearsal and accommodation space for actors and dancers. The distinctions between
vate and public space are blurred. The multiplicity of the views cancels all the boundaries. A performance stage stands at the core of the
posal while prismatic volumes, resembling the folded human body, constitute the background stage element.

City
Glasgow

Country
United Kingdom

101

Alumna

For her graduation project, Thomai Pnevmonidou created 'The Chamber of Wishes,' a structure built from 13 conceptual stories based on memories.

Name Thomai Pnevmonidou
Residence Glasgow, United Kingdom
Year of birth 1987
Year of graduation 2013
Current job Visiting lecturer at
the Glasgow School of Art

Why did you choose this school?
I had this insightful thought – a vision – that it would be an artsy experience and I went for it. My aim was to choose a school that would allow me to enjoy knowledge without competing with other people; a school that would offer me an experience that could lead me to a deeper understanding of my conceptual concerns.

What was the most important thing you learned here?
That art school is much more than education. I had the opportunity to express myself creatively – which is almost overwhelming – and convey ideas or even emotions on some projects that helped me broaden my horizon and, at the same time, become confident.

Was there any class you found particularly difficult?
Initially, I felt completely overwhelmed because of my language skills and everything seemed to be more difficult. Thus, I had to try a new approach; Instead of just getting worried about this, I had to convey carefully my thoughts developing a visual language, in a way that can be read by every viewer of my work. In doing so, I must say that I truly enjoyed all the classes (both studio projects and electives).

What was your graduation project?
It was called The Chamber of Wishes and it was an effort to describe the personal experience of space as a process of human consciousness perceived through my interpersonal relationships – memories and spatial experiences – rather than a series of physical spaces. An exploration of different worlds consisting of my past experiences with people from the academic environment, represented by spaces that live through 13 stories, which are linked in a range of literature, friendship, and movies.

What was your favourite place to hang out?
The 78 in Finnieston in the West End of Glasgow. It is a great spot with a comfortable and cosy interior that also promotes live music performances and events with different kind of music during the week.

Was the transformation from graduation to working life a smooth one?
In my case, it was very smooth indeed. After graduating from school, I had the opportunity to remain in Glasgow and work as a visiting lecturer within the Interior Design department.

If you were to do the course again, what would you do differently?
I wouldn't change any of my design processes because for that specific time period each strategy was mainly driven by personal needs for expression and personal thoughts. Every context has a story.

Course
Interior Design

School
Glasgow School of Art

'A really interesting elective course that I chose, called Analysis and Self-Analysis, helped me to understand and analyse how people act and perceive space based on the unconscious. This has influenced the way I design.'
Marianna Kapsimali

'What is really important for me is to be free to do things the way I imagine them. This school offers me that freedom. The tutors are about raising questions rather than giving answers. So as a student you make your own decisions and at the end of the day each project is unique and personal.'
Andriana Themeli

'I wanted to find my identity in design and wanted to do something different in order to express myself.'
Min Seok Seo

'You can expect an inspiring environment here which encourages you to explore the interior design challenges more deeply, and gives you the freedom to express your creativity.'
Konstantina Tsirogianni

'Glasgow is an incredible city, with such a large variety of things to do and enjoy, ranging from art galleries to the beautiful diversity of the West End. The quirky bars on Bath Street are superb.'
Claire Sheffield

City Life

Glasgow School of Art is at the heart of one of the most important cultural cities in Europe, with a wealth of heritage and contemporary happenings. Glasgow has a rich architectural legacy and was home to Scotland's best-known architect, Charles Rennie Mackintosh, GSA alumnus and designer of the famous Mack Building. The city's architecture ranges from grand Victorian tenements that line the city streets, to contemporary structures such as Zaha Hadid's breathtaking design for the Riverside Museum and the GSA's own Steven Holl Architects' designed Reid Building.

Artist-run spaces such as Transmission and The Duchy are located a short walk away from larger galleries such as Tramway and the Gallery of Modern Art, with a multitude of public and temporary artworks to see along the way. Spaces such as SWG3, CCA and the Glue Factory are one-stop destinations for design pop-up shops and exhibitions, gigs, fashion shows, club nights, performances and film screenings.

The vibrant and inclusive spirit of Glasgow creative scene is also present in the design sector. In the city's studios, boutique agencies rub shoulders with international design successes; GSA alumni such as high-end interiors giants Timorous Beasties and fashion superstar Jonathan Saunders have helped place Glasgow on the international style map.

Glasgow is home to Scotland's principal contemporary art gallery, the Gallery of Modern Art, which is housed a grand neoclassical building in Royal Exchange Square

United Kingdom

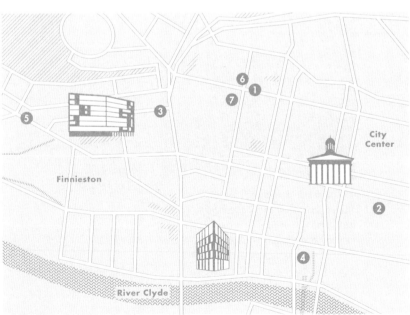

Finnieston

City Center

River Clyde

Glasgow

1 GSA
2 GoMA
3 Mitchell Library
4 The Arches
5 Crabbshakk
6 The Art School
7 Centre for Contemporary Arts

 Park

 Water

Railway

Main road

Course
Interior Design

School
Glasgow School of Art

City Facts

oMA (2)
Scotland's most visited contemporary art gallery, the Gallery of Modern Art, hosts a lively exhibition programme devoted to international artists.
glasgowlife.org.uk

itchell Library (3)
Europe's largest public reference library with over 1 million items in stock in an iconic green-domed 1911 building.
glasgowlife.org.uk

e Arches (4)
Underground (literally) club and arts venue housed in the city's old railway arches, also hosts pop ups and installations, events and concerts.
thearches.co.uk

Riverside Museum
Zaha Hadid's zinc-clad, five-pointed roof lures visitors to the engaging displays of the transport museum.
glasgowlife.org.uk

Tramway
Tramway plays host to art, design, music and dance performances, is a place for coffee and enjoying its Hidden Gardens in the heart of the south side of Glasgow
tramway.org

Crabbshakk (5)
This Argyle Street eatery is one of Glasgow's many fine independent restaurants in the up-and-coming Finnieston area. It's run (and the interior was designed by) architecture alumnus John MacLeod.
crabshakk.com

The Art School (6)
The GSA's legendary students' association now back in its original home on Renfrew Street. Glasgow's best-known bands and DJs, including Orange Juice, Belle and Sebastian, Franz Ferdinand and Frightened Rabbit have their roots in the Art School, where art and music collide. Club nights, cafe and street food, cinema screenings, and much more.
theartschool.co.uk

Centre for Contemporary Arts (7)
The CCA is a one-stop shop for exploring Glasgow's vibrant cultural scene, complete with art, shop, gallery space, cafe and food.
cca-glasgow.com

Loch Lomond
The beautiful countryside of Loch Lomond and the Trossachs, a national park, is just 45 minutes away from Glasgow by bus or train. At 39 km long, Loch Loman is the largest freshwater loch in Scotland.
lochlomond-trossachs.org

w to get around
Glasgow is a compact and walkable city. Built on a grid system, it is easy to navigate on foot or by public transport. As well as a bus system, Glasgow has Scotland's only underground system – the circular route is a fast and efficient way to travel around particularly in the city centre, west end and south side areas. A great way to see, get around, and learn about the city when you first arrive is to jump on the City Sightseeing bus tour that leaves from George Square. The rest of Scotland is within easy reach of Glasgow by bus or rail – Scotland's capital Edinburgh is only 45 minutes away by train.

Arranging housing
Quite easy

Housing support by school
Yes

Cost of room in the city
GBP 300 per month
(approx. EUR 376)

Cost of campus housing
Between GBP 92 and GBP 106 per week (approx. EUR 115 to EUR 132)

City
Glasgow

Country
United Kingdom

HEAD – Genève

Bikes are a popular way for students to get around, thanks to many mile of cycle paths.
Photo Rebecca Bowring

Geneva University of Art and Design (HEAD – Genève)
Boulevard James-Fazy 15
1201 Geneva
Switzerland

T +41 22 388 5100
info.head@hesge.ch
head-geneve.ch

Students can enjoy working in light-filled studi

Course
Spaces and Communication

School
HEAD – Genève

'The school, like the city it is based in, is thoroughly international'

Jean-Pierre Greff, director of HEAD – Genève

What is studying at this school all about?
Our mission is a simple one: to train and challenge top-flight professionals who have already acquired credibility and a degree of recognition by the time they graduate, so that they can make their dreams come true, become leading designers and build up projects and careers at the highest level and often in an international setting.

What kind of teaching method is applied here?
Our teaching methods are highly varied, but the emphasis is often on sessions designed as a moment of intensity, focusing on a specific project and run by prominent international figures from the relevant fields, as well as workshops geared to 1:1 scale projects, work commissioned from HEAD by leading industry players and institutions, or HEAD projects that will be shown to the general public and professionals at the many fairs, competitions and exhibitions we successfully take part in. Our school encourages interdisciplinarity and we endeavour to build bridges between the many fields we teach in.

Why should students choose this particular school?
We offer a wide range of multiple experiences at the highest level. Both the school and the city it is in are thoroughly international. We have teams of international teachers, all of them recognised professionals in their fields. Our premises and facilities are of outstanding quality. Geneva is a highly stimulating, internationally oriented place to work and offers all kinds of opportunities. Finally, the main focus of our day-to-day work is on our students' projects and successes – and those of our alumni, with whom we maintain close links. We create a structure that allows our students to develop their full potential.

What is expected from the students?
What we expect from our students (besides, of course, creative talent) is strong motivation and ambition, consistency and maturity in their projects, a critical mind and a strong, free personality – in short, all the qualities and skills that go to make an author-designer.

What kind of jobs do your former students generally go on to do?
Our students are trained for the most varied jobs. Many set up their own studios, often in teams possessing complementary skills. Others join often prestigious architecture and design agencies. Some opt for less typical professions, such as working in cultural design centres, galleries or for magazines. We especially encourage the pursuit of adventurous entrepreneurial careers, through our Excellence Awards and our establishment of a Design Incubator for four to six graduates a year. The idea is that within 12 to 18 months they should be running viable businesses of their own.

Programme

The Spaces and Communication programme is headed by the designers of El Ultimo Grito. It offers an international training programme. It is intended for space and interior architects, product designers and graphic designers. Most of the teachers are renowned designers, graphic designers, interior architects, exhibition curators, artistic directors or journalists.

The unique combination of the Spaces and Communication specialisation reflects the identity of today's designer, involved in the development of a global design, from its conceptualisation to its design, from small to large scale, from the object to the city. Space design, exhibition design, signage systems, urban signs, corporate design, labelling, catalogues and showcases, all projects are based on real-life situations and built on a 1:1 scale.

From the first year of their training onwards, in addition to commissions and projects for partner institutions and prestigious companies, students develop a personal project, the backbone of their work, with the support of their tutors and coaches, which leads towards their diploma project. Through targeted apprenticeships, study tours and workshops, students acquire and develop the in-depth knowledge and strong technical skills required for their future practice, enhance their awareness, construct their networks and complete their project as author-designer.

The building offers a reflective space for study and work.

State of the art facilities with a wood and metal workshop. Photo courtesy HEAD – Genève, S. Poin

Programme
Spaces and Communication

Leads to
Master of Arts

Structure
The teaching is organised into three types of modules that cover 4 semesters and total 90 ECTS:
- A studio/laboratory, devoted to specific areas of teaching and to carrying out a digital design project (30 ECTS)
- Optional theoretical and technical classes (30 ECTS)
- A theoretical and practical master's thesis (30 ECTS).

Head of programme
Alexandra Midal

Mentors and lecturers
Ruedi Baur, Nitzan Cohen, Damian Conrad, Matali Crasset, El Ultimo Grito (Rosario Hurtado and Roberto Feo), Marteen Gielen (Rotor), Tristan Kobler and Maki Suzuki (Åbäke).

duration of study
2 years

full time
Yes (40 hours a week)

part time
No

Female students
50%

Male students
50%

Local students
50%

Students from abroad
50%

Yearly enrolment
18

Tuition fee
CHF 500 per semester
(approx. EUR 410)

Funding/scholarships
No

Minimum requirements for entry
Bachelor's degree

Language
French and English

Application procedure
The following documents must be
submitted in order to complete the
application:
a completed online application form
your portfolio (PDF or DVD)
your copy of degree/diploma
a text outlining your artistic and
intellectual position
description of your planned study
outline and research project
two letters of recommendation.
Short-listed candidates will be invited
for an interview. There is an application
fee of CHF 150 (approx. EUR 123).

Application details
head-geneve.ch/admissions

Application date
Before 28 March

Graduation rate
90%

Job placement rate
High

Memberships/affiliations
None

Collaborations with
Local, national and international
higher education institutions,
museums, galleries and business
partners including RCA, EnsAD,
ENSCI, Swissnex and others.

Facilities for students
Printshops, 3D prototyping, wood and
metal workshops, library, audiovisual
borrowing facilities and a cafeteria.

Student Work

Bedroom (2014)
By Jessica Brancato and Amélie Freyche

Within a simple block of paper, we discover the intimate space of the bedroom, where the sleeper interweaves reality and dreams. Photo courtesy of HEAD – Genève, Dylan Perrenoud

Heroic Simulator (2013)
By Wendy Gaze

A series of nine devices for recreating space as it is experienced by film heroes. For example, 001 I'm Flying offers the exhilarating experience of Rose on the bow of the Titanic. Photo courtesy of HEAD – Genève, Raphaelle Mueller

Padpad (2012)
By Jeremy Lasnier

Padpad is a smart cushion that reduces the amount of time that users spend sitting immobile – which is a known health risk. Padpad monitors the sitter's activity level and gives feedback, enabling users to be more aware of their posture and movement levels. Photo courtesy of HEAD – Genève, Sandra Pointe

Course
Spaces and Communication

School
HEAD – Genève

Living Room: La Vie est Rose or Prospective Archaeology of the Domestic (2014)
By Aurélien Reymond and Gaspar Reverdin

Objects are filled with a poetry of daily life far removed from glossy magazine pictures. In everyday life, does our domestic environment influence our relationships and interactions, and does our behaviour also modify our domestic environment?
Photo courtesy of HEAD – Genève, Dylan Perrenoud

...aisons & Ambiances (2014)
...v 2nd year students of HEAD – Genève

...isons & Ambiance Magazine Scenography and booth ...cept conceived by second year students for the Habitat et ...din Fair in Lausanne 2014. Photo courtesy of HEAD – ...nève, Sandra Pointet

Entrance (2014)
By Antoine Guay and Barbara Jenny

...long corridor in the form of a library, around which the ...artment rooms are distributed. Its repetitive and geometrical ...ucture acts as a framework for the whole apartment. This ...m plays with the ambiguity between apartment and ...ibition spaces; it lies at the boundary between public and ...mestic space. Photo courtesy of HEAD – Genève, Dylan Perrenoud

Couture Graphique (2014)
By students of HEAD – Genève

Scenography of the room dedicated to HEAD's Fashion Departement during the MUDAC, Museum of Design in Lausanne Exhibition: Couture Graphique, 2014. Photo courtesy of HEAD – Genève, Sandra Pointet and Baptiste Coulon

Alumnus

Name Mathias Zieba
Residence Geneva, Switzerland
Year of graduation 2012
Current job Co-owner of preorder&soldout
Website preorderetsoldout.com

Photo preorder&soldout

Why did you choose this school?
Having studied graphic design for 4 years,
I wanted to extend my skills into signage
or stage design. HEAD was the only one to
propose this perspective.

What was the most interesting project you did?
For 2 years I took part in a lot of workshops,
collective projects, and cross-over projects for
prestigious exhibitions like the Salone in Milan
or for the Pompidou Centre in Paris. All these
projects were very interesting and supervised
by well-known designers. But ultimately my
graduation project was the most personal and
the most intense. Everything I had learned
throughout the course was applied in a
personal project achieved in accord with these
deep reflections.

What was your graduation project?
I worked around the aesthetic of the ruin and
the attraction it can exert, especially for urban
explorers. The project was realised in two
steps: first the writing of a master's thesis
about the chosen subject, and then a project
which is linked to this theory.This equipment
I designed, allows to reproduce forms or
animated images which are both those of the
ruins and of the action produced by the
explorer. It is made of three steel balls named
Hubert, Alfred, Gordon (HAG). They produce
respectively video footage, surface captures
and volume recordings by the means of video,
scan and sonar.

Any words of advice for future students?
I would quote Anthony Burrill: 'Work hard and
be nice to people!'

What was your favourite place to hang out?
There is a music venue in Geneva called The
Zoo. It's equipped for the practice of mapping
and thus enables the VJs to work along with the
DJs who appear on stage. This energy is linked
to the creators of softwares like Modul8 and
Madmapper based in Geneva.

Are you still in contact with the school?
After passing the master's, I applied with
another student, Alexandre Burdin, for the
AHEAD design Incubator. This is a foundation
which helps you to create a studio – and thanks
to AHEAD we have been able to take
advantage of a coach and a workshop for more
than a year while we launched our office. I also
keep a close link with the school by working in
workshops or organising exhibitions.

One of preorder&soldout's first realisations after Zieba
and Burdin's graduation: An interactive showcase for
Romain Jerome watches at Baselworld 2013.

Current Students

'Until I arrived in Geneva, I never cycled as much as I do now. It's great for the mind, and the body, a perfect balance to studying for a master's at HEAD!'
   Wendy Gaze

udying at HEAD, you develop ritical spirit and learn how defend and present your ncepts with a personal and sponsive approach.'
   Juliette Rambaud

hroughout the course, students at HEAD are ven the opportunity to work on important sign projects worldwide with renowned ists and designers.'
Alexandra Loader

'I love the Bains des Paquis, a jetty in the port of Geneva. This is a very cosmopolitan town, where everyone is very hard-working, but the lakeside is where people relax together. After work, you come with your picnic or eat at the bar, and catch the last rays of sun with a beautiful view.'
   Cécile Guichard

City Life

Geneva is a great location for living, studying and working. It has cultural variety, a beautiful location on the shores of Lake Geneva and next to the Alps, and an innovative environment. HEAD is ideally located in the heart of the city. Its five buildings and exhibition space, LiveInYourHead, are part of the city's cultural life.

Known both as the 'smallest of big cities' and the 'city of peace', Geneva is home to the European headquarters of the United Nations as well as many other NGOs. With far greater international influence than any other city of 200,000, Geneva is focused on both the international economy and the world of research, education and science: it is home to CERN, the European Organization for Nuclear Research, where physicists and engineers are probing the fundamental structure of the universe.

Geneva is also a city of arts and culture, counting more than 30 performance venues and 11 museums. In addition, it is one of the greenest cities in Europe. Numerous parks and green spaces contribute greatly to the quality of life of its citizens. Above all, Geneva is a fun place to live, with a lot of bars and attractive nightlife (including L'Usine and Motel Campo) plus great beaches in the summertime and superb wintersport opportunities – the city is just a one-hour drive from the best ski locations in the world.

Switzerland

Lake Geneva. Photo by Patrick Nouhailler.

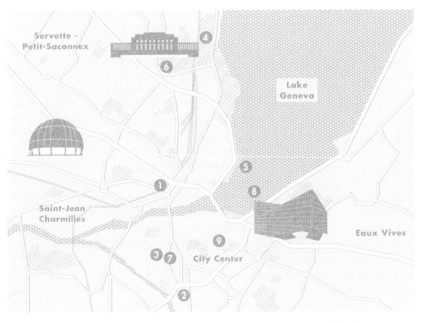

Servette - Petit-Saconnex

Lake Geneva

Saint-Jean Charmilles

Eaux Vives

City Center

Geneva

1 HEAD
2 Plainpalais Flea Market
3 Centre d'Art Contemporain Genève
4 Jardin Botanique
5 Bains des Pâquis
6 Place des Nations
7 Mamco, Musée d'art Moderne et Contempor
8 Jet d'Eau
9 St. Peter's Cathedral

Park

Water

Railway

Main road

Course
Spaces and Communication

School
HEAD – Genève

City Facts

e Old Town
The atmospheric Old Town is a maze of cobblestone streets and little squares filled with quaint shops, bars and cafes.

ainpalais Flea Market 2
Mingle with the locals at Geneva's largest outdoor flea market (open Wednesdays and Sundays from 8.00 to 17.00 rain or shine). Antiques, records, vintage clothing and other curios await savvy bargain hunters.

ntre d'Art Contemporain Genève 3
Founded in 1974, the centre became the first contemporary-art institution in French-speaking Switzerland. A space for production, research and experiment, the centre is the place for intriguing exhibitions of contemporary art.
centre.ch

Quartier des Bains
The Quartier des Bains Association, 12 galleries and four cultural institutions, aims to encourage and promote contemporary art in Geneva, in particular in the Quartier des Bains area. It organises three Nuits des Bains art events, in March, May and September.
quartierdesbains.ch

Jardin Botanique 4
Renowned for its conservatory, the botanical garden houses magnificent collections of plants. Ideal for a walk or a contemplative retreat from everyday life.
ville-ge.ch

Bains des Pâquis 5
A few francs gets you access to a great 1930s bath with beach and piers. Swim in the lake, steam in the sauna or enjoy the view of Jet d'Eau opposite. The food is good – especially the winter fondue.
buvettedesbains.ch

Place des Nations 5
The Place des Nations is the heart of international Geneva and features the famous 12m-high Broken Cair, designed by Geneva artist, Daniel Berset and symbolic of the fight against anti-personnel mines.

Mamco, Musée d'Art Moderne et Contemporain 7
The largest and youngest museum of contemporary art in Switzerland, with a collection of 4000 items and changing exhibition programme.
mamco.ch

Jet d'Eau 8
Located in the heart of La Rade, this giant fountain is the symbol of the city of Geneva and its main tourist attraction. Every second, 500 litres of water are jetted some 140 m into the air.

St. Peter's Cathedral 9
The 12th-century cathedral in the Old Town houses a collection of archaeological treasures from pre-History to the Middle Ages but remains best known for its association with John Calvin, whose wooden chair is still here.
saintpierre-geneve.ch

w to get around
It's very easy to explore Geneva by tram, bus and even by boat. Geneva's public transport (TPG) network links bus, trams, some trains and the yellow taxi-boats of the Mouettes Genevoises that regularly cross to the other side of the lake. Tickets are available at every stop in the city. The country buses have ticket machines on board. Prepaid cards can be bought at the TPG agencies, the railway station's ticket office and authorised retailers. Cycling is a popular alternative, due to the short distances, miles of cyling lanes and free-to-use bikes (mid-April to mid-October).
There is free public transport from the airport to the city centre.

Arranging housing
Difficult

Housing support by school
No

Cost of room in the city
CHF 600 per month (approx. EUR 425)

Cost of campus housing
n/a

Hochschule für Technik Stuttgart

Hochschule für Technik Stuttgart,
University of Applied Sciences
(HFT Stuttgart)
Schellingstr. 24
70174 Stuttgart
Germany

T +49 (0)711 8926 2883
imiad@hft-stuttgart.de
hft-stuttgart.de

The colourful facade of the HFT's architecture libr[e]

Course
Interior Architectural Design

School
Hochschule für Technik Stuttgart

'Our Interior Design department profits from a very technical and practical context'

Prof. Wolfgang Grillitsch, dean of the IMIAD course

When was the school founded?
Our university was founded in 1832, originally as a school for construction workers to bridge the winter when there was no work possible.

Has it changed much over the years?
We have progressed from a technical school for craftsmen during bad weather, to a university for applied sciences, still with a focus on architectural and constructional competences.

What is studying at this school all about?
The profile of our university is very technical and grounded in practical issues. Our Interior Design department profits from this context. Our creativity mixed with all the opportunities of our university makes complex projects achievable. Networks with different leading international universities gives our students the chance to optimise their skills and communication techniques.

What kind of teaching method is applied here?
We have a close connection to industrial partners and networks. The general focus on practical experiences and knowledge is fundamentally important for us. Our teaching philosophy tries to connect practice, research and learning methods. All other ways would be too academic for our aims. We aim to make the students 'feel' materials and structures and go deeply into details.

Why should students choose this particular school?
We teach how to do and how to manage. How to see and analyse things. How to realise complex tasks, how to work and make things or change them with the maximum output.

What is expected from the students?
That they can develop their technical skills and knowledge in combination with their creativity, as well as being interested in international cultures.

When did you start offering the master's degree course in interior architecture?
The programme was founded in 2005 and is being continuously optimised and developed.

What is the most important thing for students to learn during this course?
Teamwork, project work and organisation in foreign countries with different laws and cultures. It's all about coming together and working in an international context. We coach our students to be able to open their own office, or to work in leading positions worldwide.

What is the most important skill to master when one wants to become an interior architect?
Learning to work with the child inside you.

What kind of jobs do your former students mostly go on to do?
Most of them work for renowned design companies for the first few years before setting up their own studios.

Programme

The 2-year master's course offers professional design and technology competences for ambitious, international-minded students. The education is practice and project orientated. The focus is on international experience and parts of the study is conducted abroad. This course is part of the IMIAD programme which comprises five cooperating universities around the world. It results a common master's degree signed by all the participating schools. For this reason, the second semester must be followed at one of the partner universities. The third semester starts with an international workshop where students and teachers from all schools gather at different locations. The programme contents are coordinated between the universities. The other schools involved in the programme in addition to HFT Stuttgart are SUPSI, Lugano, Switzerland; CEPT, Ahmedabad, India; Istanbul Technical University, Istanbul, Turkey; Edinburgh College of Art, Edinburgh, United Kingdom.

An exhibition space during a light workshop presentation.

Students trying out their practical skills in the wood workshop.

Programme
Interior Architectural Design

Leads to
International Master of Interior Architectural Design (IMIAD)

Structure
The 2-year master's course consists of 4 semesters. The first semester is held at the home university. At HFT Stuttgart, the first semester is held in the German language. The second semester is abroad, at one of the partner universities, were classes are given in the English language. The third and fourth semester are at the home university again, with master thesis in both languages. The curriculum is divided into design, social, technical and management modules. The main teaching focus is on cultural knowledge and international experience.

Head of programme
Wolfgang Grillitsch

Mentors and lecturers
Klaus-Peter Goebel, Eberhard Holde Thomas Hundt, Karsten Weigel, Eberhard Winkler and Diane Ziegle

Notable alumni
Simone Völcker and Christoph Völk

118   Course
Interior Architectural Design   School
Hochschule für Technik Stuttgart

School Facts

Duration of study
2 years

Full time
Yes (40 hours a week)

Part time
No

Female students
–

Male
–

Local students
70%

Students from abroad
30%

Yearly enrolment
25

Tuition fee
Free

Funding/scholarships
Different local and international
scholarships available.

Minimum requirements for entry
Bachelor's degree in a relevant
subject. Proficiency in German
and English.

Language
German and English

Application procedure
The following must be submitted in
order to complete the application:
a filled application form with a photo
certificate of entitlement to be
admitted to higher education (certified)
graduation certificate of first studies
(certified)
proof of any vocational qualifications
(certified)
proof of any job activity (certified)
for international applicants:
certificate showing skills in German
(DSH 2 or TestDaF 4)
for international applicants:
certificate from ASK proving
graduation
a handwritten, tabular curriculum vitae
portfolio containing applicant's
individual work
your letter of motivation in English
and German.
A second application round follows,
with a personal interview for all
selected applicants.

Application details
imiad@hft-stuttgart.de

Application date
Before 15 June

Graduation rate
99%

Job placement rate
100%

Memberships/affiliations
Erasmus

Collaborations with
ITU Istanbul Technical University,
Istanbul, Turkey; CEPT University,
Centre for Environmental Planning and
Technology, Ahmedabad, India; SUPSI,
Scuola universitaria professionale
della Svizzera italiana, Lugano,
Switzerland; and ECA, Edinburgh
College of Art, Edinburgh, UK.

Facilities for students
Material lab, Styro lab, metal-,
wood- and modelling workshop.

Student Work

Un/Places – Context and Creative Potential of Spatial Fragments (2013)
By C. Lars Schuchert

The project revolves around a theory that defines a spatial typology along the prefix 'un'. Particularly recognised since the Facebook generation, the *unlike* button has become part of our general knowledge. After choosing to *like* something, it is possible to undo this action by one more click. Exploring the concept as a design strategy, an 'unplace' is directly generated as anti-matter in the Weissenhof Settlement in Stuttgart.

1966 | Neues Grünes Herz | 2016 (2013)
By Lillian Wagenblast

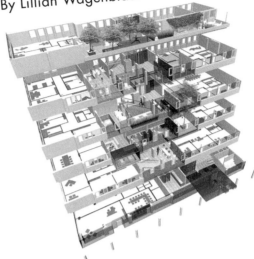

How indoor landscaping – sustainable, healthy and employee-friendly – can be used for the renovation of the cell office architecture of the post-war period so as to contribute to a significant revaluation of the occupational quality and the appearance.

er Einfluss von Raum auf Körper und Geist (2013)
y Andrea Nothelfer

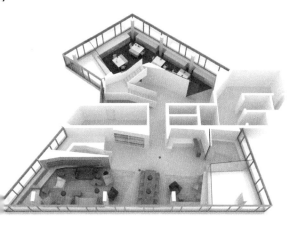

there an influence of space in all its facets on body and mind? This work deals with the issue of atmosphere in space and the question of how
an have a favourable effect on the healing process of a patient by the design parameters. The result is the planning and design of an urban
ychosomatic treatment centre.

Möbeldesign 2020 (2013)
By Christoph Völcker

As a prognosis of furniture design in the year 2020 Völkers thesis analyses the
history of design. The relative technologies, social and economical
circumstances are taken into account. Technical innovations have gained market
maturity under the postulate of ecology and will play an important role in
2020. 3D print and nano-technologies open the way to a new freedom in
design. A rethinking in design domain seems to be within grasp.

Alumnus

Name C. Lars Schuchert
Residence Lucerne, Switzerland
Year of birth 1981
Year of graduation 2010
Current job Researcher and teaching assistant at the Lucerne University of Applied Sciences and Arts
Clients Private and public clients for research projects
Website craftcube.net

Why did you choose this school?
I had completed an architecture degree at the HFT Stuttgart, and realised that I wanted to learn more about spaces. I was already familiar with the university's staff and resources, so I could focus entirely on studying.

What was the most important thing you learned here?
To draw from the existing context as much as from inspirational shapes or the written word, and to design great spaces before filling the

perimeter with functions – function follows form. This seems quite simple, but experiencing the power and consequence of this approach totally transformed my former way of designing that I had developed during my architecture studies.

What subject do you wish you paid more attention to?
We had some classes on sociology and philosophy. I wish I had tried to include social factors in my design projects more.

Was there any class you found particularly difficult?
The most difficult part was the outgoing semester that I spent at SUPSI in Lugano, Switzerland. We had two parallel design projects and an Italian language course.

What was your graduation project?
For my graduation project I covered Un/Places – Context and Creative Potential of Spatial Fragments. It started with the idea of activating gap spaces but turned into a theoretical contribution to spatial nomenclature. The thesis defines 'unplaces' in the conceptual context of space/place, time/perception, non-places, and utopia.

What was your favourite place to hang out?
In general, I really enjoyed the atmosphere at the school's studio. There was a certain vibe of teaching and working, and the other students motivated me to invest in the projects as much as possible. Off campus, I was playing bass in a band, and practice became my favourite thing to do at night.

Are you still in contact with the school?
Currently I am co-advising an IMIAD master's thesis that explores the aesthetics of decay. It great to work together with former teachers and to get to peek behind the curtain.

Are you still in contact with your fellow students?
Every so often I am happy to read some Facebook updates, but contact is rather spars. Moving to Switzerland probably didn't help.

Was the transformation from graduation to working life a smooth one?
While I was still studying, I was offered a teaching assistant job in Lucerne, Switzerland where I am working right now. Only 6 weeks after graduation, I was already living and working there. It was a bit of a close call with all the moving and immigration but it turned out quite well.

If you were to do the course again, what would you do differently?
I would leave the studio more often to enjoy time with my fellow students.

For his graduation project, C. Lars Schuchert created a theory of the 'unspace' and then applied it to a real-wo situation. Here seen the 'after' situation.

Course
Interior Architectural Design

School
Hochschule für Technik Stuttgart

'The most valuable class for me was Tanja Fury's class on soft skills, which are often ignored in the design profession. Real-life factors like teamwork, time management and presentation skills are one of the key factors for a project to be successful. This class helped me to understand the positive and negative aspects of my own nature and pushed me to challenge myself to be a team leader.'
Manushi Mathur

'The main focus of this course is group work. You have to expect working in groups, pretty much as in an office with designers, a materials team or construction team. Teamwork is an essential skill in workspaces and this course emphasises that.'
Sinan Sever

chose this school because the IMIAD course offers you an ernational exchange with students from different countries d the opportunity to go abroad for 1 semester. I also ed that you are not only doing typical interior architectural ojects but also taking a look into other subjects.'
Sabrina de Kruyff

'My favourite class was the one on materials; to understand how materials behave gives you greater opportunities for your work.'
Philipp Grem

City Life

The special fascination of Stuttgart is its hilly topography – it fundamentally characterises the atmosphere of the city. Few other cities have more fabulous and inspiring views. Built environments and spaces that capture this atmosphere and use its potential are all around, often with an extraordinary quality regardless of their genesis in time. The campus of HFT Stuttgart is located right in the city centre.

Stuttgart is the economic capital of south-western Germany. It has a special genius for engineering and is home to world-leading companies in technology. Different cultural and natural regions are just around the corner and include the Black Forest, Lake Constance, Switzerland and French border. In the nearer surrounding of Stuttgart there is also a lot of beautiful nature with excellent opportunities for biking, hiking and climbing. The city itself is known for its excellent state opera, two automobile museums of international importance, exclusive art exhibitions and exciting concerts and subculture: Stuttgart is an cultural metropolis with a heart open to anyone and everyone.

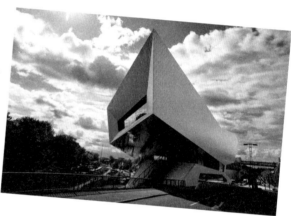

The remarkable building of the Porsche Museum is part of the Stuttgart appearance. Photo Barnyz

Germany

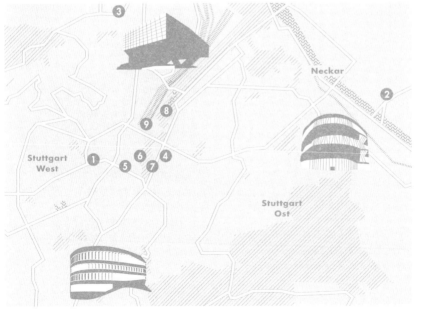

Stuttgart

1 HFT Stuttgart
2 Mercedes-Benz Museum
3 Weisenhof Siedlung
4 Neue Staatsgallerie
5 Kunstmuseum Stuttgart
6 Künstlerbund
7 Staatsoper Stuttgart
8 Schlossgarten
9 Main train station

Park

Water

Railway

Main road

Course
Interior Architectural Design

School
Hochschule für Technik Stuttgart

City Facts

ercedes-Benz Museum ②
Stuttgart's rich engineering legacy is on show here in a spectacular UN Studio building. Exhibits document the history of the car and marque in the form of 160 vehicles and other displays.
mercedes-benz-classic.com

rsche Museum
More fascinating car history, this time in a stunning Delugan Meissl building.
porsche.com/museum

eisenhof Siedlung ③
A housing estate built for the Deutscher Werkbund exhibition of 1927 and showcasing modernist homes by Mies van der Rohe, Le Corbusier, Walter Gropius and others.
weissenhofmuseum.de

Neue Staatsgallerie ④
Housed in a controversial masterpiece by James Stirling, the museum combines a 20th-century collection with contemporary art exhibitions.
staatsgalerie.de

Kunstmuseum Stuttgart ⑤
A spectacular glass cube houses the world's most important Otto Dix collection and much more.
kunstmuseum-stuttgart.de

Künstlerbund ⑥
Contemporary arts institute with exhibitions, events and a popular cafe with a terrace outside.
kuenstlerbund-stuttgart.de

Staatsoper Stuttgart ⑦
Stuttgart has been an important centre for opera since the 17th century. That heritage is alive and well in its huge 1912 neoclassical opera house.
oper-stuttgart.de

Schlossgarten ⑧
A large and beautiful park with a 600-year history and a central location.

Cannstatter Volksfest
This autumnal beer festival is second in size and revelry only to the Munich Oktoberfest.

w to get around
Through the rail network (ICE, IC, InterRegio), Stuttgart is directly connected with 13 European capitals, while Stuttgart Airport offers flights to 110 destinations in 33 countries. From the airport, the S-Bahn, which connects with terminal 1, brings you to the city centre and main train station ⑨ in 25 minutes.

Getting around the city itself is easy thanks to suburban trains (the S-Bahn), trams, light rail and bus connections. Cycling and walking are both possible due to the fairly small distances in the city centre.

Arranging housing
Difficult (centre) to never a problem (outskirts)

Housing support by school
Yes, student dormitories are available

Cost of room in the city
EUR 400 per month

Cost of campus housing
Between EUR 200 and EUR 400 per month

City
Stuttgart

Country
Germany

125

The courtyard of the School of Design is an informal meeting point for all creative disciplines. Photo Katharina Dubno

Hochschule Mainz University of Applied Sciences

Hochschule Mainz University
of Applied Sciences
Holzstraße 36
55116 Mainz
Germany

T +49 (0)6131 628 2430
assistenz-ia@hs-mainz.de
ia.hs-mainz.de

Students outside the main entrance of the School of Design. Photo Katharina Dubno

'Our master's programme is focused on comprehensive projects: experiment and research drive innovative solutions'

Klaus Teltenkötter, programme director in Kommunikation im Raum (Spatial Communication)

What is studying at your school all about?
As our course is part of the School of Design with its departments of interior design, communication design and media design, our master's programme is embedded in an ideal environment for interdisciplinary exchange and creative projects. The small numbers of students in each class allow for individual and personal care. There is a lively exchange among students and teachers and the atmosphere is friendly.

What are the advantages of your school's location?
In Mainz, the university can look back on 250 years of tradition. The city was actually the birthplace of Johannes Gutenberg. Mainz is the state capital of Rhineland-Palatinate, a media city and a university town. It's also a stronghold of carnival, and it's well located in the economic and cultural centre of the Rhine-Main region. Being close to Frankfurt, our beautiful medieval town next to the river Rhine offers ideal conditions for an intense, inspiring and creative study, and of course high potential for international exchange through its central location in Europe.

What is the focus of your master's degree programme in interior design?
It deals with a variety of topics and tasks concerning spatial communication. We work on spaces where communication and information are expressed in innovative and creative ways. With each and every project, we are looking for an additional value and relevance in our design task in the context of architecture and design. This focus is the basis for a unique profile with innovative project work. We frequently offer collaborations with industry partners in the design and realisation of student projects. The results of these projects are well published and rewarded.

What do you expect from the students?
A basic requirement is a previous education in the context of interior architecture, architecture or design. From our students we expect curiosity, dedication, initiative and enthusiasm. Our master's programme is focused on comprehensive projects. Experiment and research drive innovative solutions. The design tasks are grounded in content, and they support both the personality and the technical skills of students.

Why should students come here?
Because they can expect a dedicated team of teachers, as well as an interdisciplinary and creative working environment. Our graduates go on to work in leading architecture and design studios.

Programme

The programme explores topics and challenges relating to spatial communication. We study spaces where communication and information is expressed in exceptionally designed ways. These include interactive spaces that respond to differing needs, as well as intelligent, communicative media installations, exhibition design and information with content on graphic surfaces

Based on our conviction that content matters and atmosphere is more important than technology, a serious reflection of the communicative aspects of spaces is the foundation for our approach to design. Students are guided and supervised by a team of professors and lecturers with core expertise in fields including architecture, art, technology, product design, material, lighting, digital media,

construction and theory. Using this interdisciplinary approach, the students' projects are discussed from a variety of perspectives and often in cooperation with professional partners from the Rhine-Main region. Interdisciplinary subjects are frequently offered in cooperation with the departments of Communication and Media Design. Students share their studio with other students (Gutenberg Intermedia) whose focus lies on various disciplines in the field of arts.

The interdisciplinary master's stud

Students working with the sunlight simulator.
Photo Katharina Dubno

Programme
Kommunikation im Raum
(Spatial Communication)

Leads to
Master of Arts

Structure
The course duration is based on 3 semesters of 16 weeks each and accounts for 90 ECTS credits. Structured into seven modules, the programme operates multiple teaching formats (lessons, seminars, presentations, placements, supervised workshops), integrating a historical approach, theory, learning and practice. The first semester is devoted to a practical team project, while the second semester explores individual design tasks. For the final master's thesis, students work on self-chosen topics in the field of innovative spatial communication.

Head of programme
Klaus Teltenkötter

Mentors and lecturers
Bernd Benninghoff, Lutz Büsing, Iris-Susan Fäth, Wolf Gutjahr, Alexa Hartig, Andreas Kaiser, Gerhard Kalhöfer, Antje Krauter, Markus Pretnar, Holger Reckter, Klaus Teltenkötter and Clemens Trop

Notable alumni
Programme started only 4 years ag

School Facts

ration of study
1.5 years

l time
Yes (26 hours a week)

rt time
No

Female students
90%

Male students
10%

Local students
80%

Students from abroad
20%

Yearly enrolment
16

Tuition fee
EUR 264 per semester (including a ticket for buses and trains, covering a large area around Mainz)

Funding/scholarships
Yes

nimum requirements for entry
Bachelor's degree in the field of interior architecture, architecture or design.

nguage
English and German

plication procedure
Apply by registering and sending an application containing:
your curriculum vitae
a portfolio with examples of recent works (prints)
a copy of your qualifying degree.
A jury will invite selected candidates for admission interviews.

plication details
hs-mainz.de

plication date
Before 15 June

Graduation rate
90%

Job placement rate
90%

Memberships/affiliations
None

Collaborations with
Industry partners include Mercedes Benz, Frankfurt Airport, Conrad Electronics. Academic partners include departments of music, business and fine arts from different universities. International university collaborations with Swinburne University of Technology, Melbourne, Australia; École Supérieure des Arts Appliqués Boulle, Paris, France; Istituto Superiore per le Industrie Artistiche, Rome, Italy; Victoria University of Wellington, New Zealand; Academy of Fine Arts in Gdansk, Poland; Escola Superior des Artes e Design (ESAD), Porto, Portugal.

Facilities for students
Individual workstations in interdisciplinary studios. There is also a wood workshop, model-making workshop (with 3D printer, laser, CNC and CNC foam-cutting), lighting laboratory, digital laboratory, photo studio, materials library and department library.

Student Work

Open Sum X (2013)
By Lea Mirbach

Sum X is a spatial representation of the so called 'open space technology', a popular method for hosting and organising large meetings or conferences of heterogeneous groups. The concentric design features a mobile and highly flexible layout that contracts or expands, using the bellows-like structures for meeting rooms.

Resonate (2012)
By Master's Team

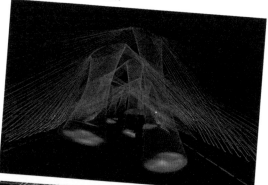

Resonate is a trans-disciplinary team project in collaboration with the Mainz School of Music, developed and realised for the international light festival Luminale. A glowing string structure floats inside the steel hull of a container ship and generates atmospheric sounds and images. By plucking the strings, visitors were able to generate individual sounds that were transformed into waves of light.
Photos Jan Philipp Ley and Martina Pipprich

Interactive Kölsch (2011)
By Master's Team

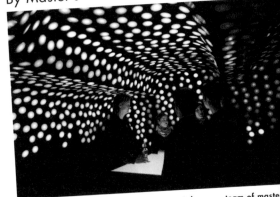

As part of the design festival Passagen in Cologne, a team of master students transformed the basement of the Hotel Monte Christo into an atmospheric and interactive space. Visitors purchasing a bottle of Kölsch beer were handed a coaster. Sliding these beer mats across the surface of an interactive table affected the position, colour and size of the lively lights – and the atmosphere of the entire interior. Photo Martina Pipprich

Tu Luz (2014)
By Stephanie Brenken and Viola Kressmann

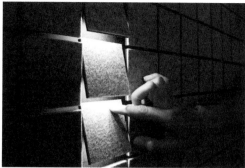

Tu Luz, meaning 'your light', describes the atmospheric possibilities and individuality of a wall element that consists of a large number of operating switches which can be tilted to project the light upwards or down. Tu Luz, a product created within the interdisciplinary Interactive Objects project, creates different lighting moods, offering countless possibilities, both for positioning and brightness. Your personal light for every mood!
Photos Stephanie Brenken

...sing Light (2014)
...y Lisa Ambach and Annika Ebbers

...sing Light is a lighting object whose folded structure can react sensitively ...d variably. Its light accompanies a person on their passage through the ...om, while at the same time creating an atmospheric background glow. ...e structure is situated above the person, giving an impression of opening ...d widening the room, where persons and space seem to be breathing.
...oto Annika Ebbers

Silence In Arrangement (2013)
By Aline Schaefer and Anne Kielenz

...ne of the most vivid places, Frankfurt Airport, travellers sometimes seek for a place to calm down and meditate. Rooms of ...ce offer an atmospheric balanced space without any religious denomination. Rooms of ...aphor of a window as a focal point for self-reflection that forms into shape through the motion of the visitor. The project was ...nised in cooperation with the management of Frankfurt Airport.

Alumna

Name Katharina Bahne
Residence Mainz, Germany
Year of birth 1986
Year of graduation 2013
Current job Interior designer
at Atelier Markgraph
Website markgraph.de

Why did you choose this school?

During my bachelor's degree in classical interior design, I discovered that I'm mainly interested in interdisciplinary design and communication spaces such as exhibitions, events, media spaces and brand experiences. Therefore I wanted to educate myself in that direction. First, I thought of taking another bachelor's in information design, communication or media design. But then, in 2010, I visited IMM Cologne and discovered the new master's Kommunikation im Raum at Hochschule Mainz, which provided the opportunity of specialising in exactly that direction.

What was the most important thing you learned here?

I learned to work with digital media and interactive, user-driven objects and spaces at the interface of architecture, design and communication. Most of all I worked on concepts. The design stands or falls with the concept.

What was the most interesting project you did?

I actually enjoyed almost all of them! Most of all the realisation projects, the best was Interactive Kölsch – an interactive space and light-installation – which we developed in our first semester as a group project for the Passagen 2011 in connection with the IMM Cologne. In it, 1600 individually controllable LEDs transformed the basement into a fantastic shared experience. We all had a lot of fun developing and realising the project and really grew together as a team. The best thing about it was to see on the spot how impressed the visitors were by our project.

What subject do you wish you paid more attention to?

I would have liked to take more courses in the other departments of media design and communication design. Unfortunately, I didn't make use of the interdisciplinarity between the departments as intensely as I planned to because I was so busy with my own projects and my side job.

Any words of advice for future students?

Always do what you feel like doing and live your own attitude in terms of design. Use your studies to broaden your horizon. The outcome is what you do with them.

Are you still in contact with the school?

I have a lot of friends who still study or work at the school and I still live in Mainz. I continue going to school events and exhibitions where I always meet former professors and friends.

Are you still in contact with your fellow students?

Yes, all of them. There were only 16 students in our class so it's not that hard to stay in touch. Plus, we grew together like a family during our studies. We frequently meet at birthdays or other events and visit each other from time to time.

Was the transformation from graduation to working life a smooth one?

Yeah, totally smooth! Directly after I finished my studies I designed a new vegetarian snack bar for friends in Mainz while also finishing my portfolio. After 3 months, I started applying and immediately found a job. So I finished the snack bar project next to my new job by working in the evenings and weekends.

Katharina Bahne's graduation project, Liebe deine Stadt, was an interactive resource, shop and meeting point for the city of Mainz.

Course
Kommunikation im Raum

School
Hochschule Mainz University of Applied Science

'Interaction is a very important topic here, between people, rooms and objects. I think it often brings interior design to another level.'
Lisa Ambach

love working in an
terdisciplinary way
d in a team – you can
eate something so
uch better when there
e a lot of different
fluences.'
Francesca Müller

'The easiest way to get around Mainz is by bicycle. Mainz is a very manageable and friendly city, that's why it feels good to live here.'
Tina Strack

'Future students can expect to work independently. There aren't too many input lectures, but more hands-on projects.'
Viola Kressmann

'The course lets you work on real projects and competitions. Working with local companies allows you to create high level objects and exhibitions.'
Julien Schaab

'In the Neustadt area of Mainz, which is actually becoming the insider hotspot, you have to visit Annabatterie for good coffee and cake and some of the world's best ice cream from N'Eis at the Gartenfeldplatz. At night lots of students meet at the club and bar Schon Schön.'
Franziska Schmidt

City
Mainz

Country
Germany

City Life

Mainz is located in the heart of Europe. Due to its position, coming from or travelling to other European cities is easy. International train stations and the Frankfurt airport provide fast transportation links. Students benefit from the culturally and economically attractive Rhine-Main region, with its international as well as cultural landscape: the ZDF headquarters (German public television channel), the Frankfurt Trade Fair, and numerous cutting-edge creative industries are all located here.

The city itself has an important history and was home to famous historical figures such as Johannes Gutenberg, who invented the movable type printing press. But Mainz also has an interesting present, with many events taking place, such as the carnival or the Johannisfest. These bring together citizens and visitors in town and create a unique atmosphere in the public spaces. Traditional taverns, cafes, restaurants and the weekly market add to the study experience.

As a university town, Mainz has a vivid and constantly growing and changing young cultural scene. For a creative person, Mainz i a good city to live in. Design-start-ups and small studios offer a perfect opportunity to work together in different creative discipline

The view over the River Rhine towards Mainz Cathedral.
Photo Katharina Dubno

Germany

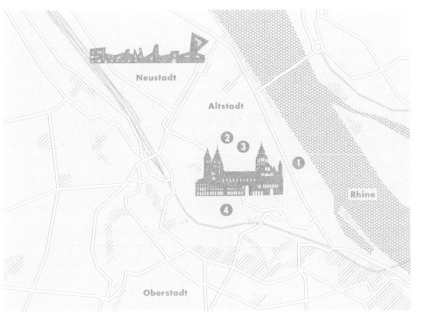

Mainz

1 Hochschule Mainz University of Applied Sciences
2 Mainzer Dom
3 Gutenberg Museum
4 Collegiate Church of St. Stephan

Park

Water

Railway

Main road

Course
Kommunikation im Raum

School
Hochschule Mainz University of Applied Scien

City Facts

Rhine Riverside
Mainz city centre is just a short walk away from the Rhine riverside, a lovely landscape and a popular location for sports and social activities. The relaxed atmosphere creates a feeling of being on vacation without travelling.

Mainzer Dom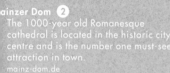
The 1000-year old Romanesque cathedral is located in the historic city centre and is the number one must-see attraction in town.
mainz-dom.de

Gutenberg Museum ③
One of the oldest museums about books and printing in the world, devoted to the history of Mainz-born Johannes Gutenberg's world changing invention.
gutenberg.de

Meenzer Fassenacht
Mainz carnival is one of the largest carnivals in Germany. It is well known for parties and parades which take place all over the city, including costumed gatherings and brass bands.
meenzer-fassenacht.de

Johannisfest
The traditional Mainz Midsummer St. John's Night Festival is a huge fair with numerous attractions, including musical and artistic performances. It takes place all over Mainz, including along the river.

Theatres
Mainz has a variety of theatres, covering all categories of performance from classical ballet to modern dance.

Collegiate Church of St. Stephan ④
This church in Mainz is best known for its nine stained-glass choir windows by Russian artist Marc Chagall.

Wine Festivals
Mainz is located in a major wine-producing region. During the year, wine festivals take place in parks and along the riverside.

How to get around
Mainz is a medium-sized town which offers good and easy public transportation links. Most places are well within walking or cycling distance. The ticket for regional public transportation around Mainz and Frankfurt is included in the tuition fee of the school. The University of Applied Sciences Mainz has two locations. Kommunikation im Raum is situated close to the River Rhine and the historic city centre.

Arranging housing
Average

Housing support by school
Yes, student dorms available

Cost of room in the city
EUR 300 per month

Cost of campus housing
Between EUR 220 and EUR 450 per month

City
Mainz

Country
Germany

A leafy courtyard occupies the heart of the building. Photo Sıla Burcu Başarir

Istanbul Technical University

Istanbul Technical University (ITU)
Taskisla Campus
Taskisla Street
34437 Istanbul
Turkey

T +90 (212) 293 1300 (ext. 2812)
icmakademik@listeci.itu.edu.tr
sbe.itu.edu.tr

An aerial view of the ITU Taskisla Architecture Faculty building in Taksim, Istanbul. Photo Oğuz Meriç

Course
Interior Architectural Design

School
Istanbul Technical University

'We offer a common platform for study which is based on international collaboration, cultural and experiential exchange, as well as design and theory'

Özge Cordan, head of programme

When was the school founded?
ITU was established in 1773, during the time of the Ottoman Empire. With the name of Royal School of Naval Engineering, its responsibility was to educate chart masters and ship builders.

How has the school developed?
With a history dating back 237 years, providing technical education within a modern educational environment and strong academic staff, ITU is strongly identified with architectural and engineering education in Turkey. Since its foundation, ITU has constantly led the way in reform movements, and in the latter era of the Republic of Turkey, ITU has assumed pivotal roles in the reconstruction, modernisation, and administration of the country.

When did you start offering this course?
Founded in 2001, the ITU Department of Interior Architecture joined the International Master of Interior Architectural Design (IMIAD) Programme in 2006. This programme allows students to study at an additional school in another country for part of the course.

What kind of teaching method is applied here?
The teaching methodology of the programme puts together theory and practise on the same spot. In addition, the programme consists of multiple teaching methods such as modular course structures, seminars, presentations, site visits and workshops in the international arena, and so on.

Why should students choose this school?
The most distinguished characteristic of the programme is that it offers a common platform for study, which is based on international collaboration, cultural and experiential exchange and partnership as well as theoretical, practical, communicative and managerial competencies.

What is expected from the students?
We look for students who are open to collaborative studies and who have curiosity, creativity, ambition and consistency.

What is the most important thing for students to learn during this course?
To combine theory and practise through applied research, innovative design methodologies and practices in a collaborative and international study environment (both academic and corporate), which we share with the other IMIAD partners.

What is the most important skill to master when one wants to become an interior architect?
Self-evaluation, self-critics, collaboration and realisation.

What kind of jobs do your students mostly go on to do?
Our aim is to help our graduates to find their own path in the early stage of their careers, all over the world. Our graduates can find job opportunities in design practice and management, as well as in academia at both public and private universities.

City
Istanbul

Country
Turkey

Programme

The International Master of Interior Architectural Design IMIAD programme is based on an agreement between ITU and Edinburgh College of Art (United Kingdom), Lahti Polytechnic (Finland), Scuola Universitaria Professionale della Svizzera Italiana (Switzerland) and Stuttgart University of Applied Sciences (Germany). The Centre for Environmental Planning and Technology University in Ahmedabad (India) joined the collaboration in 2011.

The main goals of the programme are to take master's-level interior architecture education to an international level, to introduce the different cultural atmospheres and professional conditions of different disciplines like interior architecture/interior design, product design and architecture, to strengthen the communicative environment and to address the global field of work. In addition, ITU's IMIAD programme answers the need for a workforce in education, research and practice in the field of interior architecture and design.

Besides developing students' spatial comprehension, presentation techniques and design skills, one of the objectives of the course is to train them for managerial functions, with particular competencies in design and decision-making processes.

A top-floor studio in the faculty building. Photo Sıla Burcu Başarir

In addition to the main library, the faculty building also offers a periodicals library on the second floor. Photo Sıla Burcu Başarir

Programme
Interior Architectural Design

Leads to
International Master of Interior Architectural Design (IMIAD)

Structure
The programme consist of 4 semesters which includes one semester of study abroad. The total ECTS credits are 120 (30 ECTS per semester). The first semester is spent at the home institution. Next, the student spends a semester at one of the partner institutions. In the third semester a workshop of 2 to 4 months is carried out in the country of one of the five institutions (a different one every year). During the fourth semester the students continue and finish their education in the home institution.

Head of programme
Özge Cordan

Mentors and lecturers
Semra Aydınlı, Banu Başeskici Garip Müge Belek Teixeira, Deniz Çalışır Pençe, Demet Dinçay, Frederico Fial Teixeira, Emine Görgül, Bahadır Numan, Leyla Tanaçan, Gülfer Oraz Topçu, Hülya Turgut, Hilal Uğurlu, Alpin Yener and Çağıl Yurdakul.

Notable alumni
Alper Akar, Demet Altunkılıç, Berna Arslan, Işıl Bilgehan Göktepe, Seze Burçe Şahinkaya Aydın, Pınar Çeler Cemal Çobanoğlu, Sule Çolak, Işıla Dikeç, Gayem Doğan, Handan Duye Bolortsetseg Enhbaatar, Müge Ertür Esin Hasgül, Esra Karagöz, Bilge Ka Nazlı Kambur, Nihan Oğuzhan, Mü Özden, Selma Özkan, Gülşen Sizye Selin Tunalı and Sabiha Yıldız Sevg

Course
Interior Architectural Design

School
Istanbul Technical University

School Facts

Duration of study
2 years

Full time
Yes

Part time
No

Female students
77%

Male students
23%

Local students
80%

Students from abroad
20%

Yearly enrolment
12

Tuition fee
- Free for local students
- TL 1600 per semester for foreign students (approx. EUR 550)

Funding/scholarships
Erasmus, TEV (Education Foundation of Turkey), Istanbul Chamber of Commerce, TOG (Community Volunteers Foundation) and Istanbul Chamber of Industry.

Minimum requirements for entry
A bachelor's degree in the field of interior architecture, architecture, industrial/product design and proficiency in English.

Language
Turkish and English

Application procedure
The following documents must be submitted in order to complete the application:
a completed online application form
your curriculum vitae
two reference letters
a statement of purpose
a master's thesis proposal
(max. 1000 words)
a copy of ALES/GRE/GPA exam
a copy of your passport or identity card
a copy of your qualifying degree
a copy of your language certificate.
For the admission interview, students must prepare a printed portfolio.

Application details
sis.itu.edu.tr/onkayitlar/lisansustu/
basvuru

Application date
Between 3 April and 20 June

Graduation rate
45%

Job placement rate
99%

Memberships/affiliations
Erasmus, Cumulus

Collaborations with
IMIAD partners, national companies and organisations such as Koleksiyon and Mardin local government.

Facilities for students
Periodical and non-periodical libraries, computer labs, carpentry workshop with laser cutter and 3D printer, material supply store, sport facilities, restaurant, cafe and studios.

Student Work

Exhibition Design Coffee (2013)
By Gökçe Evren

An old car park in Çukurcuma is given new functions and facilities, becoming a public art gallery which includes exhibition places, a stage and also a coffee centre. The project is intended to attract more artists and creatives to the area.

Opus #1 (2013)
By Didem Acar

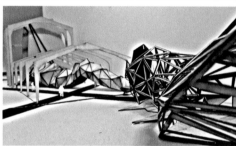

Music and architecture have made use of mathematical proportions throughout the history for the purpose of creating acoustic and visual forms. This study combines the frequency intervals of a piece of classical music with those of a digital design environment to create geometrical architectural forms focused on acoustic performance.

Churrascaria Çukurcuma (2013)
By Nazım Kahraman

An old production facility is converted into a restaurant and a workshop space, with a brutalist theme to express the nature of the restaurant (an Argentine churruscaria).

Course
Interior Architectural Design

School
Istanbul Technical University

ame Çukurcuma (2014)
y Tiffany Halbritter

A plan for a former garage creates an urban garden for the local community, while the interior provides space for local designers to work and exhibit their designs.

Balat Houses (2013)
By Pelin Uyar

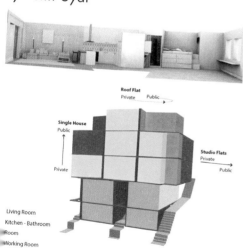

Living Room
Kitchen - Bathroom
Room
Working Room

roject to create modern living environments while serving the historic architecture of Levantine houses of nbul's Balat district.

Layers of Interiors and a New Approach to Old Bedesten (2013)
By Nazlı Sağlam

A modern spatial design for the world's first known bank, Cevahir Bedesten, inspired by the densely layered urban fabric of Istanbul's Grand Bazaar.

Alumnus

Name Cemal Çobanoğlu
Residence Istanbul, Turkey
Year of birth 1985
Year of graduation 2011
Current job Interior designer and furniture designer
Website coroflot.com/cemalcobanoglu

Why did you choose this school?
Because of the IMIAD programme which offers an opportunity to study at different universities in different countries. Within the context of this programme, I had the chance to study and take part in workshops at Istanbul Technical University in Turkey, Lahti University of Applied Sciences in Finland and the Edinburg College of Art in Scotland.

What was the most important thing you learned here?
Thanks to the travel aspect, I realised the importance of different factors on design, such as social lifestyle, climate, geography and so on, and I learned to deal with different local inputs as a designer.

What was the most interesting project you did?
The main subject of my furniture class in Finland was designing and manufacturing an ecological chair. In my design, Belt Chair, the process was as satisfactory as the result itself. Belt Chair creates a connection with the basic elements of interior space such as walls, columns and furniture. It can also be used as a low table and a sledge. It was a great fun to 'ski' with my friends on a snowy day in Istanbul with Belt Chair.

What was your graduation project?
We had to write an extensive thesis, including a project, as part of our graduation project. My subject was: 'Overview of Furniture Design after World War II: Finland 1945-1960'. As the additional project of my thesis, I redesigned the stools which we use in our design studios d ITU according to the principles of Scandinavic design. Therefore, I paid extra attention to the connection of my design to users and space.

Any words of advice for future students?
Each student has to select a subject for the thesis, so be sure to pick one you will enjoy doing. I first chose the connection between cinematography and space, but after 5 month I realised I was not having enough fun and I decided not to continue with it.

Was the transformation from graduation to working life a smooth one?
I had a chance to work for several companies before I started the course, and I continued to do freelance work during my studies. So I got through the transformation from school to working life pretty smoothly.

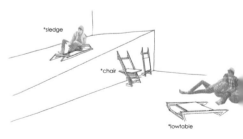

*sledge
*chair
*lowtable

Cemal Çobanoğlu travelled to the IMIAD partner school in Finland where he studied sustainable furniture design and produced the Belt Chair, inspired by Scandinavian design.

Course
Interior Architectural Design

School
Istanbul Technical University

'I avoided using the bus since there is too much traffic. Instead, I recommend taking the tram or metro, which are the most practical ways to save time here.'
Enes Can Kılıç

'I chose this school mainly for the exchange opportunities of the IMIAD programme. Students can choose one of five foreign countries and study there for a semester.'
Bürde Gültekin

'Thanks to the cultural richness of the IMIAD programme, the different perspectives and understandings broaden your experience and your views, and not just in an educational way – I gained some new friendships that brought me so much.'
Nazlı Sağlam

e attitude of the tutors is
t stereotypical instructor
haviour – they try to help
u like a friend.'
Cansu Köksal

'Methodology and Techniques in Digital Design was the most valuable class for me. Through it, I could understand the relationship between architecture and other disciplines like biology and mathematics.'
Pelin Uyar

'I live in Beşiktaş and I love to hang out here during the day. There are many cafe's and shops with good prices and products for students. On Saturday, there is a bazaar.'
Pınar Önal

City Life

Istanbul is the largest city in Turkey with a population of 14.1 million and it forms one of the largest urban agglomerations in Europe as well as the third-largest city in the world by population within the city limits. It is also the only city in the world to straddle two continents.

Founded around 660 BC as Byzantium, it has served as the capital of four empires: the Roman Empire (as Constantinople), the Byzantine Empire, the Latin Empire and the Ottoman Empire. The old city of Istanbul boasts some remarkable relics of this rich history: Hagia Sophia, dating from the days of Byzantium, the Ottoman-era sultan's palace complex of Topkapi and the 16th-century Sinan mosques and baths, to name only a few. But Istanbul is a modern city too, with one of the world's fastest-growing economies in recent years. Contemporary culture is well represented at Istanbul Modern, Sakip Sabanci Museum, Koc Museum, Miniaturk and Salt Istanbul.

The ITU Architecture Faculty is located in Beyoglu, which consists of two historic area Pera and Galata. Taksim Square, Cicek Passage and Galata Tower are the most important tourist spots nearby. Nightlife is well represented with Babylon, Asmali Mese and Nevizade on Istiklal Street, while the chic Nisantasi and Istiklal Street shopping areas are within close walking distance of the faculty.

Istanbul hosts many international design and culture events annually, including IKSV Istanbul Biennale, IKSV Istanbul Film Festive Istanbul Design Biennale, Istanbul Design Week and Alldesign.

Turkey

The panoramic view of Istanbul from Galata Tower, taking in the Bosphorus, the Golden Hor and Sultanahmet. Photo Ivan Mlinaric

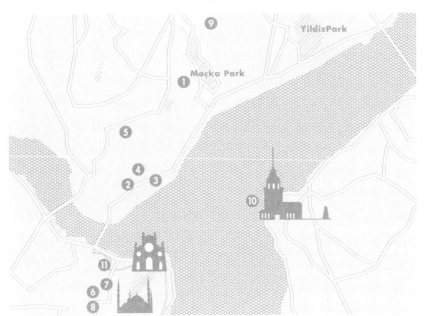

YildizPark

Maçka Park

Istanbul

1 ITU
2 Istanbul Design Week
3 Istanbul Modern
4 Blue Mosque
5 Mama Shelter Istanbul
6 Sultanahmet Square
7 Hagia Sophia
8 Non
9 Soda Istanbul
10 Maiden Tower
11 Sirkeci Station

Park

Water

Railway

Main road

Course
Interior Architectural Design

School
Istanbul Technical University

City Facts

ksim Square (2)
The bustling heart of modern Istanbul
is the place to go for shops,
restaurants and people-watching.

anbul Modern (3)
The Istanbul Museum of Modern Art,
Turkey's first private museum to
organise modern and contemporary
art exhibitions, was founded in 2004
and occupies an 8000-m² site on the
shores of the Bosphorus.
istanbulmodern.org

e Mosque (4)
So-called because of the blue tiles
adorning the walls of its interior,
the beautiful Blue Mosque was built
for Sultan Ahmed I between 1609
and 1616.
bluemosque.co

Mama Shelter Istanbul (5)
You don't have to stay here to enjoy
the huge, open-plan public space –
lounge, bar, pizzeria, restaurant,
performance area and terrace –
in Philippe Starck's lively Mama
Shelter Istanbul – one of the social
hubs of the city.
mamashelter.com

Sultanahmet Square (6)
The centre of the historic old city, and
once the Hippodrome of
Constantinople, Sultanahmet Square
is a tourist magnet as it's just a stone's
throw from all the major sights.

Hagia Sophia (7)
A masterpiece of Byzantine
architecture, Hagia Sofia has been a
church and mosque, but is now a
museum. Its beauty inspired the
architecture of the great Ottoman
architect, Sinan.
hagiasophia.com

Non (8)
Non gallery is devoted to artists who
embrace non-disciplinary art
practices, resulting in new languages
and artistic experiences.
galerinon.com

Soda Istanbul (9)
Soda is a contemporary art and
design space that focuses on artists
and designers using different
materials and medias from various
disciplines and especially supports
contemporary art jewellery, which is
a globally rising trend.
sodaistanbul.com

Maiden Tower (10)
On a small in the Bosphorus, the
Maiden Tower ('Kız Kulesi' in Turkish)
features a restaurant and a cafe.
kizkulesi.com.tr

w to get around
Most planes arrive at Istanbul Atatürk
Airport, 20 km west of the city centre.
From the airport, there are various
options for getting into Istanbul: you
can take a taxi, the express bus service
or the metro. For heading deeper into
the old city, the tram is recommended.
International trains from across Europe
arrive at the station in Sirkeci (11),
close to Sultanahmet. Asian trains
arrive at Haydarpasa Station. To get
between the two, catch a ferry across
the Bosphorus.

Traffic in Istanbul can be manic;
expect a stressful drive because you
will be cut up and honked at
constantly. If you've arrived in
Istanbul by car, and you're not
familiar with the streets, it's better to
park up your car in a safe place and
take public transportation to get
around. Istanbul Technical University
is located in Beyoglu, an area in the
European part of the city.

Arranging housing
Average

Housing support by school
No (but if necessary, they will do
their best)

Cost of room in the city
TL 700 per month (approx. EUR 250)

Cost of campus housing
Between TL 240 and TL 540 per month
(approx. EUR 80 to EUR 180)

The tall school building sits between the many fashion boutiques, designed by famous architects, that the Shibuya district is known f

Kuwasawa Design School

Kuwasawa Design School (KDS)
1-4-17 Jinnan, Shibuya
150-0041 Tokyo
Japan

T +81 (0)3 3463 2431
kouhou@kds.ac.jp

The school has its own shop that stocks many of the materials that students may need to create their products.

'Our mission doesn't change: to teach the essence of design which will not be influenced by trends'

Toshiki Omatsu, chief tutor of the Space Design course

When was the school founded?
The full-time course started in 1955, followed by evening classes in 1956.

Has it changed much over the years?
Our mission doesn't change: to teach the essence of design which will not be influenced by trends. If you achieve the basic and essence of design you will be able to adapt to social changes. For this reason we put emphasis on teaching basic plastic skills.

What kind of teaching method is applied here?
We teach design of interiors, residential projects, and architecture. We also teach design that relates to furniture, lighting and products, these subjects we call 'element design' at Kuwasawa; things that are close to the human body. Going from micro level to macro level in design is important. When designing products or furniture, it is important to think from a personal, micro perspective, but we encourage students to look at design from a macro perspective, placing those products or furniture in an urban scale as well. To achieve architectural thinking is important. This means that no matter how small the object is, it needs to be considered in relation to society and the city.

What is expected from the students?
During the course students will be immersed in CAD and 3D technologies. The school places much importance on achieving these skills. More important however is design thinking

where students come up with new concepts or ideas and figure out how to realise those new ideas. Students are encouraged to practice full-scale spatial design in relation to furniture design. Spatial design is a culmination of furniture and various elements of design and will extend to larger city design.

What is the most important thing for students to learn during this course?
In designing a space for living, designers need to be capable of abstract thinking. Residential design needs to be considered in relation to where it will be placed, and thinking on city scale is abstract.

What is the most important skill to master for an interior architect?
Instinct and objective thinking. Instinct is crucial to come up with designs. However, an idea that comes merely from instinct is art. Being a designer you need to be able to revise, improve and develop that instinct.

What kind of jobs do your former students mostly go on to do?
Our students end up as furniture designers, interior designers, architects, photographers, design directors or magazine editors.

Programme

Whilst the product design course is focused on cars, electronics and industrial design, it is the space design course that focuses on products that adorn our living environment, as well as space design for residential housing. The course is structured around learning fundamental plastic skills which form the basis for any course at Kuwasawa. This foundation can be described as searching for the aesthetic value of form. Students will take intense classes on this during the first year. Gaining a deep understanding of these fundamental skills will enable students to further develop their design skills when they proceed to the space design course.

In the second year, students will take studio workshops on element design, interior design, and residential environment design. These workshops are not in the form of classes but tutorials in which a teacher comments and advices on the students work progress. Complementing three studio workshops, are classes on drawing, CAD, 3DCG, as well as model making, a history class on furniture, interior design and architecture. Designers working in different fields are invited on a weekly base to give lectures.

In the third year, students will study in lab seminar format. Over that one year, students will take part in the spatial design lab run by Shigeru Uchida, and the element design lab run by Keisuke Fujiwara, allowing them to prepare for their graduation project.

Through workshops, students develop technical skills to enhance the composition of their products.

Students can make use of a richly-stocked library.

Programme
Space Design

Leads to
Specialist Diploma

Structure
The 3-year course is structured into an intensive 21 hours of lectures per week plus assignments. Each year is divided into two semesters of 14 weeks each, with the first semester starting in April and the second starting in September.

Head of programme
Toshiki Omatsu

Mentors and lecturers
Yoko Kinoshita, Keisuke Fujiwara, Toshiki Fujiwara, Mikio Tai, Shigeru Uchida and Makoto Watanabe.

Notable alumni
Hisae Igarashi, Yukichi Kawai, Takao Kawasaki, Setsuo Kitaoka, Shiro Kuramata, Takanori Urata an Tokujin Yoshioka.

Course
Space Design

School
Kuwasawa Design School

School Facts

uration of study
3 years (3 x 28 weeks)

ll time
Yes

rt time
No

Female students
60%

Male students
40%

Local students
98%

Students from abroad
2%

Yearly enrolment
60

Tuition fee
- JPY 1,580,000 for the first year
  (approx. EUR 16,350)
- JPY 1,280,000 for the second and
  third year (approx. EUR 13,250)

Funding/scholarships
Yes, partial funding and scholarships
are available from the Tokyo
metropolitan government fund,
Japanese student support
organisation, Kuwasawa Design
School scholarship and Kuwasawa
Gakuen educational scholarship.

nimum requirements for entry
High school degree and proficient
spoken Japanese

nguage
Japanese

plication procedure
Apply by sending application form
containing:
a copy of your accreditation from the
latest educational institution
an essay outlining why you have
chosen a particular course as well as
describing what you wish to pursue
during this course
your Japanese proficiency test
a photo
a receipt of payment of the non-
refundable application fee of JPY
30,000 (approx. EUR 310).
If you are selected, you will be invited to
either present your portfolio if you have
previous work to show or, if you don't
have any experience or a portfolio,
you will be invited to undertake an
assignment to prove your skills which
will be followed by an interview.

plication details
kouhou@kds.ac.jp

plication date
Before 1 November

Graduation rate
82.5%

Job placement rate
45%

Memberships/affiliations
None

Collaborations with
Pierre Herme

Facilities for students
Workshop facilities, computer rooms
and a library.

City
Tokyo

Country
Japan

149

Student Work

Leaf Arrangement (2013)
By Kasumi Nakagawa

This shelf unit is made in the form of a gingko leaf. It can be made in pewter, tin or wood. It shows Japanese aesthetics of yearning to bring ephemeral nature to the interior.

Zag (2013)
By Tatsuya Kishioki

This low-seat chair was inspired by the shape of superimposing layers of a flat surface.

Glasswall (2013)
By Eiko Hosoda

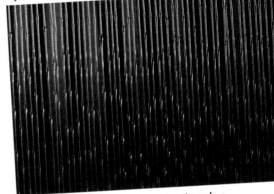

A glass screen with a special treatment on the surface.

The Edo Pop Hotel (2013)
By Kae Ishii

Hotel for tourists from overseas. The interior and furnishings incorporate motifs popular in the Edo period, here adopted into a contemporary setting.

150   Course
Space Design   School
Kuwasawa Design School

One's Final Abode (2013)
by Kotone Kawata

...ouse for a retired couple. The Interior has subtle curves to be ...xible to the lifestyle of a retired couple.

Tokaikko Menbow (2013)
By Takahiro Saito

The Shibuya scramble intersection is one of the most fluctuating places in the world. Continuous emission of information and its consumption take place at this intersection. Information is accumulated in the form of billboards and advertisements on the building forming the space. This relation between information and people that come and go changes endlessly, which shapes Shibuya itself.

Dress Up (2013)
By Midori Suzuki

...is DIY shop is aimed at a fashion-conscious clientele and offers not just products but gives a hint on lifestyle. The concept of the shop dressing up one's room. The design of the shop revolves around the scenario of picking out a dress from the wardrobe and drawers ...d then getting dressed, while customers will walk around different areas of the shop that are designed like rooms in a house.

Alumnus

Name Takanori Urata
Residence Chiba, Japan
Year of birth 1974
Year of graduation 1996
Current job Director Takanori Urata Design
Website urata-design.com

What was the most important thing you learned here?
One of important asset I've gained at Kuwasawa is meeting with people with character. Those people opened my eyes to see things in wider perspective.
As for my philosophy on design, I try not to be adamant on having my own style, but listen to the client and be adaptive to the client's need when I design. Working this way always gives me a fresh approach and makes the client happier.

What was the most interesting project you did?
That was an assignment I did during the first year. We were to design a house collectively with a group of 5 students. All of us got really into the project and we put way too much effort into things that got off track.

Was there any class you found particularly difficult?
The teachers' demand on the level of precision in projects is very high, which meant that I had to revise my work persistently. This allowed me to become very tough and thrive on adversity. You have to be tough to work in the design industry.

Any words of advice for future students?
As I now teach part time at Kuwasawa, I get to talk to many students. They are very diligent and hard workers, however, there are very few with an edge. When I was a student, Kuwasawa was famous for its strange and funny students. I remember there were many students with outrageous ideas and personalities. I do encourage students to get out of the norm and be more eccentric. Don't be afraid. Take pride in your own character and be funny. I think that is something that is only allowed while you are a student.

Was the transformation from graduation to working life a smooth one?
I finished school in 1996, after which I got a job at a constructer where I stayed for 7 years. Then I was so lucky to get a job at Tokujin Yoshioka's office where I worked for 8 years as an assistant designer. Working under Yoshioka gave me many experiences which otherwise I could not have got. However, there was a desire inside me to create things out of my own idea rather than designing under the direction of someone else. This pushed me to become independent at the age of 36.

If you were to do the course again, what would you do differently?
Looking back at my school days, one thing I regret is that I wish I had entered more competitions.

A 40-year-old building was planned to have facelift and Takanori Urata was commissioned to design the entrance. It proved how positive the impact is on people working in a positive environment.

Current Students

'Benefitting from the location of being in the centre of Shibuya, we often go visit newly opened retail spaces.'
Kouhei Aiba

'The school has a close link with design industry allowing us to be involved in what is happening in the field.'
Meng-Ying Chung

'Teachers encourage us to think outside the box.'
Kenjiro Kitamura

'One of the challenges studying at the school is that there are so many assignments to work on at the same time that I do need to organise very systematically.'
Hiroaki Ogihara

'Currently, I live in the Chiba prefecture, which is more than an hour from the school. However, Chiba is close to the international airport and sea, which is great to shift my mind.'
Mikiko Yamasawa

City Life

Shibuya is one of the 23 wards of Tokyo, located on the southwest side. There are more than 200,000 inhabitants living in the 15-km² area which make it one of most cosmopolitan districts in Tokyo. With more than 1600 hair salons, Shibuya claims to be the mecca for beauty seekers. The locality is also the epicentre of youth culture as well as being one of the busiest shopping districts in Tokyo. It is a test case for any commercial retailer to survive in a fast-changing market like Shibuya. In such an environment, students can observe people's buying trends, as well as come across ideas of what to design for eternal purpose in such an ever-changing market.

Neighbouring Shibuya, Omotesando is a showcase of contemporary architecture wher you can find jewels of buildings. Tadao Ando Omotesando Hills, Herzog & de Meuron's Prada shop, Jun Aoki's Louis Vuitton shop an Toyo Ito's Tods shop adorn the main boulevard. Once you get into small mews, yo come across time-honoured buildings used fo cosy cafes and organic restaurants that cater for even the most discerning palate.

With more than 130 live music venues and 14 cinemas, Shibuya offer many attractions for students.

Japan

The campus is based in the Shibuya area, the epicentre of youth culture in the heart of Tokyo.

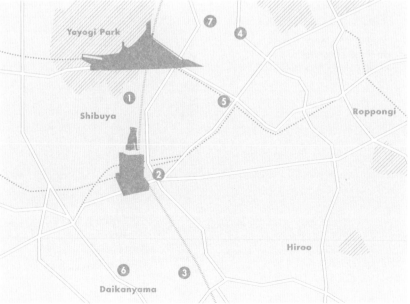

Tokyo

1 KDS
2 Hikarie
3 SML
4 Watari-Um Museum
5 Gallery Rocket
6 Daikanyama Tsutaya
7 Bunkaya Zakkaten

Park

Railway

Main road

Course
Space Design

School
Kuwasawa Design School

City Facts

yogi park
In the heart of Tokyo, just a few minutes' walk from Harajuku, is a park covering over 540,000 m² with seasonal floras, a soccer ground and a cycling course. Once a military parade ground in the late 19th century, Yoyogi park is now an oasis for the Tokyoites. Every weekend there are festivals featuring everything from music to eco-friendly events with organic food stalls.
tokyo-park.or.jp

iyashita park
Sitting next to Shibuya Station, Miyashita park used to be the hang-out for homeless people in Tokyo. But Nike has bought the land and converted it into a hidden sanctuary for the city dwellers. It doesn't have as much greenery as Yoyogi park, but creatively designed by Japanese architectural practice Atelier Bow-Wow, you can sit quietly on a deck or watch youngsters on their skateboards.

karie ②
This new shopping complex, spanning over 16 floors, entices you with gourmet food, fashion, furniture and household items and a state of the art musical theatre. But the must see for design students is the 8th floor, where anonymously designed everyday

goods selected from 47 different prefectures in Japan are showcased, as well as the ladies' restrooms which must be the most entertaining toilet in the world.
hikarie.jp/en/index.html

SML ③
Craft and design shop focusing on Japanese contemporary handcrafted pottery, celadon porcelain and free-blown glasswares. Exhibitions are often held on the shop at which the artists will be at present.
sm-l.jp

Watari-Um Museum ④
Museum designed by Mario Botta with a focus on contemporary art. The museum also places emphasis on architecture and garden design having held exhibitions on Luis Barragan, Sou Fujimoto and garden designer Mirei Shigemori in the past.
watarium.co.jp

Gallery Rocket ⑤
Exhibition platform for experimental art and food experiences. Tucked away in an alley in the Harajuku neighbourhood, the gallery is extremely difficult to find but worth the search. Some of the past exhibitions include Broken Heart Restaurant and Cinema Canteen.
rocket-jp.com

Daikanyama Tsutaya ⑥
Bookstore with impressive stock of world magazine, and more than 140,000 books on design, art, cuisine, cars and travel. The premises also houses a huge stock of movie DVDs as well as music CDs, and it also has a cafe inside. Designed by English practice Klein Dytham architecture, it is open from early morning until midnight, becoming more than just a bookstore.
tsite.jp/daikanyama

The Terminal
Opened in 2011, the space is a combined working space/cafe/meeting place for creative people. The space is equipped with Mac computers, each installed with all the programs a creative can need. Anyone can use them once you pay JPY 190 for 30 minutes or JPY 1050 for the whole day.
theterminal.jp

Bunkaya Zakkaten ⑦
Like a modern 'cabinet of curiosity', the shop sells amazing items which the owner makes at his atelier, as well as funny items picked up on his journeys around the world. Opened in 1974, in Harajuku, and now in its 38th year, the shop defies ages.
bunkaya.co.jp

w to get around
Tokyo is Japan's largest domestic and international hub for rail, ground and air transportation. Haneda Airport offers domestic and international flights, while Narita International Airport is the major gateway for international travellers. A train service is available from Narita Airport to Shibuya on the Narita Express. Trains run every 30 to 60 minutes and make the journey to Shibuya in 70 minutes.

Public transportation within Tokyo is dominated by an extensive network of clean and efficient trains and subways – one of the most extensive urban railway networks in the world. So by the far the best way to get around in Shibuya is by train. Shibuya Station is served by five lines, with frequent services that are extremely punctual and used by nearly 1,200,000 passengers every day. There are also 50 bus routes terminating in Shibuya that connect to all areas of Tokyo, some of which run after midnight.

Arranging housing
Difficult

Housing support by school
No

Cost of room in the city
JPY 50,000 per month (approx. EUR 515)

Cost of campus housing
n/a

Kyoto Institute of Technology

Kyoto Institute of Technology (KIT)
Matsugasaki, Sakyo-ku
606-8585 Kyoto
Japan

T +81 (0)75 724 7131
ses@jim.kit.ac.jp
kit.ac.jp

Located in a beautiful natural setting, the university is surrounded on three sides by mountains. Photo Yasushi Ichikawa

'With their own vision, students are encouraged to challenge new vocabulary of interior design'

Yoshiro Ono, dean of the Design and Architecture programme

When was the school founded, and how has it changed over the years?

Precursor of Kyoto Institute of Technology, Kyoto College of Technology was founded in 1902. Undergraduate school of Architecture and Design was founded in 1949, followed by Graduate School of Engineering and Design in 1965. We started offering the master's programme in Design in 2006 which was restructured in 2014 in order to adapt to ever changing technological, social environments of current society. Furthermore, in March 2014, the Kyoto Design Lab. was founded as an affiliate to support the master's programme adopting new teaching and research methods that reflect the current needs of our society.

What is studying at this school all about?

In an information-driven society, there is a demand for skills to be able to adapt to constantly changing phases of 'Practical Intelligence'. In our course we strive to find problems in social, global, environmental, business, and technological changes and to come up with innovative solutions to those problems through design. With this in mind our teaching focuses on basic skills in interior, architectural, product and graphic design as we exercise Project Based Learning with both Japanese and overseas companies and institutions.

What kind of teaching method is applied here?

Working with specialists in interior design as well as other related fields is very important in order to meet various needs and to offer new solutions. Our goal is to nurture talent of students that can bring innovation using design as an efficient tool.

What is expected from the students?

We think that interiors become truly meaningful as they mature through good use and maintenance of people, and that the role of interior designers is to help this process, rather than making individual 'works'. This is the key. In the Interior Design laboratory, run by Professor Kiyoshi Noguchi, students are expected to approach space design from a broad perspective, not just from functional and aesthetic points of view. Especially thinking about ethical and environmental issues, as well as symbiosis with nature is important.

What is the most important thing for students to learn during this course?

In addition to acquiring the basic knowledge of interior and architectural design, students are expected to form their own critical vision of designing and maintaining interiors. Here, awareness of the current problematical state of interior design is very important. With their own vision, students are encouraged to challenge a new vocabulary of interior design and find the way to negotiate such new vocabulary of design with their communication skills.

Programme

Interior design education is incorporated in the programme of which the concept is as follows. We see designers as visionaries, critical thinkers, and vital members not only of corporations but also of communities. Designers as concept builders and strategists will create and shape a wide range of cultural trends. The master's programme of Design offers specialisation across a wide spectrum of design field subjects for such applicants.

Through course work and practical research the programme aims to develop qualified creative designers who will have the power to contribute to the needs of the 21st century. Since the world is changing rapidly in nearly every direction, the master's programme of Design was designed to train students through the study and application of economic, technological and cultural point of views. Designers in particular, have to come to appreciate their role and responsibility in a society that is becoming increasingly information and knowledge oriented.

The programme consists of progressive design theory and project-based design practice. In the project-based design practice class, students are planned to collaborate with companies and students from other fields, aiming to come up with demanding solutions that meet social needs. The well-balanced education of both theory and practice will nurture expert skills necessary become a designer. The programme also aim to nurture future designers who are capable of working in highly professionalised teams.

Installation by interior and graphic design laboratories in the Honen-in Temple.

Professor Kiyoshi Noguchi, who mastered interior design in Japan and the UK, is the head of the Interior Design Laboratory.

Programme
Design

Leads to
Master of Design

Structure
The curriculum of the 2-year, full-time Master of Design programme offers both theoretical instruction and practical research activities. The programme is categorised in six different fields: Product design for everyday use; Communication design, including visual design planning and image analysis of commercial messages; Interaction design through methods found in various design fields such as web design; Interior design for enriched life environment; Emerging design themes such as design management; and Scientific analysis of the relationship between the physical properties of design wo (colour, shape, texture etc.) and human perception.

Head of programme
Katsuhiko Kushi

Mentors and lecturers
Yasushi Ichikawa, Takayuki Ikegawa Kanako Murayama, Sosuke Nakabo Yoshito Nakano, Masanobu Nishimu Kiyoshi Noguchi, Eizo Okada, Keita Tatara and Kentaro Yamamoto

School Facts

...ration of study
...2 years

...ll time
...Yes (30 hours a week)

...rt time
...No

Female students
50%

Male
50%

Local students
90%

Students from abroad
10%

Yearly enrolment
25

Tuition fee
JPY 535,800 per year
(approx. EUR 3920)

Funding/scholarships
Yes

...nimum requirements for entry
Bachelor's degree. Proficiency
in Japanese.

...nguage
Japanese and English

...plication procedure
Application materials should be sent
in a single package containing all the
following documents:
your applications form
a recommendation letter
your academic transcript
your curriculum vitae
a photocopy of your passport
your portfolio with three recent
and meaningful works.

...plication details
innyushi@kit.ac.jp

...plication date
Before 1 January or 15 July

Graduation rate
95%

Job placement rate
95%

Memberships/affiliations
None

Collaborations with
Rahti University of Applied Science,
Finland; Aalto University, Finland;
Stuttgart University of Applied Science,
Germany; National Superior School
of Architecture Versailles, France; and
University of Leeds, United Kingdom.

Facilities for students
Library, Museum and Archive,various
workshops, University Co-op retail
store, a bookstore, restaurants and
cafeterias, a healthcare service centre
and the travel tickets and housing
service offices.

Student Work

Puwa a Puwa (System Kitchen) (2013)
By Akiko Kadowaki

Kitchen aimed for shared houses for residents with various life-sty▶

Kahaful (Incense) (2013)
By Tomoya Kan

Incense paper for any mood or taste. You can rip off the incensed pieces of papers from a little booklet, each booklet has a different scent and different graphics.

Perori (Wall Display) (2013)
By Eriko Yoshio

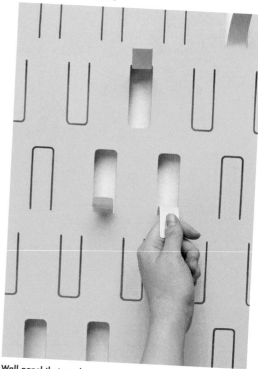

Wall panel that can be used for display, storage and decoration.

...old (2013)
...y Tao Tanaka

Furniture which outlines space in itself. A solution for small size housing in urban cities.

...e Shared House (2013)
... Kim Hyongchol

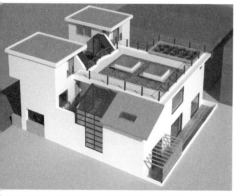

...se based for interchange between residents.

Tension Furniture TUG (2013)
By Keita Yamashita

Furniture composed of wooden frames and ink jet film with tensile force.

Lämpö (2013)
By Shiho Kataoka

Dining table designed to encourage close communication between a busy working mom and her kids.

Alumnus

Name Yuta Nonogaki
Residence Osaka, Japan
Year of birth 1984
Year of graduation 2009
Current job Interior coordinator
at Cassina IXC
Website cassina-ixc.jp

Why did you choose this school?

The school offers an environment to study architecture, product, industrial, graphic and interior design as an integrated field.

Were there any classes you found particularly difficult?

The Industry-University partnership and Government-University pilot programme. Because it involves money, we were expected to make evidence of result. Both projects were intense and proved practical in the end. I participated in a project to revamp tourism in one of the villages in Kyoto. Through field research we found what was the current problem and discussed with the people in the village as to what is needed to revamp local tourism. Also I participated in a pilot program initiated by the Kyoto government to expand the pedestrian walkways of one of the high streets in Kyoto.

What was your graduation project?

I made a light fixture using hand blown glass. While mastering the craft of hand blown glass making, I had to develop industrially feasible design to glass making which is primarily determined by craft.

What subject do you wish you paid more attention to?

I wish I had participated more in student competitions. At the school there were many opportunities to challenge not only in interior design competition but also on architectural, product, industrial and graphic ones.

Where were you living while being a student

I went to school from my home in Nara, another ancient and historical city. As Nara is a bit far away, I often stayed over at my class mate's room in Kyoto.

What was your favourite place to hang out?

Tadasuno Mori forest in Shimogamo Jinja in Kyoto.

Are you still in contact with the school?

Yes, with teachers from the master's programme of Design.

Any words of advice for future students?

How you spend 2 years at the graduate course will determine what you will be in the society. Whether it is your belief, your approach to work or what you value in your life, it will sure be an enormous asset for your future. With thi in mind, I encourage future students to always question why you are working on that project and what the objective is of the class. Try to fi your own answer and try to realise the solutio

For Nonogaki's graduation project, he made a light fixture using hand-blown glass.

Course
Design

School
Kyoto Institute of Technology

Current Students

is rare to have a design
urse at a national
iversity like Kyoto Institute
Technology, and we are
owed to explore wide
lds of design, not only
erior design.'
Satsuki Kakutani

'My German professors told me that KIT is a very good university to follow an exchange seminar in architecture and design. It gives me a great chance to learn a lot about Japanese architecture and interior design.'
Anselm Büchler

'I benefit from getting to know people from different backgrounds, like the product, graphic and architectural design students at the school.'
Mina Goto

'The course approaches design from a scientific point of view, meaning not only the teaching of aesthetics of form and colour, but methodology of design thinking down to the user experience.'
Maasa Kurachi

he school takes advantage
being in Kyoto. We go on
ld trips to experience the
ditional culture or visit
cal manufacturers.'
Kanako Togo

'I am an oversea student from Thailand. I've always wondered how Japanese design can still reflect the identity of its culture even in the modern design. It made me start looking back at the Thai culture.'
Tent Pattrawoot

'I think it is very special to study contemporary interior design in a city with such historical buildings.'
Ayaka Okada

City Life

Kyoto is a compact city surrounded by mountains. Being an ancient capital, Kyoto's government policy is to keep its historical landscape and traditional culture, making the city function like an interior space where old and new elements coexist. If you go out into the suburbs, Kyoto boasts with mountains in the north area and a seascape. One will come across how tradition, innovation, nature, man-made landscape, urbanism and the countryside are designed into a harmonious entity which makes Kyoto a 'one and only' city.

The school maintains close contact with crafts people from traditional industries such as *Karakami* (handmade paper often covering sliding doors)

and imbricated tile roof and metal work. The school initiates projects to combine these traditional cultures and industries with new creativity.

What makes Kyoto interesting is that there are buildings with traditional ornaments and decoration and workshops with ancient crafts while there are also companies that merge state-of-the-art technology with engineering. These companies include game maker Nintendo, electronic manufacturer Kyocera and innovative textile manufacturer Wacor. In addition, there are many universities in Kyoto pulling academics and researchers from around the globe to the city as well as attracting intellectuals to live there.

Japan

The Rakuhoku section, in the northern part of Kyoto, has a history of 1200 years. Photo Yasushi Ichikawa

Kyoto

1 KIT
2 Anteroom
3 Kyoto International Manga Museum
4 Kyoto Art Centre
5 Tukuru Building
6 Kyoto Imperial Palace
7 Kyoto Botanical Garden

Park

Water

Railway

Main road

Course
Design

School
Kyoto Institute of Technology

...teroom ❷
A creative hub which comprises of a hotel, residential apartments and a gallery. A space bringing together art and culture expressing the essence of contemporary Kyoto.
hotel-anteroom.com

...oto International Manga Museum ❸
Developed as a joint project of Kyoto City and Kyoto Seika University, the Museum acts as a venue for the collection, preservation and exhibition of manga and animation materials, which have been accumulated through generous donation from both individuals and companies.
kyotomm.jp

Kyoto Art Centre ❹
The Kyoto Art Center converted an old primary school into an art space in 2000. They promote arts in Kyoto in a comprehensive way by collaboration between the city of Kyoto, artists and other people related to art.
kac.or.jp

Tukuru Building ❺
A creative space that offers upcoming designers shared office space. The building also features a bookshop.
tukuru.me

Asahi Beer Oyamazaki Villa Museum of Art
A former residential house renovated by Tadao Ando. The museum houses one of the greatest collection of Mingei arts and craft in japan.
asahibeer-oyamazaki.com

Kyoto Imperial Palace ❻
The Imperial Palace is the former residential palace of the successive Tokugawa Shoguns in the Edo Period. The Palace preserves the look and ambiance of that time.
sankan.kunaicho.go.jp

Kyoto Botanical Gardens ❼
Located on the east bank of the Kamo-gawa River, the Kyoto Botanical Gardens rival the Kyoto Imperial Palace Park as the single best park in all of Kyoto. Often overlooked by visitors, the Kyoto Botanical Gardens is one of the city's hidden treasures. It's great for picnics, strolling or cherry blossom viewing.
pref.kyoto.jp/plant

Parasophia
Kyoto's International Festival of Contemporary Culture is to be held for the first time in Spring 2015.
parasophia.jp

...w to get around
Kyoto is Japan's most visitor-friendly city, with lots of English-language signs and an easy-to-navigate transportation system. The airport is about 100 km from Kyoto Station, which is 75 minutes by train or 95 minutes by bus. From Kyoto Station to the university is about 30 minutes using the metro. Get off at Matsugasaki Station.

Major attractions are centred around four stations which are Kyoto, Karasumaru, Kawaramachi and Sanjo Keihan. The bus and metro are easy to use in the city, but a bicycle is the most convenient way of getting around.

Arranging housing
Average

Housing support by school
Yes

Cost of room in the city
Between JPY 50,000 and JPY 60,000 600 per month (approx. EUR 365 to EUR 440)

Cost of campus housing
Between JPY 5900 and JPY 14,200 per month, excluding electricity, water, cleaning, etc. (approx. EUR 45 to EUR 105)

NABA's modern campus is located in Milan's atmospheric Navagli district. Photo Sette Secondi Circa

NABA – Nuova Accademia di Belle Arti Milano

NABA – Nuova Accademia di Belle Arti Milano
Via C. Darwin 20
20143 Milan
Italy

T +39 02 973 721
info@naba.it
naba.it

Some 2700 students attend the 17,000-m² university.

Course
Design – Interior Design

School
NABA – Nuova Accademia di Belle Arti Mil

'NABA places students at the centre of an educational process based on direct participation in the everyday practice'

Luca Poncellini, course leader of the MA in Design – Interior Design

When was the school founded?
NABA was founded in 1980 to cultivate artistic practises, culture and criticism in Italian design.

Why should students choose NABA?
While we offer a specific and updated programme in design, students learn in an art-school environment and are exposed to a rich and interdisciplinary academic context.

NABA is based in Milan and most of the teachers are prestigious and well-known professionals with extensive experience and contacts in the design field. NABA students have the opportunity to collaborate with leading companies and institutions in Italy and abroad, among them are Abitare, Alessi, Diesel, Giorgio Armani, Saatchi & Saatchi, The Swatch Group and IKEA. Furthermore, NABA offers huge opportunities to participate in valuable international competitions. Thanks to the recognition by MIUR (Italian Ministry of Education, University and Research) NABA degrees are internationally recognised.

What is studying at NABA all about?
NABA places students at the centre of an educational process based on direct participation in the everyday practice and professional excellence of the faculty. Students work with a recognised network of companies of national and international importance and therefore have access to unique opportunities.

When did you start offering the master's degree course in interior design?
The 2-year MA in Design – Interior Design was launched in 2012. It has replaced the former 1-year Interior Design programme, which had been running since 2008.

What is the most important thing for students to learn during this course?
The ability to deal with any design task and to successfully tackle any design challenge, relying on a solid methodological approach.

What is the most important skill to master when one wants to become an interior designer?
The complete understanding of the multiple parameters of a project (conceptual, aesthetical, technical and economical) and their mutual interconnections, in order to always be able to make informed decisions.

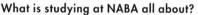

Programme

The master's programme leads students to develop an experimental, investigative and innovative approach to interior design, and a self-challenging attitude towards the discipline. The course aims to provide students with a solid methodological background that supports the pursuit of the most important skill for a designer: the awareness of his/her capacity to deal with any design task at any professional level. Students are exposed to different design experiences, through a combination of integrated project workshops design courses, theoretical courses and extra-didactical activities. The ultimate aim o the course is to allow students to be empowered by their own design talent.

NABA enjoys a diverse student population, with over 60 nationalities represented. Photo courtesy of NABA

Student theses written as far back as 1980 can be found in the university's library. Photo Sette Secondi Circa

Programme
Design – Interior Design

Leads to
Master of Arts

Structure
The first year includes modules such as the history of design, project methodology, new materials technology, product design, light design, 3D rendering and integrated new media. In the second year, students take modules such as design management, brand design, interaction design, exhibition design, decoration and multimedia design. In addition to these programmes, students can partake in Erasmus exchanges, cross-disciplinary seminars, conferences, internships and work experience.

Head of programme
Luca Poncellini

Mentors and lecturers
Joseph Forakis, Stefano Giovannon Migliore+Servetto Architects, Denis Santachiara and Mario Trimarchi

Notable alumni
Vera Gapon, Dmitry Aleksandrov, Francesca Bassi Longton, Julie Wimmerova, Emily Cheng, Davide Gamba and Lene Utbjoe.

Course
Design – Interior Design

School
NABA – Nuova Accademia di Belle Arti Mil•

School Facts

Duration of study
2 years

Full time
Yes (40 hours a week)

Part time
No

Female students
81%

Male students
19%

Local students
38%

Students from abroad
62%

Yearly enrolment
23

Tuition fee
• EUR 9790 per year for EU citizens
• EUR 12,990 per year for non-EU citizens

Funding/scholarships
NABA offers scholarships for talented students requiring financial support, based on the evaluation feedback provided by the course leader.

Minimum requirements for entry
A degree in design or architecture. Applications by students with a different degree or diploma may be taken into consideration if the applicant is motivated by a significant interest in the programme topics. Proficient written and spoken English.

Language
English

Application procedure
The following documents must be submitted in order to complete the application:
a completed online application form
your portfolio
your curriculum vitae
a copy of degree/diploma
academic transcripts
your motivation letter
a copy of your CEFRL B2 level certificate (if applicable).
All admissions are based on a personal evaluation by the course leader.

Application details
naba.it

Application date
Before 30 November

Graduation rate
High

Job placement rate
100%

Memberships/affiliations
IDSA, ADI

Collaborations with
Abitare, Bosch, ComTech, Comvert, Electrolux, ENI, Fondazione Pirelli, Giochi Preziosi, IKEA, Industreal, Jannelli & Volpi, L'Oreal, Material Connexion, Momo Design, Orange, Parco Nord Milano, Pininfarina Extra, Samsung, The Swatch Group, Tupperware, Vinavil and Waril, and Zanotta.

Facilities for students
A design lab (equipped with a 3D printer, laser cutting machine, and thermoforming and blender machine), knitting labs, a textile library and a fashion lab.

Student Work

Outré (2013)
By Dilara Guneri and Benguhan Ozis

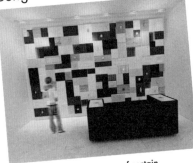

Tasked with creating a space of certain dimensions – namely, 600 x 600 x 480cm – on the ground floor of a building in a Western city, students designed Outré, a chocolate shop in Paris, which features a patchwork system of drawers on the store's back wall.

House of Awareness #1 (2013)
By Sebnem Kut, Minh Minh Le, Benguhan Ozis, Anna Popova and Ege Uzrek

In this collective research project investigating the complex relationship between human life and the environment, students designed a dwelling space for humans, animals and vegetation to coexist together. Energy i the basic ingredient for the interaction between species.

Architecture as a Self-Portrait (2013)
By Ezgi Nazli

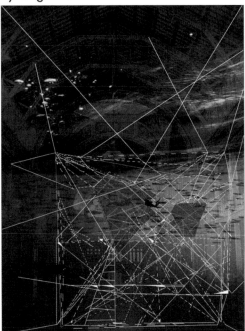

An experimental project that blurs the line between design and art and examines the idea of architecture as a self-portrait.

House of Awareness #4 (2013)
By Szilvia Bugner, Paola Ferraresso, Ivan Korlat, Matteo Maggiolo, Fatimas Taracido and Pavlina Tzovar

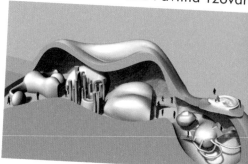

Dedicated to the theme health, this house is an exhibition centre which takes the shape of a human body prone on the ground. Visitors are led on a journey inside the body, through smaller pavilions dedicated to the parts of the body that provide physical and emotional balance.

Course
Design – Interior Design

School
NABA – Nuova Accademia di Belle Arti Mile

Permeability (2013)
By Anne-Sophie Gauvin and Andrea Monedero

A modular system was designed by this student duo for an apartment in Milan. With a variety of levels and an assortment of compartments, the structure accommodates a huge storage space while successfully dividing up the room into two floors.

Office Space (2013)
By Emmy Taimour and Ulviyya Javadova

Students chose Sydney as the city to base their design of an office. The open-plan workspace allocates various dedicated areas for work and relaxation.

House of Awareness #2 (2013)
By Anne-Sophie Gauvin, Dilara Güneri, Abdul Mayouf, Andrea Monedero, Maged Raphael and Emmy Taimour

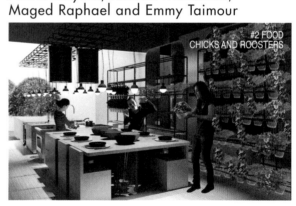

Designed with the set of a reality television show in mind, this house has a focus on food. Then people – all from different countries – gather around a huge dining table and a hydroponic plantation where plants are grown using mineral nutrient solutions in water, without soil. By growing, cooking and consuming food, the guests and their audience will discover the different cultures and rituals associated with food.

Alumna

Name Paola Ferraresso
Residence Singapore, Singapore
Year of birth 1983
Year of graduation 2012
Current job Interior designer
at Kemistry of Style
Website kemistryofstyle.it

The most interesting project Ferraresso did at NABA was an interior design project with Piero Lissoni. The client needed a very functional living space. The concept was to emphasise 6 x 6 m-space through the clever use of intelligent design.

Why did you choose this school?
In Milan, you are absorbed by design. You have the opportunity to attend important events, meet famous designers, visit some of the most prestigious furniture production houses and, of course, attend the Salone del Mobile. The other advantage is the team of tutors. The year I attended, I studied under Italo Rota, Piero Lissoni, Andrea Branzi, Denis Santachiara and Ernesto Gismondi. I already knew all of them through their work, so it was a great inspiration to have them as teachers.

What subject do you wish you paid more attention to?
The project workshop. It was the most complex class, because you had to face challenging design tasks that had to be developed from an interdisciplinary perspective under the supervision of a small team of professors, each responsible for a distinct aspect of the project. It was quite close to the realities of the profession.

Was there any class you found particularly easy?
No class was easy, as each one presented unique challenges. However, one of the classes I was most passionate about – and which therefore became easier – was design history. I already had a good background on the subject, so the class presented a fabulous opportunity to enhance the knowledge I had already acquired. The way that Andrea Branzi and Angela Rui ran it was very different from my past experience, but it really helped me understand the process of producing ideas.

What was your graduation project?
The House of Awareness: a journey in search Euphoria. The project developed a new way t create an exhibition experience between art and architecture. The exhibition path was a personal experience that made use of all the senses. The main idea was to make the visitor feel like an explorer, discovering the space through a free path. This complex system translated into a colourful, fluid space with a special lighting installation.

What was your favourite place to hang out?
During the summer, I loved to drink a spritz in the garden of the Triennale Design Museum.

Are you still in contact with the school? How
I live in Singapore now, but every time I go back to Milan I call in to say hello to my professors and the staff. It was thanks to Luca Poncellini – the new course leader – that I got the chance to work in Singapore. One day he asked: 'Who would like to go to Singapore? There is a job opening for an exhibition designer.' After a couple of months – and interviews – I arrived in Singapore.

Current Students

'Listening to the stories of failure and success from the esteemed architects and designers who teach at NABA makes me feel closer to succeeding.'
Cagda Akten

'Alzaia Naviglio Grande is a street full of bars, clubs and restaurants, and it's ten minutes away from the school!'
José Raúl Zuleta Pérez

'My advice to future students? Don't be afraid of failure. The more you fail, the more opportunities you will have to succeed. I believe that genius is born from mistakes.'
Anastasiia Loboda

'Finding an apartment is pretty easy thanks to some specialised websites, but also the university helps you.'
Laura Scapin

'We worked with students from Beijing's Tsinghua University on an exhibition during Design Shanghai. The most valuable thing, for me, was that we saw our ideas, the ones that usually remain as drawings, become reality.'
Erica Fornara

City Life

For students of design, studying in Milan is an obvious choice. Hailed as a major world fashion and design capital, the city hosts two of the biggest events in these fields: Milan Fashion Week and Milan Design Week. So, while students can soak up the Italian culture and cuisine all year round, in these 2 weeks, they can witness – from the comfort of their own city – the best from the rest of the world. Design aside, Milan is a bustling city with plenty on offer. Take in the *Last Supper* at the church of Santa Maria delle Grazie, relax in Parco Sempione, the 116-acre park located behind the impressive Castello Sforzesco, and enjoy Milan's famous *aperitivo* – a pre-dinner drink accompanied by complementary nibbles – at any number of establishments.

Italy

Housed within a four-story double arcade in central Milan, the Galleria Vittorio Emanuele II is one of the world's oldest shopping malls. Photo Andrea Raffin

Paolo Sarpi

Porta Venezia
6

Brera

3

5
7

2

Zona Tortona
4

Navigli
1

Milan

1 NABA
2 Duomo
3 Triennale Design Museu
4 Navigli Area
5 Quadrilatero Della Moc
6 Bar Basso
7 Panzerotti Fritti

Park

Railway

Main road

Course
Design – Interior Design

School
NABA – Nuova Accademia di Belle Arti Mil

City Facts

See more Milan City Facts on p.56 and p.256

Duomo 2
Ascending the steps of the metro at the Duomo stop, visitors are struck by the sight of the towering Gothic cathedral. After taking over 5 centuries to complete, the beautiful and imposing Duomo is the fifth largest cathedral in the world.
duomomilano.it

Triennale Design Museum 3
Surrounded by the lush Parco Sempione, the Triennale is a design student's dream. Featuring a permanent collection of significant contemporary Italian design, a series of temporary exhibitions and an event space, the museum is great for getting inspired or just having a coffee in the design cafe.
triennaledesignmuseum.it

Navigli Area 4
Near the Porta Genova station, this canal district is instantly appealing. The streets are lined with a variety of cafes and bars as well as an assortment of galleries and design shops. The perfect place to enjoy an *aperitivo*.
navigli.milano.it

Salone del Mobile (Milan Design Week)
The most important event on the design calendar worldwide, Salone is *the* place to see design and, of course, to be seen. During this week, Milan is packed with press, designers and design worshippers from the world over. The main fair takes place outside Milan in Rho, while fringe events, parties and talks are spread across the entire city.
cosmit.it

Quadrilatero Della Moda 5
Literally translated as the 'quadrilateral of fashion', these four streets are a high-end shopping paradise with stores such as Alexander McQueen, Armani and Jimmy Choo. While students might not find much in their price range here, at least the windows displays can inspire.

Idroscalo
Originally dug out as an airport for seaplanes, Milan's man-made lake is reachable by public transport and offers a varied timetable of sporting activities, as well as hosting important national sporting events.
idroscalo.info

Bar Basso 6
Truly an institution, this cocktail bar is perched on the corner of a roundabout on the east-side of Milan. The classic cocktail venue draws large crowds, particularly on the nights during the Salone del Mobile when it inevitably becomes the fair's unofficial after party.
barbasso.com

Panzerotti Fritti 7
If it wasn't for the huge queues outside, you might just miss this unassuming take-away near to the Duomo. While they sell a variety of baked goodies, they are most famous for their *panzerotto* – similar to a small *calzone*, but fried.

How to get around
In Milan, buses, trams, metro (underground) and trains are run by the same company, ATM (Azienda Trasporti Milanese). With more than 50 urban bus routes, the bus system sometimes offers a more direct route than the underground. The fare costs EUR 1.50 and you can get on and off as many times as you want for 90 minutes. The metro system consists of three lines: M1 (red), M2 (green), M3 (yellow). There is also a blue line, the *passante ferroviario*, which is a railway but can be used with the same ticket as the urban tracks.

Arranging housing
Quite easy

Housing support by school
Yes, full support

Cost of room in the city
Between EUR 300 and EUR 600 per month

Cost of campus housing
Between EUR 300 and EUR 600 per month

The school site next to a waterfall forms a bridge with both nature and the building's industrial past. Photo Toni Kauppi

Oslo
National
Academy
of the Arts

**Oslo National Academy
of the Arts (KHiO)**
Fossveien 24
0551 Olso
Norway

T +47 22 995 500
postmottak@khio.no
khio.no

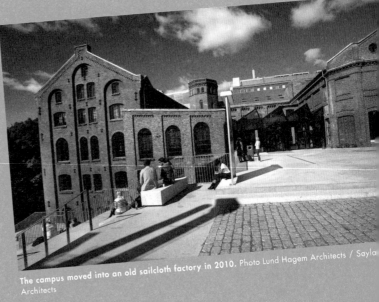

The campus moved into an old sailcloth factory in 2010. Photo Lund Hagem Architects / Sayla
Architects

**Course
Interior Architecture and Furniture Design**

School
Oslo National Academy of the Arts

'Our programme operates in between several disciplines, taking advantage of a rich dialogue with multiple voices'

Toni Kauppila, head of the Spatial and Furniture Design programme

When was the school founded?
The school was originally founded in 1818 as the Royal Norwegian Drawing School. Today, it is a contemporary, multidisciplinary art institution with departments in Design, Crafts, Fine Arts and Performing Arts, and an emerging collaboration with the Oslo School of Architecture and Design. We find this set up inspiring, since the programme of Spatial and Furniture Design operates in between several disciplines, taking advantage of a rich dialogue with multiple voices. Rather than having a fixed framework, we are constantly evolving the curriculum to be agile in the face of current and future developments in our fields.

What is studying at this school all about?
The school and class sizes are very small. We have a common agenda around social and human-centric design. Within that, individual concerns are nurtured and progressed to a diversity of undertakings. Rather than making fixed definitions of our disciplines, we challenge our students to investigate the peripheries.

What teaching approach is taken here?
The pedagogical approach is based on critical dialogue and collaborative learning. Students enter the programme with certain skills and experiences, only to be pushed forward by the collective provocations. At the MA level we emphasise nurturing dispositions for learning beyond specific skills or knowledge. We aim to prepare the students for an uncertain future, for which we don't yet know all the needed expertise. We want to facilitate the explorations for these emerging territories.

Why should students choose this school?
We want to position the school in the intersection where Scandinavian design's craft tradition meets 21st-century social responsibility. The great heritage of Norwegian craftsmanship is updated by a commitment and passion to enhance the good life for the future. Through the art school configuration, we can provide generous facilities exploring the multiplicity of creative processes.

What is expected from the students?
We are interested in curiosity and a passion to explore the unknown. We consider the students to be privileged on entering the programme, which requires commitment and responsibility. In return, we hope to equip them with the confidence to establish and position themselves as proactive designers in a super-complex world.

What kind of jobs do your former students mostly end up?
The work situation in architecture and interior design has been exceptionally good in Norway over the past years. We have a strong emphasis on entrepreneurship, on developing a new practice in newly surfacing areas of interest. We try to give students the confidence to pursue their work to its full potential, to see opportunities and go beyond conventional constraints.

Programme

The MDes Interior Architecture and Furniture Design is a 2-year full-time programme. The main agenda is to investigate the social urban cultures; the spaces and the objects related to it. The academy operates with a broadened definition of the disciplines. They position the programme in-between urbanism, architecture and product design. The courses are structured on the basis of shifting perspectives; the holistic understanding is in the core, yet different themes are brought in to the foreground. They orbit around concerns of the Context, the Social and the Material. The studio courses are built around these themes benefiting on variety of experts from specific fields. The Context webs issues such as global mega-trends, systemic thinking, and cultural diversity as the framework for design interventions. The Social begins with the human body and the encountering of the other to unfold the communal networks. Here the programme collaborates with the performing arts paralleling the dynamic design practices for space, time and action. The Material expands the understanding of the production practices as laboratories of design research. Courses collaborate with the industries both locally and internationally. The courses make every year excursions to gain first-hand experiences to the related topics.

The discipline specific, studio-based courses coincide with the trans-disciplinary theory and method courses. These are well integrated with the ambition of establishing new intellectual design research practices. Entrepreneurial thinking penetrates through all the courses with a specific intensive perio focusing on emerging new models of practic to enable the novel interests to surface.

The multi-disciplinary school provides the students with access to a wide range of workshops and resources for their design tasks. Photo Charlotte Kristiansen

The students have their own house by the river w a bar for social activities. Photo Oda Hveem / Javialbiennalen

Programme
Interior Architecture and Furniture Design

Leads to
Master of Design

Structure
The 2-year full-time course (120 credits) begins with 2.5 semesters of studio-based, research-orientated courses on the themes of the specialisations paralleled with trans-disciplinary design theory and method courses. Studies vary betwe longer projects, intensive workshop and seminars both as individual an group works. Thesis work occupies 1.5 semester long (45 credits).

Head of programme
Toni Kauppila

Mentors and lecturers
Theodor Barth, Bjørn Blikstad, Terje Hope, Toni Kauppila, Ellen Klingenberg, Maziar Raein, Vigdis Ruud, Sigurd Strøm and guest teachers.

Duration of study
2 years

Full time
Yes (40 hours a week)

Part time
No

Female students
60%

Male
40%

Local students
61%

Students from abroad
39%

Yearly enrolment
8–10

Tuition fee
Free

Funding/scholarships
Norwegian students are entitled to loans and grants from the State Educational Loan Fund (NSELF). Foreign students can apply for grants from the Quota scheme or Norad Program in Arts and Cultural Education (ACE).

Minimum requirements for entry
Bachelor's degree in design, architecture or art. Working experience in a similar business sector/industry is also acceptable.

Language
English and Norwegian

Application procedure
You can apply digitally through the online application service. The following documents must be submitted in order to complete the application:
a completed and signed application form
a copy of your curriculum vitae
a copy of your qualifying degree (if appropriate)
your portfolio
references
a project proposal
a copy of your language certificate (if appropriate).
Shortlisted candidates will be interviewed in the first week of March. Before the end of March some candidates will be offered a study place.

Application details
opptakdesign@khio.no

Application date
Before 1 February

Graduation rate
High

Job placement rate
High

Memberships/affiliations
Norwegian Centre for International Cooperation in Education, Cumulus, Cirrus (Nordplus) and Erasmus.

Collaborations with
Oslo School of Architecture and Design, Aalto University School of Arts, Design and Architecture, Lahti University of Applied Sciences, Central Saint Martins, L'école nationale supérieure d'architecture de Paris La Villette, Tama Art University, the Royal Danish Academy of Fine Arts, Design School Kolding, HDK School of Design and Crafts, Konstfack, Iceland Academy of the Arts and Institute Superiore de Artes e Cultura.

Facilities for students
Dedicated personal studio space, multiple contemporary workshops for different materials with both traditional and computer-controlled machinery, and workshops for 1:1 experiments, including a space lab.

Student Work

'Små Rom' (2014)
By Martin Ramstad Rygner

Out of the Blue (2013)
By Eva de Moor

A study about colour in interior architecture focused on the connection between colour and daylight. This research project consisted of small independent projects which concluded with a colour palette for a swimming pool, Sagene Folkebad, in Oslo which completed by the skin colour of the swimmers.

Mindful Eating (2014)
By Camilla Akersveen

Små Rom is a project on how we should develop the future city and investigates the quality of small spaces. The transformation of the old tower at Briskeby fire station lies on the border of furniture design and interior architecture.

A product series aimed at enhancing the sensory experience related to eating and drinking, these pieces incorporate surprising playful and social elements to build an emotional bond with the user. Over time and through continued use, the products should stimulate secular rituals in context of food.

Course
Interior Architecture and Furniture Design

School
Oslo National Academy of the Arts

earing the Scenery (2014)
y Ma Lina

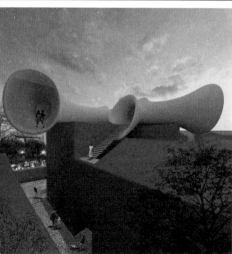

a specific site, trumpet structures add a voice to a space.
sounds are about the value of a past that is rapidly
appearing in Shanghai's Longtang and in the grassland of
er Mongolia. A soundscape tells people of the way things
e – complete with a patch of grassland to show them, too.

Sense of Place (2014)
By Margrethe Hvesser

How can 'the character of a place' be brought into and conveyed
through new spatial design? The project is located in an existing meeting
place in one of Oslo's largest parks, a place said to have lost contact
with the character of its surroundings. The design solution explores how
a location can be transformed into a symbol of its surroundings.

Låven (2014)
By Hege Grøholt

Based on analysis, research and documentation of the
architecture of a traditional Norwegian barn, this building type
is re-functionalised with the aim of retaining is authenticity.
The design balances between facilitating reuse and preserving
the barn's integrity.

Alumnus

Name Bjørn Jørund Blikstad
Residence Oslo, Norway
Year of birth 1981
Year of graduation 2009
Current job Independent designer and lecturer
Clients Contract and private
Website worksby.com

For his graduation project, Bjørn Jørund Blikstad created the geometrical storage solution Imeüble as 'a non-symbolic design for the storage and retrieval of personal flat stuff'.

Why did you choose this school?
After graduating with a bachelor's degree from this school, I wanted to continue with a master's degree because of the staff. There is a very exciting mix of tutors here. On one hand you have the Norwegian and Scandinavian design tradition, with a strong anchor in arts and crafts, and on the other hand there's an international staff with more focus on academic rigour. The mix of these and addition of an anthropologist makes it an exciting place to study to become a designer of artefacts and spaces.

What was the most important thing you learned here?
Discursive discussion, and craft techniques.

What subject do you wish you paid more attention to?
A difficult question because the study was very self-driven and artistic. It's based on different projects with particular deadlines with the different subjects woven into each delivery. There were perhaps one or two projects I didn't like doing – but I don't think I should have paid more attention to them.

Was there any class you found particularly difficult?
The hardest part of the 2-year programme was when I received a travelling stipend from the Federation of Norwegian Industries with a subsequent internship at a Norwegian Furniture manufacturer. It was difficult to mentally manage the different levels of emphasis from the academic world and from the business world.

What was your graduation project?
A search for a non-symbolic design for the storage and retrieval of personal flat stuff

(books, texts and imagery). A conceptual comparison of the link between physical storage capabilities and mental storage capacity resulted in various designs, including the geometrical storage solution Imeüble.

Any words of advice for future students?
Listen to all your tutors and make consistent decisions based upon your intuition.

What was your favourite place to hang out?
The student bar on Friday evenings from six to midnight.

Are you still in contact with the school?
I'm a fill-in lecturer on the BA programme, teaching construction, ergonomics/human factors and conceptual thinking and design thinking.

Are you still in contact with your fellow students?
Yes. Four of us are doing design projects together when convenient. It's both idealistic and professional.

Was the transformation from graduation to working life a smooth one?
Smooth if you think about the constant increa in the amount of work to be done. Not so smooth if you think about it as a level of comfort in terms of a ride.

182   Course
Interior Architecture and Furniture Design

School
Oslo National Academy of the Arts

Current Students

'Good design depends on discussions around ideas and opinions. During the course, we have had many interesting discussions with our tutors, fellow students and ourselves.'
Hege Bøhmer Grøholt

'I ride my bike almost everywhere in Oslo. It's not famous for facilitating for this but you get used to how it works soon enough.'
Åsmund Wivestad Engesland

'The choreography course was the most interesting and valuable for me. The project involved workshops with choreography and dance students, where we looked at the social aspect of design and choreography. We observed people and spaces and analysed them, then choreographed performances and worked with making manuals and descriptions.'
Veronica Skogvold Navekvien

'The school emphasises the role of design as a social intervention to change people's behaviour. You have many opportunities to contemplate what design can contribute in terms of benefits to individuals and society as a whole.'
Taeho Noh

'I chose this school because of its incredible and new facilities!'
Antonio Cascos Chamizo

City Life

Oslo, the capital of Norway, was founded in 1048. The city is surrounded by nature, with forests and fjords close to the city centre. The school is located in Grünerløkka, a formerly industrial, now hip district renowned for its vibrant local life. In this neighbourhood, there are independent galleries, design studios and bookshops, and nearby is Birkelunden park, with its weekend flea- and farmer's markets.

Just a short walk away from the school, Olaf Ryes Square is surrounded by cafes, galleries and unique bars and restaurants.

At the north end of the square is Parkteatret, which has recently evolved into one of the most interesting concert venues in Oslo. The city is famous for its cafe culture and there are about 70 coffee shops in town.

Oslo National Academy of the Arts is a part of a growing creative area beside River Akerselva. Our closest neighbour is the Oslo School of Architecture and Design. Not far down the river, there is another old industrial area called Vulkan which is now home to various cultural attractions.

Norway

The iconic Norwegian Opera House designed by Snøhetta. Photo VisitOSLO

The school is located in Grünerløkka, a formerly working class area that is now one of Oslo's hipster districts. Photo Charlotte Kristians

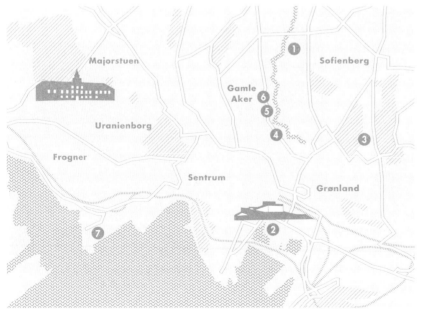

Majorstuen

Sofienberg

Gamle Aker

Uranienborg

Frogner

Sentrum

Grønland

Oslo

1 KHiO
2 Norwegian Opera House
3 Munch Museum
4 DogA
5 Blå
6 Dansens Hus
7 The Astrup Fearnley Museum

Park

Water

Railway

Main road

Course
Interior Architecture and Furniture Design

School
Oslo National Academy of the Arts

Norwegian Opera House ❷
A wonderful landscape of a building by local architects Snøhetta, also worth visiting for the opera and ballet inside.
operaen.no

Munch Museum ❸
Dedicated to the life and work of the famous Norwegian artist Edvard Munch. The museum has the world's largest collection of his paintings – including the iconic Scream.
munch.museum.no

gA ❹
The Norwegian Centre for Design and Architecture, housed in a cool industrial complex, is a lively meeting place hosting a variety of events and facilities.
doga.no

Blå ❺
A dark and industrial jazz club known for booking some of the best jazz and electronica live acts in the world.
blaaoslo.no

Dansens Hus ❻
The national stage for contemporary dance, housed in a former industrial building.
dansenshus.com

The Astrup Fearnley Museum ❼
A great private collection of contemporary art in a brand-new Renzo Piano building. Includes works by Damien Hirst, Matthew Barney, Cindy Sherman, JeffKoons and Takashi Murakami.
afmuseet.no

National Museum of Art, Architecture and Design
In four different locations in the centre of Oslo, with a varied exhibition programme as well as permanent collections.
nasjonalmuseet.no

Designers' Saturday
Oslo's biggest design event spreads itself all over the city every other September – foot-saving free buses circulate around the different venues.

Holmenkollen and Oslo Winter Park
Oslo's biggest ski resort, at Tryvann, is only 20 minutes by metro from the city's Central Station.
oslovinterpark.no

Vigeland Park
The world's largest sculpture park made by a single artist, Gustav Vigeland. is one of Norway's most-visited tourist attractions.

How to get around
Oslo is not a very big city, which makes it easy to get around by foot and bicycle. However, there is good public transport provision, with trams, metro and bus. City Bikes are places all around the city, and around EUR 12.50 buys you a card to get access to these.

The major train stations in Oslo, Central Station and National Theatre, are both about 3km from Oslo National Academy of the Arts. The nearest tram and bus stop are at Birkelunden, just a few blocks away from the school.

Arranging housing
Average

Housing support by school
No

Cost of room in the city
NOK 5500 per month (approx. EUR 650)

Cost of campus housing
Between NOK 3000 and NOK 3500 per month (approx. EUR 355 to EUR 415) for housing from the student organisation (SIO).

The exterior of The New School's new University Center
exemplifies the school's commitment to creativity,
innovation and social engagment. Photo Martin Seck

Parsons The New School for Design

The New School has a stunning new University Center – a forward-thinking design
opened in January 2014. Photo James Ewing

**Parsons The New School
for Design**
72 Fifth Avenue
New York, NY, 11216
United States

T +1 800 292 3040
thinkparsonsgrad@newschool.edu
newschool.edu/parsons

Course
Interior Design

School
Parsons The New School for Design

'We seek students with an insatiable curiosity who are committed to making a better future for people on this planet'

Jonsara Ruth, director of the MFA Interior Design programme

What is studying on this programme all about?

This programme was initiated to advance the study and the discipline of interior design. We aim to expand the definition of interior design. Challenging assumptions is a core principle. The programme is built on rigorous inquiry, exploration and experimentation. We understand that interior designers help to shape the experiences of others. It is the designer's responsibility to understand subtleties of human perception, sensation and cognition. We believe in design as an agent of social change, and as an act of environmental stewardship.

What is expected from the students?

We seek students with an insatiable curiosity who are committed to making a better future for people on this planet. We welcome students from a wide variety of disciplines and encourage them to bring knowledge from other fields to the study of Interior Design. We look for students who want to explore and invent and who aren't afraid of hard work.

When did you start offering the master's degree course in Interior Design?

The first 12 students arrived in August 2009.

What is the most important thing for students to learn during this course?

An understanding that the design of environments can affect the way that people feel, and that a designer has a direct effect on culture and on the environment.

Why should students choose this school?

We're always looking for students who share our vision of sustainable, provocative, and thoughtful design. This is greatly influenced by our location in one of the world's greatest metropolises. In the heart of Greenwich Village in New York City, we use our immediate surroundings as an urban laboratory.

What kind of teaching method is applied?

The programme has a studio-centred, research-oriented focus. Our lecturers are prominent design practitioners, as well as experts in the field of history and theory specific to interior design. Ethnographers, material and fabrication specialists, and environmental consultants are also regular faculty practitioners. In our teaching, we aim to encourage students to use the most current thinking in these fields to question and reimagine possibilities. Our methods of teaching combine research with lab work. Hands get dirty and discussions are heated. Writing is used to further comprehension and thought, and drawing is a tool to analyse, imagine and refine thought into design propositions.

Where or in what kind of jobs do your former interior design students mostly end up?

Most students take jobs in large and small firms running research or design projects. Others have gone on to design furniture or events. Still others are now in-house designers for major retail brands.

Programme

The MFA programme in Interior Design at Parsons is uniquely positioned to lead the discourse and address the practice of interior design in the 21st century. Inaugurated in September 2009, at the very school where formal Interior Design education began in 1906, this graduate programme builds upon 100 years of our history and leadership in the field. The MFA programme offers instruction of incomparable depth with links to the school's other graduate programmes in architecture, product design, and lighting design.

Distinguished practicing professionals work with students to explore and question: material applications and their environmental impact; craftsmanship and manufacturing processes; building systems and operational energy consumption; digital representation technologies and drawing as means to gain insight; principles of using natural and electr light; fundamentals of colour; and the effect indoor air pollution on human health.

Taking a fundamental role in influencing habitation and social culture, the interior design student is challenged to analyse human behaviour, comfort, and the direct relationship of human perception to the built interior. Design as a social practice is the continuous underlying discussion. Graduates are positioned to become exceptional practitioners and knowledgeable educators.

Some vibrant colours are just inside the school's building.

Inside the Sheila C. Johnson Design Center at Parsons, where exhibition galleries blur the educational boundaries. Photo Michael Moran

Programme
Interior Design

Leads to
Master of Fine Arts

Structure
The 2-year full-time MFA Interior Design degree is awarded for completion of 60 credits. The programme is spread over 4 semesters. The first 3 semesters consist of a combination of classes and studio work while during the last semester students work on their thesis.

Head of programme
Jonsara Ruth

Mentors and lecturers
Alice Chun, Luben Dimcheff, Erica Goetz, Lorraine Karafel, David Leve David Lewis, Joanna Merwood Salisbury, Daniel Michalik, Derek Porter, Mark Rakatansky, Glenn Shrum, Ioanna Theocharopoulou, Allan Wexler, Peter Wheelwright, David White, Alexa Winton and Alfred Zollinger. Plus many guest an part-time lecturers.

Notable alumni
Zachary Barr, Greg Diedrich, Lee Gibson, Kimberly Kelly, Anne-Mette Krolmark and Cristina Noguer Guardiola.

Duration of study
2 years

Full time
Yes

Part time
No

Female students
82%

Male
18%

Local students
48%

Students from abroad
52%

Yearly enrolment
45

Tuition fee
USD 21,585 per semester
(approx. EUR 15,900)

Funding/scholarships
Three scholarships are given
annually to promising applicants of
the MFA Interior Design Program:
Jamie Drake Scholarship, Victoria
Hagan Scholarship and The Donghia
Foundation Scholarship. Graduate
students are automatically
considered for merit scholarships
as part of the admission process.

Minimum requirements for entry
Bachelor's degree

Language
English

Application procedure
Applicants must submit their
application form online and then mail
any supplemental application
materials to the Office of Admission.
The following documents are required:
a completed application form
USD 50 application fee
(approx. EUR 37)
USD 15 slideroom fee
(approx. EUR 11)
transcripts of previous institutions
attended
current curriculum vitae
a statement of interest
two letters of recommendation
portfolio which best exemplifies your
individual perspective and creative skills
GRE scores if you are a native
English speaker
TOEFL, IELTS or PTE proficiency test
(if appropriate).
The Admission Committee will make
acceptance decisions only after all the
required materials have been received.

Application details
newschool.edu/parsons/admission/
interior-design-graduate-programs

Application date
Applicants who wish to be considered
for a Dean's Scholarship must submit
a complete application packet by
1 January. Applications received later
will be considered on a rolling basis.

Graduation rate
94.5%

Job placement rate
High

Memberships/affiliations
ASID, IIDA, NY11+

Collaborations with
Carnegie Fabrics, Homosote
Company, Ashton Keefe (Food
Designer), Metropolis Magazine,
Charlie Morrow (Sound Designer)
and David Stark (Event Designer).

Facilities for students
Students at Parsons have access
to extensive studio facilities and
professionally staffed model-,
fabrication- and print shops,
including rapid prototyping,
photography and imaging labs,
metalworking, jewellery and
woodworking facilities. Also a
library and a computer lab is
available for students.

City
New York

Country
United States

Student Work

Food for the City (2012)
By Paolo Agostinelli

Ingestion of the Interior (2012)
By Kimberly A Kelly

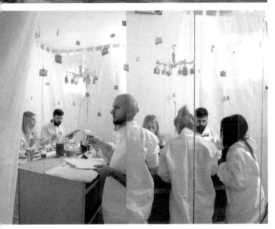

Taste is the culmination of all of the senses. Sensory stimuli are simultaneously produced by food, inhabitants and the interior. Six experimental interior experiences were created to emphasise and explore one of the senses in relation to taste perception. Research from food science, human physiology and sociology helped explore the question: How can we design for the multiple sensory experiences of food and interior environments?

The current global food system, developed to support mass urbanisation and a growing population, has resulted in high energy consumption, food waste, land degradation, health issues and hunger. This thesis brings food, cooking and dining, usually confined to the domestic space, back into the urban social life, celebrating rituals and traditions.

Entropic Decadence: A Retreat In Time (2012)
By Molly Page Prickitt

This project proposes an interior informed by the temporal nature of space and celebrates the inevitability of deterioration and change. Beyond nostalgic stagecraft, it explores the materialist and formalist qualities of entropy as a way to encourage a meaningful re-connection with natural rhythms – incomplete, imperfect, and impermanent. The interior renovation unfolds at a pace equal to that of the deterioration already underway.

Sounding Domestic (2013)
By Zachary Barr

nsorium (2013)
Renee Burdick

sorium is a teahouse and garden located in a historic tobacco ehouse on the Brooklyn waterfront, which offers a respite from over-stimulating environment of New York City which can dull ory receptors, which results in a loss of the connection with the environment. Can the senses be re-engaged by physically oving the body from this stimulation? Sensorium was created to this question.

Instead of engaging with sound, interior designers have largely concerned themselves with suppressing it. What might be possible if sound were made central into the practice of interior design? This proposal for a two-person, live/work loft was used as the platform for exploring how an interior designer might shape the way we live with sound in a domestic space.

Alumna

Name Anne-Mette Krolmark
Residence Stockholm, Sweden
Year of birth 1971
Year of graduation 2011
Current job Store Development
Architect at H&M
Website krolmark.dk

For her thesis project, Anne-Mette Krolmark designed an upmarket men's fashion store.

Why did you choose this school?
Because of its great reputation and the quality of Parsons' former students which includes Tom Ford, Marc Jacobs and Alexander Wang. Plus, the amazing location on Manhattan Island in New York City.

What was the most important thing you learned here?
I learned a lot about sustainability as it is integrated in all aspects of study at Parsons.

What was the most interesting or fun project you did?
My thesis project, which was a concept store for an avant-garde menswear brand.

What subject do you wish you paid more attention to?
I wish I had dared to play and experiment more.

Was there any class you found particularly difficult?
The Master's in Interior Design programme is super-intense. It completely takes over your life in the 2 years you are there. That is amazing and scary at the same time.

What was your graduation project?
I looked at how to combine sustainability with retail design.

Any words of advice for future students?
Try to lose yourself...and not worry so much.

What was your favourite place to hang out?
I really enjoyed doing my reading for my Interior Design Survey classes at the tea parlour in the basement of the now sadly clos Takashimaya department store.

Are you still in contact with the school?
Yes, I always visit the school when I am in Ne York. I still keep in contact with my fellow students, my thesis instructor and the director of the Interior Design programme.

How do you keep in touch with your former classmates?
I believe only half of our class stayed in New York City, and the rest of them are now sprea out all over the world, so I mostly follow them all on Instagram. But they are all very welcon to visit me when (and if) they come to Scandinavia.

Was the transformation from graduation to working life a smooth one?
Actually, it took me quite some time to find th right job after completing the programme, because I knew I definitely wanted to work in international retail design.

Course
Interior Design

School
Parsons The New School for Design

Current Students

'Students who study at Parsons can expect to leave the school as strong conceptual design thinkers. The way the school helps you think about ideas continues to inspire. This is what gives Parsons students an edge over students from other programmes.'
Rachel Miller-Crews

'The most useful class for me was Studio 03 – a collaborative project between an interior design student and a lighting design student. Collaboration is valuable training for an interior designer.'
Areum Park

Ian Wexler's first semester Design dio is over the top! He blew mind with ways of representing, ative process, experimentation, nds-on work, poetics, sensibility, ssion and care for my work.'
Cristina Noguer Guardiola

'The MFA Interior Design programme at Parsons teaches you the importance of materiality and fabrication within interior environments and how you can create important and memorable experiences for people.'
Samantha Elese Obell

City Life

New York City is an internationally acclaimed resource for scholarly and applied research in the interior design industry and the urban context. Students benefit from Parsons' longstanding connections to the spectrum of industry partners: interior design and architecture firms, media, manufacturers, and academic and institutional exhibitors. Rich sourcing options exist in the city's large trade showrooms such as the Decoration & Design Building the New York Design Center and the Manhattan Art & Antiques Center as well as the endless small galleries, studios, showrooms and auction houses which populate the streets of New York City. Annual gatherings such as the International Contemporary Furniture Fair provide students with opportunities to network with those who are shaping the industry and framing important debates.

Parsons is located in Manhattan, this long thin island is only one of New York City's five boroughs, but it's Manhattan that has the concrete canyons and the inimitable skyline; Manhattan that has the world's brightest and most renowned theater district; Manhattan that has Central Park, Rockefeller Center and the Guggenheim Museum; and Manhattan th comprises iconic neighbourhoods like Harler the Upper East Side, Times Square, and Greenwich Village.

United States

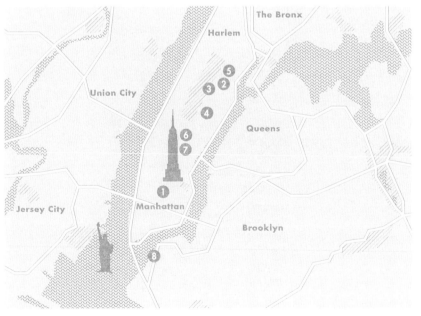

The New School's campus sits near New York's historic Union Square Pe
Photo Jacob Pritchard

New York City

1 Parsons
2 Cooper-Hewitt
3 The Metropolitan Museum of Art
4 Frick Collection
5 Neue Galerie
6 Material ConneXion
7 Grand Central Station
8 Brooklyn Bridge Park

Park

Water

Main road

Course
Interior Design

School
Parsons The New School for Design

ooper-Hewitt, National Design useum 2
Housing a comprehensive collection of decorative arts, furniture, wall coverings, and textiles, the museum is Parsons' institutional partner for the MA in History of Decorative Arts and Design programme. The museum hosts industry-related symposia and workshops and is a key resource for interior design students.
cooperhewitt.org

e Metropolitan Museum of Art 3
The largest art museum in the United States, its permanent collection is an extensive survey of art history and includes works from antiquity, paintings and sculptures from European masters, American art, and modern art.
metmuseum.org

ck Collection 4
European paintings and decorative arts beautifully presented in a neoclassical building.
frick.org

Neue Galerie 5
An unparalleled collections of decorative arts and period rooms from early 20th-century Austria and Germany (1890-1940).
neuegalerie.org

Material ConneXion 6
An industry consultancy for materials research which compliments Parsons' own collection in the Angelo Donghia Materials Center.
materialconnexion.com

The High Line
Originally an elevated freight rail line, the High Line is one of New York City's newest parks, opening in 2009 to visitors. The historic rail line has been transformed with walkways, gardens and seating.
thehighline.org

Central Park
At the heart of the city, Central Park is a dynamic and vibrant manmade wonder. This green space for leisure or activity offers a number of walkways, fountains, sculptures, bridges, and recreational facilities to park visitors.
centralparknyc.org

Grand Central Station 7
America's greatest rail hub with an iconic Beaux-Arts facade offers plenty of places to eat and shop while admiring the zodiac ceiling.

Brooklyn Bridge Park 8
This great waterfront destination draws a lot of the Parsons community to the river's edge. There are spectacular views of the city skyline and the Statue of Liberty.
brooklynbridgepark.org

w to get around
New York City's rail and bus system is run by the Metropolitan Transportation Authority (MTA). It's inexpensive, environmentally friendly and a great way to see sights throughout the five boroughs. It operates 24 hours a day, seven days a week. Alternatively, take one of New York's iconic fleet of yellow taxicabs. To get to Staten Island, board the free Staten Island Ferry and enjoy the views of the Statue of Liberty, New York Harbour and Lower Manhattan.

Within Manhattan, one of the five New York City's boroughs were Parsons is located, the best ways to get around are on foot, by cab, or by taking the subway or bus. Driving is strongly discouraged.

Arranging housing
Average

Housing support by school
Yes, campus accommodation is available.

Cost of room in the city
USD 16,875 per year (approx. EUR 12,462)

Cost of campus housing
Between USD 15,000 and USD 19,750 per year (approx EUR 11,100 to EUR 14,670)

Piet Zwart Institute

All students have access to their own studio
Photo Ojodepez Photography

Piet Zwart Institute
Willem de Kooning Academy
Rotterdam University
of Applied Sciences
Blaak 10
3011 TA Rotterdam
The Netherlands

T +31 (0)10 794 4716
pzwart-info@hr.nl
pzwart.nl

The Blaak 10 building, a historical building in Rotterdam, Photo Ojodepez Photography

Course
Interior Architecture & Retail Design

School
Piet Zwart Institute

'**Our focus is on the advancement and recasting of the interior by exploring its parameters, technologies, histories and theories'**

Alex Suarez, course director

When did you start offering this course?
Officially, the new programme MIARD started in 2011. We are young, progressive and experimental. When shaping the programme, we questioned the future of design, the changing role of the designer, and the knowledge, skills and networks necessary for a student exploring and researching the Interior.

What is studying at this school all about?
Our focus is on the advancement and recasting of the interior by exploring its parameters, technologies, histories and theories in the built environment at various scales. Our curriculum is structured with a diversity of thematic design projects that are crafted to explore contemporary themes in interior architecture and related fields. Critical studies in analogue and digital processes of design, making, materiality and applications are employed as a means to experiment and shape projects.

What kind of teaching method is applied here?
A bottom-up, hands-on, research experimentation and making design methodology. We are studio based and the programme maintains small class sizes to ensure in-depth interaction with teachers. Our teaching and learning environment unfolds through an array of contemporary methods and contexts.

Why should students choose this school?
We are motivated by a collective interest to expand the definition and practice of interior architecture and the calibre of the work our

students achieve is outstanding. The teachers, researchers, scholars, and professionals that form our community are first-rate professionals from a diversity of disciplines. Every year, we exhibit student work at various local and international design events. Our students get to exhibit their projects during the Salone in Milan – which is an amazing opportunity to reach a global audience. This is representative of the quality of work that is expected. Our annual graduation show is also organised as an important public event, held at cultural venues in Rotterdam. We recently implemented a teaching assistant sub-programme for students interested in a career in teaching. Our facilities are state of the art, with valuable resources and technical assistance available for realisation of projects. All students are provided studio spaces for the length of the academic year. Finally we are located in the centre of Rotterdam – a dynamic international design, art and architecture city, with a large student population, and some of the world's most notable ateliers.

What kind of jobs do your students mostly go on to do?
We prepare students for a diversity of careers; our alumni are very active in their professions. A number of our designers open up their own practices, independently or with partners. Some work in the cultural sector or academia. Many find jobs working for studios such as Marcel Wanders, Inside Outside, Mecanoo Architects, Arne Quinze and others.

Programme

The course is firmly based in applied research, critical reflection and the professional field of interior architecture. It operates from the point of view that an educational master's programme must be adaptable to a variety of external forces and should resist institutional idleness.

The course aim is to educate students in the field of interiors and whose practice can modify to cultural, technological and industry changes and set precedents for new and innovative methods of working. Intrinsic to this masters is a specialisation in retail design. In reality, the profession of the interior architect is a young practice, historically framed between the disciplines of architecture and product/furniture design and the course reflects this. As the discipline matures, the programme plan is to contribute to its emerging identity as a relevant and necessary profession with its own theoretical, historical and research policies.

The programme contributes to the professional field by working with noted and award-winning international staff and guest tutors. Students participate in national and international design events, conferences, competitions, and there is an active public lecture series throughout the academic year. Student and alumni work has been presented at international design and architecture platforms, such as Milan Design Week, Dutch Design Week, Sunlab, TENTLondon, and received extensive international press recognition with publications in *Domus*, *Frame*, *Dezeen*, *Archinect* and *Designboom*, among others.

Materials and making are explored in the metal workshop. Photo Ojodepez Photography

The plastics and ceramics workshop are just some of the many facilities available for students. Photo Ojodepez Photography

Programme
Interior Architecture & Retail Design

Leads to
Master in Interior Architecture

Structure
The curriculum employs a modular and flexible structure, where each class is designed to support the others. It's a full-time, 2-year course, divided into 6 trimesters of 12 weeks. The total course consists of 120 ECTS earned credits and is taught in English. Underlying the master's programme is a structure that combines critical analysis, experimentation and making. The programme employs a core design research/making methodology of actively studying and making explicit the design process and creating a dialectic between different forms of thinking. Three core educational threads (Design, Research and Industry) provide the basic structure for trimesters one through four. During the last 2 trimesters, students work independently on their graduation project and written report. The final graduation projects are presented a public graduation exhibition.

Mentors and lecturers
Max Bruinsma, Sander Boer, Brende Cormier, Gabriella Fiorentini, Laura Lynn Jansen, Marta Male-Alemany, Mario Minale, Lutz Müra Yukiko Nezu, Mauro Parravicini, Brian Peters, Catherine Somzé, Füs Türetken, Thomas Vailly, Aynav Ziv, among others.

School Facts

Duration of study
2 years

Full time
Yes

Part time
No

Female students
75%

Male students
25%

Local students
5%

Students from abroad
95%

Yearly enrolment
15

Tuition fee
• EUR 1906 for EU students
• EUR 9600 for non-EU students

Funding/scholarships
No

Minimum requirements for entry
Bachelor's degree in the field of
architecture, interior architecture,
interior design, spatial design or
other artistic and creative disciplines.

Language
English

Application procedure
All applications should include:
a portfolio
a motivation statement
your curriculum vitae
a certified copy of bachelor's degree
a certified copy of transcripts
a copy of your passport
two passport photographs
the results of the TOEFL/IELTS test
(only for international students)
the completed application form.

Application details
pzwart.nl/nl/courses/miard/Apply

Application date
Before 31 January or 3 March
(EU and NON EU)
Before 1 April or 1 May (EU)
Based on merit, places will be filled
from the first deadline onwards,
therefore early submissions are
encouraged. When all course places
are filled, applications will be closed.

Graduation rate
100%

Job placement rate
High

Memberships/affiliations
BNI, Dutch Association of
Interior Architects

Collaborations with
Post-Office, Ventura Lambrate

Facilities for students
Working studios, dgital technology
lab, wood workshop, metal workshop,
plastics and ceramics workshop,
textiles workshop, media studios,
edit studios, sound studios, AV
recording studios, computer studios,
photo studios (analogue and digital)
and libraries.

Student Work

ChromaThick (2013)
By Maddalena Gioglio

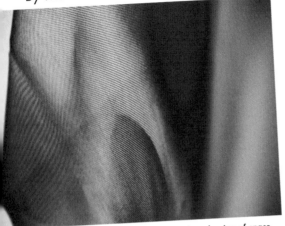

ChromaThick presents a new aproach on the colouring of space. The project offers the possibility to manipulate generic liquid paint to obtain a solid thick matter, which becomes autonomous from any surface and support. The manipulation of a spray paint tool enables this application; creating gradients, from microscopic pigments to solid erratic matter.

Sonicf.lux (2013)
By Marco Busani and Natalie Konopelski

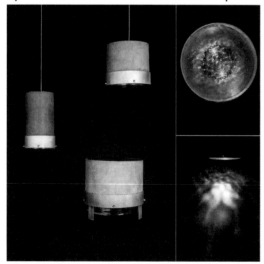

Sonic f.lux is a set of lights that reinterprets the idea of listening by extending the aural domain to the visual realm. It creates a new audio-visual experience by projecting continuous fluctuations of sound into space.

Rollware (2013)
By Joanne Choueiri and Giulia Cosenza

Rollware is a set of laser-cut rolling pins designed as a tool for the production of bread-based edible dishware, adorned with customised patterns. The sustainable products merge traditional crafts, tableware production and cooking with digital technology.

My City is my Home (2013)
By Natalie Konopelski

With this project Konopelski is rethinking strategies for residential design, from the macro to the micro scale. By interpreting the urban, public and private spaces in a new way, she wishes to create a higher density and physical interconnectivity throughout the city, and thus to build an (interior) urban landscape of coexistence.

City Pulse (2013)
By Egle Jacinaviciute

City Pulse is a long-term indoor installation, which reflects the daily flow of Rotterdam in motion by using real-time data to investigate and visualise constant changes in the city environment.

Course
Interior Architecture & Retail Design

School
Piet Zwart Institute

Interiors of Memories (2013)
By Joanne Choueiri

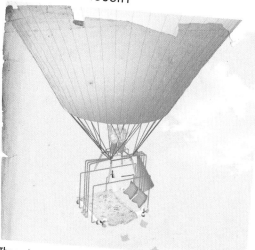

The project is a collection of spaces based in the domestic that allows for the exploration of memories as a source material for the creation of new forms of interiors, attempting to redefine the existing programmatic and experiential elements of the home.

Timeless Refraction (2013)
By Bianca Yousef

Experimentation with optical effects explores the potential for a new storefront that becomes a timepiece. Light is used to connect with the consumer as the retail storefront extends beyond the store and onto the street.

omestichordophone (2013)
Egle Jacinaviciute and Savvas Laz

nestichordophone is a playful cabinet with the features of assical string music instrument. The furniture is accessible n two sides, giving two people the opportunity to access use it simultaneously.

The Paperscape (2013)
By Albina Aleksiunaite and Devika Mirawitani

The Paperscape installation refers to sound as air in motion. Air works as a medium for sound to travel. The design itself is inspired by domestic clothes hangers and the easing sound created by the movement of air through paper. Paperscape provides a relaxing aural atmosphere within the domestic realm. It inhabits domesticity as a sonic drapery that is activated by the fluctuation of air.

Alumna

Alexandra Georgescu's graduation project,
PullOver, was a convertible conversation room
where users customise their own personal space.

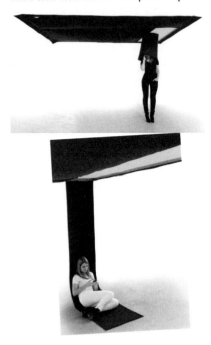

Name Alexandra Georgescu
Residence Torino, Italy
Year of birth 1986
Year of graduation 2012
Current job Interior designer
at Spark Architects Beijing
Website sparkarchitects.com

Why did you choose this school?
For the city of Rotterdam and the country of the
Netherlands – a great location for innovative
architecture, interior design and art. Also it
had interesting classes and collaborations with
big names in the field of interior architecture.

What was the most important thing you learned here?
To try and push the boundaries of interior
design to another level.

What subject do you wish you paid more attention to?
Ha! All of them! Being in the
working environment makes
me aware of the great impact
some teachers had on me and I
wish I had listened more
carefully to their precious
advice.

Was there any class you found particularly difficult?
I had some difficulties with the classes that
required model construction and working in
the workshops. I didn't have much experience
in those, but I ended up loving it. It was easier
for me to follow those classes in which concept
development was given more importance.

What was your graduation project?
PullOver – a convertible conversation room
where users can customise their own personal
space by pulling down parts of the ceiling.
PullOver is rectangular in dimension and can
be attached to any ceiling. It's made out of
navy blue pure wool felt and is connected to
the steel frame with velcro pieces. Separate
pieces can be pulled down and shaped to
create difference spaces.

PullOver was created for interior spaces that
are not defined by a specific function but whe
people assign them specific programmes by
their actions. It responds to the needs of
semi-public spaces where behaviours such as
private phone conversations in a quiet corner
group conversations in transit areas take plac

Any words of advice for future students?
Do your thing and dive deep into it! And belie
in it even if everyone else thinks it is silly.

What was your favourite place to hang out
On the riverside behind the school on a sunny
day, a beautiful spot.

Are you still in contact with the school?
Yes, I keep in contact with some of the teache
director and with my diploma project tutor. W
talk mainly via email about our work and futu
perspectives.

If you were to do the course again, what would you do differently?
I would do even more projects and crazier on

'The theory seminars taught by Füsun Türetken are not only a great inspiration on critically reflected design – they also help you find your personality and voice as a designer.'
Natalie Konopelski

'Future students can expect to be inspired and gain knowledge from many practiced, international tutors. MIARD and its tutors are dedicated in promoting the school and its students. They actively set up opportunities for us to exhibit at external events, publicise our designs and work on real-life projects.'
Bianca Yousef

'The school offers many workshops and the staff is professional and friendly, willing to help and guide you. It is a great opportunity to experiment with new techniques and materials and discover, maybe, new interests.'
Savvas Laz

think the multidisciplinary pproach is relevant owadays as it trains udents to face the allenges of their future ofessional practice.'
Giulia Cosenza

'Having worked previously in the field, I found the program at the Piet Zwart to be very enriching in various areas that are not experienced elsewhere. For instance, the research through making approach challenged my perception of design.'
Joanne Choueiri

'The product design trimester, for Salone del Mobile, was extremely stimulating, challenging and intense. We spent a lot of time in the workshops trying out different materials, from metals to wood and from ceramics to plastic.'
Marco Busani

City Life

Rotterdam is the second-largest city in the Netherlands and one of the largest ports in the world. Although founded in the 12th century, heavy bombing during World War II meant that the city had to completely rebuild itself. The result is that today Rotterdam is a young and dynamic city, a vibrant metropolis whose magnificent skyline is easy to recognise from afar. It's a city of modern architecture, innovation, creativity, events, leisure and recreation. More than one million people from at least 160 countries live in the Rotterdam region. This creates a truly global vibe. Rotterdam attracts a great deal of international interest as a city of architecture and it also is

the home of some of the world's best architecture and design firms. A few square kilometres of the city centre offers a complete overview of what the 20th century has produced in terms of modern architecture. The innovative and adventurous period after the war is expressed in structures such as the Erasmus Bridge and the Luxor Theatre. In Rotterdam, historical and modern buildings stand side by side.

Rotterdam has a deserved reputation for exciting modern and contemporary architecture, including its new Central Station building. Photo Ojodepez Photography

The Netherlands

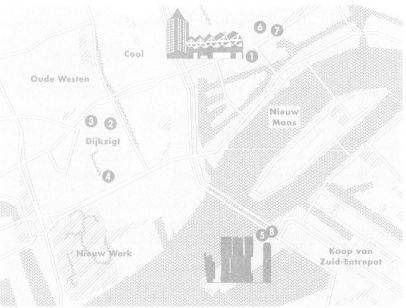

Rotterdam

1 Piet Zwart Institute
2 Museum Boijmans van Beuningen
3 Het Nieuwe Instituut
4 De Kunsthal
5 De Rotterdam
6 Markthal
7 Cube Houses
8 Art & Object Rotterdam

Park

Water

Main road

Course
Interior Architecture & Retail Design

School
Piet Zwart Institute

useum Boijmans van Beuningen 2
This museum has a diverse collection ranging from medieval to contemporary art, with a focus on Dutch art. Artists represented include Hieronymus Bosch, Pieter Bruegel the Elder, Rembrandt, Claude Monet, Wassily Kandinsky, Vincent van Gogh, and many more.
boijmans.nl

t Nieuwe Instituut 3
Following a merger with other arts organisations, the former architecture institute now focuses on design and e-culture as well as architectural innovation, with an exciting programme of events and exhibitions.
hetnieuweinstituut.nl

Kunsthal 4
A wide range of art (in its broadest sense) exhibitions are held here (25 shows per year) in a Rem Koolhaas-designed building.
kunsthal.nl

De Rotterdam 5
Supposedly Europe's biggest building, this dramatic Rem Koolhaas monolith is largely residential but also houses space for a hotel, restaurants and bars, offices and shops.
derotterdam.nl

Markthal 6
Heaven for foodies, in the form of a massive horse-shoe shaped arched structure (comprising living units) sheltering 100 fresh produce stalls plus related shops and restaurants.
markthalrotterdam.nl

Cube Houses 7
Piet Blom's innovative 1974 high-density houses look like a row of tumbling dice. One house (the 'show cube') is open to visitors.
kubuswoning.nl

The International Architecture Biennial Rotterdam
Founded in 2003, IABR offers a thought-provoking series of conferences, debates, lectures, exhibitions and more each summer. Past themes have included 'Power' and 'The Flood.'
iabr.nl

The International Film Festival Rotterdam
After 40-odd years, IFFR has grown to become one of the largest audience-driven film festivals in the world, while maintaining its focus on innovative filmmaking. Held every January.
filmfestivalrotterdam.com

Art & Object Rotterdam 8
Contemporary design fair held in De Rotterdam with the focus on the latest limited editions and one-offs – and so the cutting edge between design, crafts, fashion and more.
objectrotterdam.nl

w to get around
Public transport in Rotterdam is well organised and efficient: the trams, buses and metro are scheduled to link up perfectly. There are also water buses and taxis serving the waterfront area. Cycling, as everywhere in the Netherlands, is a good way to get around thanks to the universal presence of bike paths.

Via train and high-speed rail links, Rotterdam is connected to all the major Dutch cities and to Belgium, Germany and France. The Fyra is a frequent high-speed link to Amsterdam. With Rotterdam Airport within 7 km, and the global hub Amsterdam Schiphol Airport only 58 km away, the city is well connected globally, too.

Arranging housing
Average

Housing support by school
No

Cost of room in the city
EUR 400 per month

Cost of campus housing
n/a

The Juliana Curran Terian Design
Center connects two older loft buildings
to consolidate Pratt's four distinct
design programmes: interior, fashion,
industrial and communications design.
Photo Josh Gerritsen

Pratt
Institute

Newman Mall and Amphitheatre are focal points in Pratt's park-like campus in the historic Clinton
neighbourhood. Photo Alex Weber

Pratt Institute
200 Willoughby Avenue
New York, NY, 11205
United States

T +1 718 636 3630
info@pratt.edu
pratt.edu

Course
Interior Design

School
Pratt Institute

'In an applicant, we look for ambition, curiosity, discipline, and intelligence'

Anita Cooney, chair of the Interior Design Department

What is studying at this school all about?
By teaching skills, values, and professional knowledge to bright and motivated students from diverse cultural, professional, and educational backgrounds, our graduate programme enriches the profession of interior design. The department's educational community encourages philosophical exploration, ethical responsibility, aesthetic expression, and practical application.

What kind of teaching method is applied here?
The graduate Interior Design programme is architecturally oriented, with an emphasis on spatial design as well as surface embellishment. Our studio sequence is the core of our programme, in which students and faculty explore both specific problem-solving strategies and the broad concerns of interior design. Studio is the place where students have the freedom and the support to develop their individual identity as a designer, to help them find and engage with the issues and interests that will sustain them as a student and a practitioner.

Why should students choose this school?
The students: in a studio-oriented curriculum, one learns as much from one's peers as from their faculty and our students are exemplary. The faculty: our location gives us access to the most prodigious talent pool possible and given that most of our faculty have active, thriving practices, professional networking begins in the classroom. The location: New York City, interior design capital of the United States. The options: our graduate students can take their electives in any academic department at Pratt – industrial design, fashion design, fine arts, architecture and of course interior design; further, summer brings opportunities for studying in Chicago, Barcelona, Copenhagen, and more.

What is expected from the students?
We do not have a preconceived notion of the ideal student with a narrowly defined set of talents or skills. That being said, aptitude for graduate study is critical, and in an applicant we look for ambition, curiosity, discipline, and intelligence.

What is the most important thing for students to learn during this course?
To actively engage with the people and things around us, never losing curiosity about the how, why, and what of the design of the interior. Our students learn to think about interaction with context, ecologies of images in media and other modes of representation, and our ever-evolving relationship to emerging technologies.

What is the most important skill to master for an interior designer?
All aspects of space – scale, proportion, configuration and light, as well as texture, material and colour – must be studied in relation to their effect on the human spirit.

Programme

The studio sequence is the core of Pratt's graduate interior design programme, where students and faculty explore both specific and broad concerns of interior design. The focus of the programme is the development of a robust problem-solving methodology, unique and specific to each student. The department's philosophy is that no design process is identical to any other, and that while instruction centres around the steps of a rigorous process, each student is encouraged to explore their own interests and issues, to become the designer they are meant to be.

The most important lesson is that designers never stop learning; Pratt teaches its students how to teach themselves, beyond the classroom and into their careers. The interior design programme is professionally-oriented, preparing students for careers in interior design, ready for board-certification and eventual licensure.

A presentation in the Interior Design Classroom.

The programme at Pratt is very much studio-focused. Photo Alex Weber

Programme
Interior Design

Leads to
Master of Fine Arts

Structure
Pratt's Interior Design Department has two full-time tracks for incoming graduate students: a 84-credit, 3-year graduate programme (Master of Fine Arts) for individuals with undergraduate degrees in unrelated fields. Those with a degree in interior design or architecture may be eligible for the 60-credit, 2-year programme.

Head of programme
Anita Cooney

Mentors and lecturers
Jon Otis, Deborah Schneiderman, Hazel Siegel, Myonggi Sul, Karin Tehve, Jack Travis and Kevin Walz.

Notable alumni
Naomi Leff, Joe D'Urso and Myonggi Sul.

Course
Interior Design

School
Pratt Institute

School Facts

Duration of study
2 or 3 years

Full time
Yes

Part time
No

Female students
85%

Male
15%

Local students
60%

Students from abroad
40%

Yearly enrolment
140

Tuition fee
USD 1530 per credit
(approx. EUR 1130)

Funding/scholarships
Merit scholarships are awarded to some students during the application process. Additional scholarships are available to matriculated students.

Minimum requirements for entry
Applicants with an undergraduate degree in interior design or architecture may be eligible for the 60 credit 2-year graduate programme and must submit a portfolio that demonstrates experience, sensibility, and skills from previous education and/or professional experience. A 2-semester qualifying programme of an additional 24 credits is required for applicants whose undergraduate backgrounds are unrelated to interior or architecture.

Language
English

Application procedure
Prospective students must file an application using Pratt's online system, and upload the following documents:
a copy of your transcript (international students must have all transcripts officially translated into English)
two letters of recommendation
your English TOEFL, Pearson or IELTS proficiency test (if appropriate)
your portfolio
your curriculum vitae.
Applicants will receive an email when their file is complete and being reviewed by the admissions committee.

Application details
pratt.edu/admissions/applying

Application date
Before 5 January

Graduation rate
85%

Job placement rate
93%

Memberships/affiliations
None

Collaborations with
None

Facilities for students
The Pratt Library, Interior Design Material Library, Electronic Design Studio Lab, The Rapid Prototyping Lab and a Wood Workshop.

Student Work

Urban Interior (2014)
By Cody Leung

An urban space that is simultaneously interior and exterior, thereby encouraging inhabitation and foot traffic, where people can rest, eat, work, and play in one location.

Lucid Dream (2014)
By Mian Deng

The designed space is in between two states (asleep and awake), or two spaces (two office buildings), to reconsider the way that we perceive or understand space. Translucent white elastic fabric fashions a dream-like interior in which one will be able to temporarily escape from hectic working life.

XS (2014)
By Allen J. Kim

Development of new rule sets for micro apartments in New York City, based on an exploration of verticality, modular design, and activity based space planning.

Course
Interior Design

School
Pratt Institute

Third Skin Habitation (2014)
By Tali Oren

An interdisciplinary project that investigates the intersection between a garment and interior spaces; to investigate when a garment becomes habitation and to test it against use in temporary housing for disaster victims.

oundaries Blurred (2014)
y Kunal Kashayp

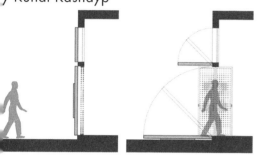

e interior and exterior are independent and impact each other in der to create balance. The design focuses on the transformation m the interior to the exterior, and the interior's adaptability to anging exterior environments.

Kitchen Club (2014)
By Marika Sorimachi

This project suggests various public shared kitchens and dining spaces for space-deprived New Yorkers to rent, as well as co-op kitchen spaces for young food business entrepreneurs.

Alumna

Name Nora Mattingly
Residence New York, United States
Year of birth 1983
Year of graduation 2012
Current job Principal of Assembly Design and D'Apostrophe Design
Clients Wythe Hotel, THE THING quartlery, private art and furniture collectors
Websites assemblydesign.us, dapostrophe.com

For her graduation project, Nora Mattingly translated the American Farm-to-Table philosophical approach into a spatial narrative.

Why did you choose this school?

I knew that I wanted a programme that emphasised technical skills while encouraging creative development. Additionally, I had been living and working in New York for several years prior with no real interest in relocating at the time. Pratt was a perfect fit and has helped me to grow the network that I had already begun building.

What was the most interesting project you did?

I began every single project I did at Pratt with an abstract collage, generally exploring an idea about colour and/or texture. This was a way for me to stay loose with my ideas and ease into each project. By the end of the programme, I had over 50 small collages and looking at them as a collection, I think it is actually the most interesting work that I did.

What subject do you wish you paid more attention to?

I would have loved to take more design history courses, more advanced colour and materials courses, a sculpture course. It is amazing how quickly the 3 years goes and how much left there is to learn.

Was there any class you found particularly difficult?

The construction courses were far more thorough than I anticipated. I am so thankful that I have the understanding of construction drawings and construction methods that I do, but at the time, it was a real challenge – it felt like learning a new language.

What was your graduation project?

My thesis project translated the American Farm-to-Table philosophical approach into a spatial narrative, showcasing the geographical, conceptual, and formal development behind both culinary and object design, in order to shift the user's traditional point of interaction from the isolated end resu to the integration of process.

Any words of advice for future students?

Learn from other disciplines. It is easy to forge that, at Pratt, you have access to gifted industrial designers, graphic designers and fine artists. Some of the most exciting ideas a born out of interdisciplinary explorations.

What was your favourite place to hang out?

I really did enjoy the being in the studio. Even if you are working independently, it is nice to be around all of the creative energy.

Are you still in contact with the school?

Yes, I have reached out on several occasions see if there are current students interested in internships and employment.

Was the transformation from graduation to working life a smooth one?

My experience was different than most of my peers in that, during the last month of my the I started a design studio, Assembly, with my partner Pete Oyler.

If you were to do the course again, what would you do differently?

Hmmm...I would take more classes in other departments.

Course
Interior Design

School
Pratt Institute

'Future students can expect to be overwhelmed, sleep-deprived and stressed-out! This programme is both mentally and physically demanding but it has its payoff in truly advancing your skills and creative problem-solving.'
Anna Grace Koerber

Living in New York for 2 years is a life changing experience; you are exposed to so many interesting things and creatively stimulated by them. Pratt has a great programme and I believe its location is part of it.'
Mariana Rocha

'The first-year studio was an amazing experience. It is designed to really push conceptual ideation and you learn how to extract those forms into an interior space. It really changed the way I approach design problems and develop appropriate solutions.'
Michael Adkins

Pratt Institute pushes you to think as a designer. It challenges you to question why we inhabit space a certain way and forces you to rethink the status quo. Pratt encourages you to take a closer look at interior design as an emerging profession.'
Nadia Shaheen

'I'd say for the 2 years you're in the programme, your favourite hang-out is going to be your studio. Otherwise, I love the outdoor fleas markets, little coffee shops and parks.'
Katherine Castaeñeda

City Life

Pratt is located in one of the world's multicultural epicentres for arts, culture, design, and business: New York City. Pratt's Brooklyn and Manhattan campuses are a short distance away from the Brooklyn Museum, The Metropolitan Museum of Art, the Guggenheim Museum, and many others.

Pratt's Brooklyn campus has grown over the last 125+ years to 25 acres in the borough's historic Clinton Hill neighbourhood. The park-like campus is a complex of green lawns, brick pathways, and 27 buildings housing classrooms, studios, a library, student and faculty housing, administrative offices, and computer, recreation, and multimedia facilities. New York is home to iconic buildings such as the Empire State Building and the Chrysler Building; landmarks such as Rockefeller Center, the Flatiron Building, and the Seagram Building; and newer buildings by world-renowned architects Santiago Calatrava and Frank Gehry. Many of Pratt's buildings have been designated national landmarks by the New York Landmarks Commission, and the Institute's Brooklyn campus was recognised by *Architectural Digest* as one of the top ten college campuses nationwide with the best architecture.

Brooklyn Bridge Park, beneath the famous bridge, offers a pleasant green space in the heart of the city.

United States

New York City

1 Pratt (Brooklyn campus)
2 Brooklyn Museum
3 The Metropolitan Museum of Art
4 The Museum of Modern Art (MoMA)
5 The Brooklyn Bridge
6 The Brooklyn Academy of Music (BAM)
7 Grand Central Station
8 Four Freedoms Park
9 Central Park
10 The High Line
11 Pratt (Manhattan campus)

Park

Water

Main road

Course
Interior Design

School
Pratt Institute

City Facts

ee more New York City Facts on p.186

ooklyn Museum ②
The museum has a comprehensive permanent collection that includes period rooms, decorative arts, contemporary art, ancient Egyptian masterpieces, African art, European painting, and more. The museum's cutting-edge exhibitions and programmes reflect a fresh view of traditional and historical works as well as engagement with today's important artists and artistic practices and ideas.
brooklynmuseum.org

e Metropolitan Museum of Art ③
The largest art museum in the United States, its permanent collection is an extensive survey of art history and includes works from antiquity, paintings and sculptures from European masters, American art, and modern art.
metmuseum.org

e Museum of Modern Art (MoMA) ④
With a collection consisting of paintings, sculptures, prints, photography, films and other art objects, MoMA creates a dialogue between the past and the present, the established and the experimental. The museum also highlights significant recent developments and new interpretations in its exhibition programme.
moma.org

The Brooklyn Bridge ⑤
Connecting Manhattan to Brooklyn over the East River since 1883, the bridge is now a National Historic Landmark and a big attraction for visitors due to its striking design and pedestrian paths that offer panoramic views of the city. Beneath the bridge, Brooklyn Bridge Park offers a green space for visitors.

The Brooklyn Academy of Music (BAM) ⑥
For more than 150 years, the Brooklyn Academy of Music has been a leader in artistic innovation. BAM is not strictly confined to presenting audiences with music, but also with theatre, dance, opera, film and more.
bam.org

Grand Central Station ⑦
America's greatest rail hub. With the architectural achievements of its Beaux-Arts facade, and main concourse, and the triumph of engineering that went into constructing the terminal, the iconic space is both magnificent and functional for transit.

Four Freedoms Park ⑧
Located on Roosevelt Island in the East River of New York City, the park celebrates Roosevelt's Four Freedoms: of speech and expression and worship, and freedom from want and fear. The waterfront space has spectacular views of the city skyline.
fdrfourfreedomspark.org

Central Park ⑨
At the heart of the city, Central Park is a dynamic and vibrant manmade wonder. A green oasis, it occupies 840 acres of city-owned land. Central park is a space for leisure or activity offering a number of walkways, fountains, sculptures, bridges, and recreational facilities to park visitors.
centralparknyc.org

The High Line ⑩
Originally an elevated freight rail line, the High Line is one of New York City's newest parks, opening in 2009 to visitors. The historic rail line has been transformed into a green space with walkways, gardens, seating, and a lawn for visitors to enjoy above the streets of its Chelsea neighbourhood.
thehighline.org

w to get around
New York city is served by three major airports: John F. Kennedy International, Newark Liberty International and LaGuardia. Both JFK and Newark serve long-distance international flights, while LaGuardia caters domestic destinations. Penn Station and Grand Central Station, both in Manhattan, are the two main stations of the city.

Brooklyn has an excellent, affordable transit system, with subway, buses and ferries. The subway is overall the best way to get around the whole of New York City, and also Brooklyn. Due to traffic patterns and transport network geometries, cycling can sometimes be the fastest way to commute. In recent years cycling has become more popular in the city.

Arranging housing
Average

Housing support by school
Yes, limited graduate housing is available on the Brooklyn campus.

Cost of room in the city
USD 16,875 per year
(approx. EUR 12,462)

Cost of campus housing
USD 15,634 per year
(approx. EUR 11,546)

City
New York

Country
United States

A campus building
seen from outside.

Rhode Island School of Design

**Rhode Island School
of Design (RISD)**
2 College Street
Providence, RI, 02903
United States

T +1 401 451 5848
admissions@risd.edu
risd.edu

Taking in the urban view from the Chase Center studio

Course
Interior Architecture

School
Rhode Island School of Design

'RISD's graduate programmes require a strong sense of focus and determination'

Markus Berger, acting department head (academic year 2013/14), Interior Architecture

How has the school developed over time?

Since the turn of the millennium, Rhode Island School of Design (RISD) has expanded both its emphasis on research and its advanced-level programmes in art and design. As a result, graduate student enrolment has more than doubled, with 425 talented master's degree candidates from around the world now accounting for 20% of the student population. More important than sheer numbers, however, is the influence they wield on our small creative community. With their energy, passion, focus and commitment, grad students palpably elevate the nature of the discourse across campus.

What is the focus of this school?

Since 1877, RISD has been a leader in art and design education, attracting extraordinary people who thrive in its creative culture. The mission of the school, through its college and museum, is to educate its students and the public in the creation and appreciation of works of art and design, to discover and transmit knowledge and to make lasting contributions to a global society through critical thinking, scholarship and innovation.

What kind of teaching method is important here?

Although they spend long hours in the studio, RISD graduate students are very much engaged in the world around them and interested in exploring the cultural, historical and social context for their work. All candidates for master's degrees complete a written thesis with the goal of both articulating and synthesising the ideas behind their studio work and of contributing to the development of a new space of knowledge.

Why should students choose this particular school?

Graduate students are drawn to RISD by the faculty – professional artists and designers working at the top of their fields – and the calibre of fellow students. They want to make work that matters and be a part of a community dedicated to developing innovative and responsible approaches to art and design. RISD's graduate programmes are challenging and demanding. They require a strong sense of focus and determination. In return, they have much to offer.

What is the most important skill for an interior designer?

To be able to re-think, re-make and re-visualise our existing built environment with an understanding of existing structures and the ability to find and draw potential of the existing to the new.

Programme

A field at the intersection of architecture, conservation and design of the built environment, Interior Architecture at RISD takes an innovative and progressive approach to addressing design issues intrinsic to the reuse and transformation of existing structures. The department offers two degrees for the exploration of this subject. As a post-professional study to a first degree in architecture, the Master of Arts (MA) in Interior Architecture is a unique specialist design education on the subject of adaptive reuse. The Master of Design (MDes) in Interior

Studies with a focus on adaptive reuse provides a unique design education on the design and alteration of existing structures and spaces through interior interventions and adaptive reuse.

Studying in the RISD's stately Fleet Library.

A student office in all its creative glory.

Programme
Interior Architecture

Leads to
Master of Arts or Master of Design

Structure
The programme has a fall and spring semesters plus a winter session. The core curriculum includes the study of history, theory, drawing, structures, energy, materials, lighting and technology, all of which ensures that students fully understand the concerns of professionals in the building industry and allied fields.

Head of programme
Markus Berger (academic year 2013/14), Liliane Wong

Mentors and lecturers
Mary-Ann Agresti, Faith Baum, Michael Beaman, Jonathan Bell, Markus Berger, Eduardo Benamour Duarte, Jeffrey Katz, Brian Kernaghe Eun Lee, Michael McGarty, MaryRo McGowan, Pari Riahi, Wolfgang Rudorf, Jonah Sacks, Barbara Steh Janet Stegman, Kurt Teichert, Lilian Wong and Peter Yeadon.

Notable alumni
Shraddha Aryal, Radika Desai, Eur Lee, Franklin Salasky, Andrew Thaemert and Andrea Valentini.

Course
Interior Architecture

School
Rhode Island School of Design

School Facts

ration of study
1 year (MA), 2 years (MDes)

ll time
Yes

rt time
No

Female students
80%

Male students
20%

Local students
40%

Students from abroad
60%

Yearly enrolment
65–70

Tuition fee
USD 44,284 per year
(approx. EUR 32,370)

Funding/scholarships
The department offers fellowships
and assistantships. The school
offers several options for grants,
scholarships and other funding
opportunities.

nimum requirements for entry
A Bachelor degree and proof of
English language proficiency.
All applicants who speak English
as a second language, including
US citizens, must also submit results
from TOEFL or IELTS.

nguage
English

plication procedure
Applicants should submit the
following documents:
a completed application form
official transcripts from all colleges
attended
your design portfolio
statement of purpose (with a project
or research proposal)
three letters of recommendation
your English TOEFL or IELTS
proficiency test (if appropriate)
a receipt of payment of the
non-refundable application fee
of USD 60 (approx. EUR 44).

plication details
risd.edu/grad/apply

plication date
Before 10 January

Graduation rate
96%

Job placement rate
98%

Memberships/affiliations
NASAD, NEASC

Collaborations with
None

Facilities for students
Interior Architectures studios are
linked to the RISD network through
wireless and hard-wired connections.
Students have access to in the
department's dedicated Studio area
with a large-format printer/plotter
and 3D printers, a fully equipped
wood shop, a 3D model-making
facility, the Shared Technologies
Program includes a CNC machine,
laser cutter and rapid prototype
machine. Interior Architecture is a
Macintosh-based department.

City
Providence

Country
United States

Student Work

All the Little Lights (2013)
By Carolina Martin

Carolina Martin's adaptive reuse of the Newport Congregational Church into a bridal shop is inspired by the 1950s boutique concept and its transformation from little hidden treasures to unique and spectacular places filled with architectural moments. The proposal is defined as a 'soft intervention' that brings new life to the space by introducing different layers of lighting (floor, nave, balcony).

Spiritual Laps: Contemporary Bath House and Spa (2013)
By Amy Selvaggio

In the face of secularisation, adaptive reuse of sacred spaces is becoming more prevalent as a means of preserving the historic and often beautiful architecture. This project presents the issue of rehabilitating not only a historic landmark but also a sacred space – the church (as both building and congregation). It proposes a new programme, including spa treatment rooms, gym facilities and a lap pool, incorporating the sacred character of the space and what many call the spiritual experience of the bath house.

In the Sanctuary (2013)
By Phawadee Pantrakul

A proposal to integrate Eastern methodology into existing sacred Western architecture to create a sanctuary. The proposed space would integrate the programme for an indoor community park and clubhouse into the church. Ultimately, the ambition of the project is to redeem the relationship between the citizen and religious architecture, by creating a space with a harmonious relationship between man and nature.

Taste, Space, Move and Deploy (2013)
By Roxanne Salceda

In her individual proposal for a non-invasive intervention fo the Newport Congressional Church, Roxanne Salceda tappe into food culture as a way of optimising on Providence's national reputation as a culinary power-house. Mirroring th vibrant and impressive arts and culinary scene of the city, Roxanne looked to food truck culture as an opportunity to generate increased traffic to the church, without compromisi it's original structure.

cotopia (2013)
y Anni Hurt

Ecotopia proposes a retrofitting of the vast and abandoned Narragansett Electric Lighting Company Building, Rhode Island. Sustainable strategies drive the design and form a community focused on a lifestyle that contributes to the net zero energy building.

Defragmenting LaFarge (2013)
By Carolina Martins, Roxanna Salceda and Mansi Tewari

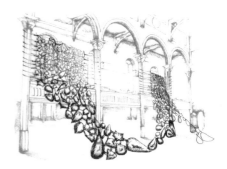

A designated US National Landmark, the Newport Congregational Church, with its La Farge stained glass windows and murals, requires that, 'No new construction, demolition or modification which would alter the relations of mass and colour must be allowed.' This group project sought to bring new life to both building and congregation, through the creation of a removable, non-invasive gesture in the space.

Fox Point Hurricane Barrier (2013)
By Yuki Kawae

his thesis project, Yuki Kawae proposed a place for gathering and rites of passage within the Fox Point Hurricane Barrier in Providence, Rhode nd. At the threshold between two worlds, the Infrastructure Intervention functions as both a mental and physical barrier between the ocean and civilisation of the city.

Alumna

Name Sui Park
Residence Brooklyn, NY, United States
Year of birth 1977
Year of graduation 2013
Current job Artist and interior architect
Website suipark.com

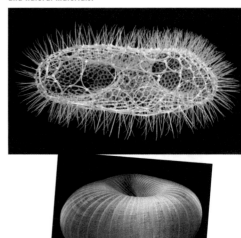

Why did you choose this school?
I was interested in adaptive reuse. Interior architecture at RISD has a great curriculum that focuses closely on this topic.

What was the most important thing you learned here?
How to approach a given design problem, or any design problems, in a way that extends and revives the special features and characteristics of the subject. I think this is what distinguishes adaptive reuse from other fields of architecture or design.

What was the most interesting project you did?
A studio class on transforming a historic building in Boston into a boutique hotel. I designed the interior with a theme of 2D design projecting into a 3D construction. Each suite in every level of the hotel features its own idiosyncratic projection combination. It was very exciting to see my projection design mixed with a historic exterior and remaining structures.

What subject do you wish you paid more attention to?
I wish I had been more creative. I had been told to be creative on designs that may not be practical, because once you graduate, everything is about practicality.

What was your graduation project?
I explored augmenting traditional rectangular spaces with dynamic structures in adaptive reuse settings. In particular, my thesis studied juxtaposing a traditional rectangular space with dynamic organic structures. The Sui Table features a sustainable organic and dynamic form. I applied traditional basketry patterns and technique (twining basketry) as units or modules to systematically construct the form. The application allows constructions of a greater flexibility and curvature, in particular an organic form. The characteristics of transparency and lightness of Sui Table reinterprets organic forms or images of natur

Any words of advice for future students?
There are a variety of art departments and resources here that can be very useful that ar not available in other schools.

Are you still in contact with the school?
Yes, I have been uploading my works on the school portfolio website. It's interesting how I get more feedback from the community after graduate. I also keep in touch with professor: When I ask for references, I always update them with my works and my proposals. Some comments have been very helpful.

Was the transformation from graduation to working life a smooth one?
Difficult. I decided not to join any firms, but t continue to work on my creative side. I think I made a good decision about this as I am getting some outcomes with good feedbacks and results.

'I loved that the programme was small, a short 2 years, and that it accepted students from alternative backgrounds and trained them to work in architecture and design.'
Katherine Porter

'At RISD, we also had a chance to participate in other classes from other departments, which opened my eyes to another art and design world that I've never experienced before.'
Tanatsha Tosayanond

he ability to explore the fferent departments, facilities, d expertise of students and ofessors, not only within but o outside of your department, a unique and important aspect a RISD education.'
Lauren McCarty

'I chose RISD because of its reputation as one of the best schools in design, and because of the adaptive reuse focus of the programme, which I found very valuable and in line with my education and career goals.'
Dina Soliman

'Go to Boston by train, go to New York by bus, go near by car and go far by air! When not travelling, my favourite hangout was my balcony which overlooked a little stream – so I could be inspired by nature.'
Yiling Chu

City Life

Located in the heart of historic downtown Providence, where cobblestone streets meet post-modern sculptures, the RISD campus boldly unites the past with the future. Providence has earned a reputation for being an arts and cultural capital. With the largest number of working artists in the country, the city boasts a vibrant mix of galleries, theatres and museums, including the RISD Museum of Art. Rhode Island's capital city is also home to seven colleges, waterfront parks and extraordinary historic architecture. At RISD, the graduate experience doesn't begin or end in the studio or classroom. In the course of walking to and from studios every day, students find that the city can have a profound effect on their state of mind and sense of wellbeing. Its

cobblestone streets, ornate architectural details, spontaneous arts installations, outdoor concerts and events create an engaging and exciting environment in which to live. Providence provides an interesting m of architecture, culture, nightlife and other urban amenities, and is easily navigable by bike, bus or car. RISD's downtown hillside campus and the neighbourhood that houses are also especially welcoming to foot traffic.

Providence is rich in atmospheric colonial architecture.

United States

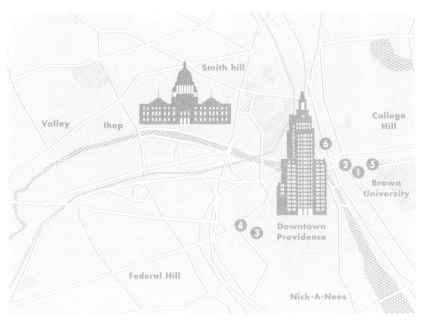

Providence

1 RISD
2 The Steel Yard
3 Trinity Repertory Company
4 AS220
5 RISD Museum of Art
6 Benefit Street

Park

Water

Railway

Main road

Course
Interior Architecture

School
Rhode Island School of Design

City Facts

e Steel Yard ②
An industrial arts space run by a
number of RISD alumni and other
community arts advocates and
occupying one of the city's many
former factories and mills.
thesteelyard.org

rinity Repertory Company ③
Trinity Rep is Providence's premier
acting troupe, putting on an average
of six productions a year – varying
from contemporary to classic – in a
beautiful theatre.
trinityrep.com

AS220 ④
Notable among the city's creative
outlets is AS220, a thriving non-profit
arts organisation that supports
gallery spaces, live/work studios,
a performance space, a community
darkroom, and a bar/restaurant.
as220.org

RISD Museum of Art ⑤
The Rhode Island School of Design's
own museum, with varied exhibitions
of art and design representing
diverse cultures from ancient times
to the present.
risdmuseum.org

Benefit Street ⑥
One of the highest concentrations
of colonial buildings in the country
makes this street the place
to experience old Providence.
rihs.org

WaterFire
Worthy of medieval Venice, the
centrepiece of the WaterFire spectacle
is a line of 100 braziers, afloat on
the water. Music also helps to light up
the night.
waterfire.org

Gallery Night
On the third Thursday of every month,
many of Providence's art galleries
stay open late for the popular Gallery
Night.
gallerynight.info

w to get around
The nearest international airport is just
19 km from Providence, Rhode Island.
The T.F. Green Airport (in Warwick) is
only 10 minutes by car away. Public
transit is managed by Rhode Island
Public Transit Authority (RIPTA).
Kennedy Plaza, in downtown
Providence, serves as a transportation
hub for local public transit as well as a
departure point for Peter Pan and
Greyhound bus lines.
Providence Station, located between
the Rhode Island State House and the
downtown district, is served by Amtrak

and MBTA Commuter Rail services.
Approximately 2400 passengers daily
pass through the station. It offers a
commuter rail route running north to
Boston and south to a station at T.F.
Green Airport and Wickford Junction.
There are three bus stops near RISD (S
Main at County Court, Tunnel NS S
Main and Memorial FS Westminster).
The entire city is easily navigable by
bike, bus or car. RISD's downtown
hillside campus and the neighbourhood
that houses it are also especially
welcoming to foot traffic.

Arranging housing
Never a problem

Housing support by school
Yes

Cost of room in the city
Varies

Cost of campus housing
Between USD 6820 and
USD 11,934 per semester
(approx. EUR 5000 to 8775)

The courtyard of the academy is often used by students to relax during lunch or in between classes.

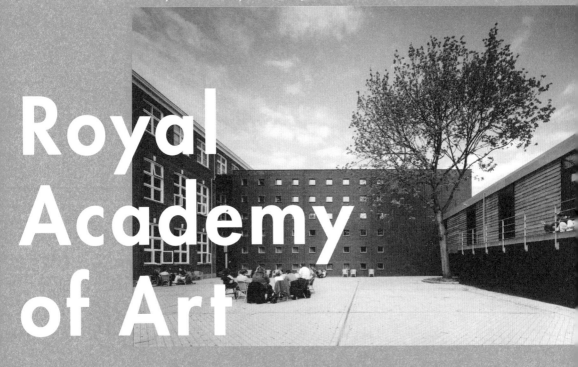

Royal Academy of Art

Royal Academy of Art (KABK)
Prinsessegracht 4
2514 AN The Hague
The Netherlands

T +31 (0)70 3154 777
info@enterinside.nl
enterinside.nl, kabk.nl

Old and new sections of the school building are juxtaposed in this hallway.

Course
INSIDE Interior Architecture

School
Royal Academy of Art

'All teaching is practice-based and supports the students to become strong, research-based and entrepreneurial interior architects'

Hans Venhuizen, head of the INSIDE Interior Architecture programme

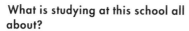

What is studying at this school all about?

With our programme we aim at reflecting on and connecting to the real world, a world that is changing. The current trend to privatise public space on a large scale calls for a metamorphosis in the discipline of spatial design. Now the primary focus is not the processes of change and growth, but people as users and 'experiencers' of the new, often large-scale, public interiors.

What kind of teaching method is applied here?

The studio takes a central position in INSIDE's curriculum. For about 40% of the time students work with architects like ZUS, OMA, Doepel Strijkers and Superuse Studios, on current topics. The studio work is supported by a theory, a skills and a flows programme that teaches the students to look at the real world not as an end product but from the perspective of all kinds of flows that surround us. The students work in groups and teams but also individually. All teaching is practice-based and supports the students to become strong, independent, research-based and entrepreneurial interior architects able to work in complex situations of spatial change.

Why should students choose this school?

The jumble of interactions that an authentic 'public' space entails gives credence to a new, unifying position for the interior architect. He/she is not yet trained to design at that level of scale and complexity, but is supremely capable of 'reading' space and shaping it from the perspective and experience of human beings – in all their complexity, not (solely) in their limited and limiting capacity as intended consumers.

What is expected from the students?

At INSIDE it is essential to be open minded, curious, focussed, involved, energetic, critical, flexible and entrepreneurial, to name a few qualities we expect from our students and ourselves.

When did you start offering the master's degree course in interior design?

INSIDE, the master's degree in interior architecture started in 2011.

What is the most important thing for students to learn during this course?

With a specialisation concerning the use of the surroundings, the interior architect can develop into a key figure within the processes of spatial change. The interior architect of the future can relate to any assignment context, from inside.

What is the most important skill to master for an interior architect?

The interior architect reads, identifies and steers the public interior from inside, based on his own observations, thorough research of the cultural, economic and political context, sociological and urban design perspectives, and his or her own artistic vision.

Programme

INSIDE is a 2-year, English-language-taught master's programme in Interior Architecture at the Royal Academy of Art in The Hague, which targets the real world. A world that is changing: large-scale interiors, the relationship between private and public space, sustainability and a greater demand for social cohesion are themes that call for new perspectives on interior architecture. The curriculum of the programme is based on two principles. Firstly, it is based on an analysis of research and design processes. Secondly, it builds on the principle of 'learning by doing'. Combined, these two principles lead to a curriculum that is divided into phases that each deal with specific stadia of research and design processes: observing, gathering knowledge, planning, research, presentation, evaluation, design, and again presentation and evaluation. These aspects are addressed all parts of the curriculum and form the criteria on the basis of which student work is assessed

The KABK gallery is meant to exhibit or present work of the students, but is also used for external exhibitions.

The academy's metal workshop is one of the facilities on offer to students.

Programme
INSIDE Interior Architecture

Leads to
Master of Arts

Structure
The total study load for the programme is 120 ECTS, equally spread over 2 years, which are divided into 2 semesters of 20 weeks each. The programme consists of five parts. The heart of INSIDE is formed by the three studios – Inter, Urban and Space – which make up about 40% of the programme's total study load. Alongside the studios, students participate in a longer research trajectory – INSIDEflows – about flows in contemporary interior architecture. In addition to this, the programme is supported by a theoretical backbone, which trains students in their reflection on and position in the field of interior architecture, as well as a Skills programme that offers students hands on experience through intensive technical workshops. Finally the Travel programme allows students to observe and reflect on the discipline, cultural phenomena and social themes.

Head of programme
Hans Venhuizen

Mentors
Doepel Strijkers (Eline Strijkers), OMA (Chris van Duijn and Mark Veldman), Superuse Studios (Jan Jongert and Lizanne Dirkx), Anne Hoogewoning, Louise Schouwenberg, ZUS (Kristian Koreman), Jan Konings, Erik Jutten, Marja van der Burgh and Hans Venhuizen. Expected 2015: MVRDV and Jeanne van Heeswijk.

School Facts

Duration of study
2 years

Full time
Yes

Part time
No

Female students
80%

Male
20%

Local students
0%

Students from abroad
100%

Yearly enrolment
15

Tuition fee
- EUR 1770 per year for EU citizens
- EUR 4500 per year for non-EU citizens

Funding/scholarships
In exceptional cases a scholarship is available.

Minimum requirements for entry
Candidates must be BA or MA graduates of an art or design academy and must present their reasons for wishing to enrol in this course on the basis of a portfolio of their work and an accompanying motivation letter. Candidates are expected to have developed an interdisciplinary approach to interior architecture, to feel a fascination for human needs and behaviour in a world where social and cultural parameters are constantly changing, and to be well informed about recent developments in the specific fields. As all courses are in English, candidates should have a sufficient proficiency in English.

Language
English

Application procedure
Candidates who wish to apply should submit the following documents:
a completed digital application form
copy of passport
copy of visa (if appropriate)
relevant diplomas
your English TOEFL or IELTS proficiency test (if appropriate)
a high resolution scan of your passport photo
your PDF portfolio

- your curriculum vitae
- your motivation letter.
  Candidates should send all the documents to marja@enterinside.nl.

Application details
enterinside.nl/apply

Application date
Before 1 May for non-EU citizens and before 1 June for EU citizens.

Graduation rate
80%

Job placement rate
High

Memberships/affiliations
BNI, Stichting Architecten Register

Collaborations with
Stroom Den Haag, The Great Indoors Award, TodaysArt Festival The Hague, Master departments KABK and various institutional clients.

Facilities for students
Workshops (media, wood, textile, 3D printing), photocopying facilities, a library, an internet wall, stores for materials and supplies and a canteen.

Student Work

Super Lucky Mall – Fortune Forest (2013)
By Yuting Guan, Klinphaka Keawcharoen and Roy Yin

Moving Wall (2013)
By Ewelina Borowiecka and Ni Nan

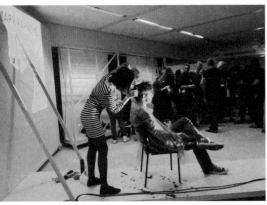

The Moving Wall, designed for a half-empty former office, combines two design projects: one in which privacy constantly needs to be negotiated, and a clockwork playground. The combined efforts led to a dynamic structure which can be freely moved. Photos Ossip van Duivenbode

The Super Lucky Mall – Fortune Forest is a proposal for a half-empty former office. The Fortune Forest triggers the hunting instincts of visitors and aims to provoke people's awareness of o of their most basic needs: food. By lifting one of the coloured cubes, one of the suspended food items will randomly come dow

Home For a Moment (2013)
By Minsun Kim

is project investigates how people perceive intimate space, by inviting
ferent people to the landscape of the installation and asking them: 'Where
you most feel at home?' During their conversation, people create an intimate
ace with miniature objects.

Sundial Yogi Bar (2013)
By Qing Liao and Joanne Smith

The Sundial Yogi Bar brings direct sunlight
into a 1970s former office building. During
the 17 hours of sunshine during the summer
solstice on 21 June, the 20th floor was
transformed from a bar into a cinema, a yoga
studio and a tea bar. For this purpose, a
mobile wooden structure is used which is
tailored specifically to move the users through
the space at the same rate and position of the
sunlight's movements.

Alumna

Name Minsun Kim
Residence Seoul, South Korea
Year of birth 1982
Year of graduation 2013
Current job Independent designer/
interior architect
Clients Several
Website minsunkim.net

Why did you choose this school?

The INSIDE programme seemed to be closed to real-life issues even though it is run by an art school.

What was the most important thing you learned here?

Don't be afraid of failure. I failed twice during 2 years. But while making mistakes, I didn't only acquire knowledge but I also learned new ways of communication, and I learned more about people.

What was the most fun project you did?

Milk Bar, the last project of first year was a group project with five classmates. It remains the most fun as well as the hardest project I did. The project was not only about space design, but also about creating a business strategy for the local economy to make a vibrant pop-up city district. We dealt with design, products, money flow, marketing and stakeholders during 1.5 months. It was really intense and also hard to manage all the different opinions as a group, but I only have good memories about it!

What was your graduation project?

It is a still ongoing research project, Home For a Moment – a participatory installation that lets people create their own intimate space scene. Since I came to study in the Netherlands, I have moved five times. This experience made me wonder how space can change to become an intimate space, and what the main elements are which make people feel at home. So I invented a kind of design tool to translate people's thoughts about feeling at home from verbal ideas into 3D-planning. I tested it during the National Day of Architecture, welcoming guests to the performance space that was designed with carpet tiles and 1:20 miniature objects. I introduced the basic rules they had to follow and assisted them translating their thoughts by asking specific questions and listening patiently. As a result, I've got 68 homes, created by 85 visitors in 24 hours.

Are you still in contact with the school?

Yes! I moved to South Korea after graduation, but I already came back to The Hague for a visit.

Are you still in contact with your fellow students?

Yes, we were quite a small group, like a family. I use social media to keep in touch, but when I visited the Netherlands we went for dinner and drinks.

Was the transformation from graduation to working life a smooth one?

To be honest, I am still settling into my working life. But it is going better than I expected.

If you were to do the course again, what would you do differently?

I was so shy in the beginning – typically Asian. But if I were to do the course again, I would act more European – real worlds are the same everywhere!

Minsun Kim's graduation project involved designing a participatory installation to address real people's ideas of what makes a home.

Course
INSIDE Interior Architecture

School
Royal Academy of Art

'I chose this school because I wanted a good compromise between thinking and doing, and also to experiment and find new methods of approaching a project while getting closer to the problems of the reality surrounding me.'
Elide Mozzorecchi

'It's important to remember that the course is on interior *architecture*. In my opinion, this is accurate because it addresses a broader context than interior *design*. We work from the urban scale downwards.'
Emilija Juodyte

'INSIDE changed my viewpoint and guided me to design in a different way. I learned how to create concepts that make sustainable design a possibility.'
Klinphaka Keawcharoen

'Feed your curiosity here and never stop questioning what happens in the design and art world. Be daring and confident in order to make the most of both studying and professional experiences.'
Junyuan Chen

'The beach is definitely the best thing about living in The Hague! There are a nice bars and restaurants in Scheveningen which are worth a visit on a sunny day.'
Joanne Smith

City Life

Stately and rather regal, The Hague is a city at the heart of Dutch politics and international diplomacy. The International Court of Justice and Peace Palace are located here, as is the Dutch King and other members of the royal family. Since 1446, the Dutch parliament has met here, at the medieval Binnenhof. Palatial architecture mixes with wide boulevards and expansive green parks to give The Hague a restfully elegant atmosphere, while top-notch museums and galleries add cultural oomph to a dynamic, multicultural city. The Hague is said to have the most shopping streets of any Dutch city, and it also has a deserved reputation for gastronomy, with an abundant supply of good restaurants.

Best of all in many people's opinion, the beach – all 11 km of it – is within easy reach, as is a wild and beautiful dune landscape. And if all else fails, Amsterdam is just a short train ride away.

The Hague is a stately and historic city, at the centre of international affairs yet with a peaceful atmosphere.
Photo Anton Sovetov

The Netherlands

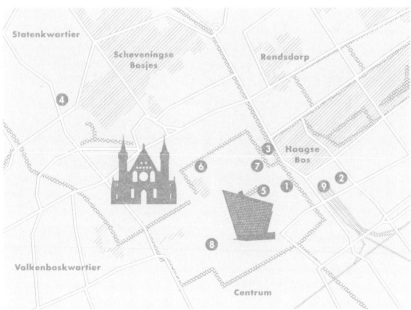

The Hague

1 KABK
2 National Library of
   the Netherlands
3 Museum Meermanno:
   House of the Book
4 Gemeentemuseum
   Den Haag
5 Mauritshuis
6 Stroom Den Haag
7 Escher in Het Paleis
8 Paard van Troye
9 Central Station The Hag

Park

Water

Railway

Main road

Course
INSIDE Interior Architecture

School
Royal Academy of Art

National Library of the Netherlands ②
Founded in 1798, the library houses 3.5 million items, from medieval manuscripts to electronic publications.
kb.nl

Museum Meermanno: House of the Book ③
Devoted to the history of the book, this museum has a remarkable collection, from medieval miniatures to modern editions, set in an 18th-century interior.
meermanno.nl

Gemeentemuseum Den Haag ④
This impressive 1935 building by architect H.P. Berlage contains the world's biggest collection of works by Piet Mondrian as well as art by Picasso, Kandinsky, Van Gogh, Monet, Toorop and many contemporary artists, plus a fine collection of Delftware.
gemeentemuseum.nl/en

Mauritshuis ⑤
The core collection at this newly restored and enlarged museum consists of masterpieces from the Dutch Golden Age, including works by Rembrandt, Vermeer, Jan Steen and Frans Hals, including the iconic *Girl with a Pearl Earring.*
mauritshuis.nl

Stroom Den Haag ⑥
A lively centre for contemporary visual arts and architecture, Stroom has an intriguing exhibition programme and provides a range of services for cultural practitioners.
stroom.nl

Escher in Het Paleis ⑦
The work of famous Dutch graphic artist M.C. Escher is on show here, housed in a former royal palace.
escherinhetpaleis.nl

Paard van Troye ⑧
Recently renovated, this legendary music venue is fun, friendly and boasts a varied programme.
paard.nl

Haagse Bos
This peaceful, leafy park in the midst of the city is what remains of the hunting grounds of Holland's medieval counts.

Scheveningen
This lively seaside resort comes complete with miles of sand, an esplanade, pier and lighthouse, plenty of restaurants and clubs, and windsurfing and kiteboarding opportunities.

How to get around
The Royal Academy of Art is situated opposite the Central Station ⑨ of The Hague. The city has a great public transport network consisting of trams and buses, but the Netherlands is very cycle-friendly, so a bike is a highly viable option.
The Hague is situated in close proximity to other big Dutch cities like Amsterdam, Rotterdam, Leiden and Utrecht.

Leiden is 16 km and takes 12 minutes by train; Rotterdam is 21 km from The Hague and the train takes 20 minutes. A train ride to Amsterdam from The Hague (52 km) takes just 40 minutes. Scheveningen (the beach) is easy to access, via tram 11 and 9 and bus 22, or by bike off course.

Arranging housing
Average

Housing support by school
No

Cost of room in the city
EUR 450 per month

Cost of campus housing
n/a

Royal College of Art

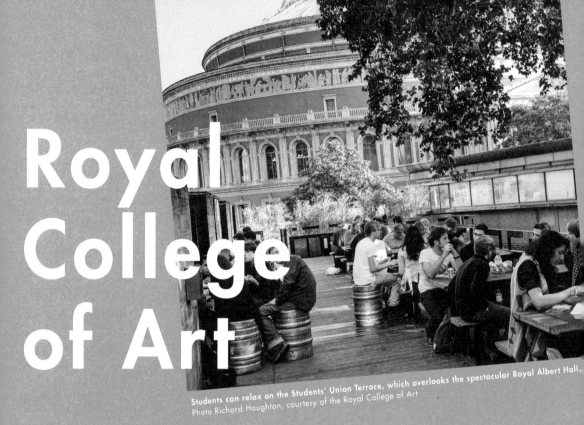

Students can relax on the Students' Union Terrace, which overlooks the spectacular Royal Albert Hall.
Photo Richard Haughton, courtesy of the Royal College of Art

Royal College of Art (RCA)
Kensington Gore
London SW7 2EU
United Kingdom

T +44 (0)20 7590 4444
info@rca.ac.uk
rca.ac.uk

The Royal College of Art Kensington campus overlooks the 270-acre
Kensington Gardens. Photo Richard Haughton, courtesy of the Royal
College of Art

Course
Interior Design

School
Royal College of Art

'Students must learn to understand the human impact of design and then deliver it with technical perfection'

Ab Rogers, head of programme

Why should students choose this particular school?

The strength of the school lies in the fact that courses are delivered by practising designers, architects and theorists, all of whom are international leaders in their fields. There are plentiful opportunities for industry-connected live projects and research. A dynamic lecture series offers talks by practitioners as well as communicators, commentators and artists from related disciplines – set design, architecture, branding, digital design, engineering, science, psychology, literature and fine art. The MA course culminates in the Royal College of Art (RCA) degree show, where completing students exhibit their work to the art and design world.

What is expected from the students?

Students are afforded the opportunity to explore the power and possibilities of the interior in its many forms. This ranges from creating new, permanent and highly integrated programmes within existing structures, derived from strictly constructed briefs, to temporary – and sometimes challenging – interventions in unusual situations on a more improvisational level.

What is the most important thing for students to learn during this course?

By its very nature, interior design involves collaboration across a multitude of disciplines. There is the overall design of a space and its infrastructure; the integration of furniture, industrial design elements, textiles, the graphic interventions of way finding, signage, moving image and illustration and the atmospheric considerations – acoustics, air and lighting. In parallel to the technical demands of a space are the emotional necessities: students must learn to understand the human impact of design, and then deliver it with technical perfection.

What is the most important skill to master when one wants to become an interior designer?

We believe that interior design occupies a unique position. Close human contact means that the balance of function, aesthetics and experience has to be carefully executed. In healthcare, hospitality, transport, industry, the office, retail and the home, the interior environment is what can most influence daily life. It has the potential to alter and radically improve the way we work, shop, relax, learn, live and die. It is a powerful commercial, political and social tool. At its best, it respects function, imagination and innovation: a place where technology, craft and poetry all have an important role to play.

City
London

Country
United Kingdom

Programme

Running alongside the Architecture course, the MA Interior Design offers both separate and related areas of study. Lectures, seminars, group work and individual thesis work are offered in the unique RCA studio context of interdisciplinary, workshop-oriented, speculative study. The programme encourages the students to develop their own solutions. It promotes design that re-invents and improves the space it occupies so as to enhance the emotional experience and shape the way its users interact with architecture.

The library has an extensive collection with over 70,000 books on art and design. Photo Richard Haughton, courtesy of the Royal College of Art

All RCA students are welcome to attend classes in the drawing studio. Photo Richard Haughton, courtesy of the Royal College of Art

Programme
Interior Design

Leads to
Master of Arts

Structure
The first year of the course will see students responding to a wide variety of live and conceptual briefs, working on a large scale and within all sectors: health, retail, leisure, education, exhibition, hospitality, domestic, etc. This will be an intense period of creative production and exploration, intended to strengthen existing theoretical, practical and conceptual sensibilities and develop new ways of thinking and working. The first year consist of two terms. During the first term of the second year students will develop a solid concept for their thesis project, creating a vision for a sensorial, crafted design that liberates their concept and clearly shows their discoveries and conclusions. In the second term, students will finalise their thesis.

Head of programme
Ab Rogers

Mentors and lecturers
Ian Higgins, Harriet Anstrusher, Tomoko Azumi, David Batchelor, Robin Blackledge, Rupert Blanchard Francesco Draisci, Chiara Ferrari, Rachel Forster, Kevin Haley, Ben Ke Pernilla Ohrstedt, Simon Pengelly, Dominic Robson, Sophie Smallthorn Zoe Smith and Jane Withers.

School Facts

Duration of study
2 years

Full time
Yes

Part time
No

Female students
69%

Male students
31%

Local students
11%

Students from abroad
89%

Yearly enrolment
18

Tuition fee
- GBP 9000 per year for EU citizens (approx. EUR 10,933)
- GBP 27,900 per year for non-EU citizens (approx. EUR 33,892)

Funding/scholarships
The College currently administers a bursary scheme for full-time students from England, Wales, Northern Ireland, Scotland and other EU countries. The amount offered for each bursary will be GBP 3000 (approx. EUR 3600).

Minimum requirements for entry
High-quality Bachelor's degree in furniture, industrial design, textiles, graphics, architecture, fashion, sculpture, theatre design, fine art, film, interactive design or any other creative field. Proficient written and spoken English.

Language
English

Application procedure
The following documents must be submitted in order to complete the application:
a completed online application form
your portfolio
a copy of degree/diploma
a statement outlining why you have chosen a particular course and what you propose to gain from your studies
the contact details of your academic referee
a copy of your TOEFL, IELTS or PTE certificate (if applicable).
Short-listed candidates will be invited for an interview.

Application details
rca.ac.uk/studying-at-the-rca/apply

Application date
Before the end of January

Graduation rate
n/a (programme has only existed since 2012, first students graduate in June 2014)

Job placement rate
n/a

Memberships/affiliations
None

Collaborations with
Arcadia Group and Save the Children.

Facilities for students
Personal work space in the studio, woodworking, metalworking, plastics and resin facilities, Apple Mac- and PC-based 2D and 3D modelling programmes and Rapidform RCA (RCA's rapid prototyping centre).

Student Work

DX Bar (2013)
By Sabrina Summer, Jakob Osterreicher and Elina Loukon

Resembling a festival stage, the two-level bar was constructed by the winning student team for the 2013 May Design Series furnishings fair at Excel, London. Inspired by the idea of a piazza, the students made the upper platform to give visitors a view over the fair. The service area below is subtly lit, with cubes providing casual seating and creating a social atmosphere.

Mary Portas Living & Giving Shop for Save the Children Fund (2013)
By Naomi Grieve (in collaboration with textiles student Flett Bertram)

Charity shops are not usually recognised as having the most stylish interiors, but this intervention certainly sets a standard. The displays are created by elevating white cubes on copper-pipe legs. Wall displays are constructed using the same piping, but with the added flourish of lengths of colourful fabric.

Course
Interior Design

School
Royal College of Art

opshop Boutique (2013)
y Rob Vinall

In the store's Oxford Street branch in London, Vinnal created a striking interior using geometric shapes and a high-impact colour scheme of hot pink, grey and white. Photo Dominic Tschudin, courtesy of Royal College of Art

Champagne Bar (2013)
By Jayoon Yoon and Eun Younghuh

Soft, tactile seating areas contrast with hard, functional surfaces in the student's champagne bar for the May Design Series furnishings fair at Excel, London, May 2013. A continuous undulating form connects tables for customers with the bar counter. The fluid design was intended to create a distinction between the bar area and the surrounding stands.

Alumnus

Name Rob Vinall
Residence London, United Kingdom
Year of birth 1987
Year of graduation 2014
Current job Freelancer
Clients Topshop, Natural History Museum
Website robvinall.com

Why did you choose this school?

I chose to study at the RCA not only for its reputation, but also for the chance to collaborate with other disciplines. I liked the idea of being influenced by other students doing work in different fields, and seeing whether this would inspire new areas in my own work.

What was the most interesting project you did?

By far the most interesting for me was the ability to indulge in a year-long thesis design project. My project was focused on the destruction of the social housing system in London, and whether or not there is a future for the buildings, which are often knocked down and replaced. Being able to address not only my political interests but also those areas of design that appeal to me most was definitely beneficial. Not only did it cultivate my understanding of the subject of social housing, but it helped me to acknowledge how rigorous and critical spatial design is and should be.

Were there any classes you found particularly difficult or easy?

There were a number of workshops dedicated to our programme that related to areas such as colour, material, light, and so on. I enjoyed the sound workshop most, but it was challenging. Sound design was tricky. Not only learning the software, but acquiring different types of sound was hard for me. There is a definite skill involved and I reckon a lot of luck, but when you get something that applies to your practise it can be very rewarding.

What was your graduation project?

My graduation project looked at how we can re-use the negative and forgotten spaces on social housing estates. I explored the future of estates through alteration, intervention and addition, instead of condemning them to demolition. The Aylesbury estate in Southwark was my site – currently a site of huge redevelopment – but it also has some really interesting spaces. Through a series of small spatial interventions on the estate, the project aims were to understand how spatial design can play a part in the longevity, regeneration and continuity of Aylesbury, and whether this could create a framework for other condemned schemes.

Any words of advice for future students?

Be in as much as you can, use all the facilities and try to cross-collaborate with the departments that interest you. Use the 2 years to develop your own understanding and stance on the subject and push yourself.

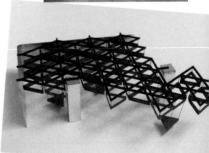

A model of an undulating triangular structure which is part of Vinall's design for the Topshop Boutique. Photo: Dominic Tschudin, courtesy of Royal College of Art

Course
Interior Design

School
Royal College of Art

Current Students

'During my time here I have met so many interesting people from different backgrounds. I hope that the friendships and connections I made here will last and, perhaps, turn into professional collaborations.'
Chiara Zambaiti

'There are lots of brilliant tutors and workshop technicians, but for me the most valuable thing is the conversation with other students.'
Atsushi Narita

'The life drawing classes reminded me of the importance of intuitive, freehand drawing. Being raised in the technological era, it's easy to forget the joys of drawing out an initial idea on paper instead of sitting before a computer straight away.'
Rosann Ling

'In my opinion, the most valuable facility is the workshops. It allows me to express my ideas from sketchbook to 3D objects. In addition, it encourages me to think about real issues and how to solve them.'
Jaekwang Lim

'The RCA programme gives students the scope to really explore what they believe interior design to be, rather than tutors dictating a set agenda.'
Naomi Grieve

'Feed your curiosity and never stop questioning what happens in the design and art world. Be daring and confident in order to make the most of both studying and professional experiences.'
Ruta Dumciute

City Life

When considering London, the words of 18th-century writer Samuel Johnson still resound today: 'When a man is tired of London, he is tired of life'. The multicultural metropolis is the most populous region in the United Kingdom and while this does make living in the city a constant battle – attempting the tube at rush hour is a reality check – what London has to offer outweighs any difficulties. Take a stroll in one of the city's impressive parks – Kensington Gardens, Hyde Park or Regent's Park – rummage through vintage clothes at Brick Lane, pick up a plant at Columbia Road Flower Market or grab a bite to eat at the covered arcade in Brixton. For students, it is certainly not the cheapest place to study, but the proximity to world-class museums and galleries, plus the wealth of free events, makes London all the more enticing.

Some impressive landmarks surround the RCA Kensington campus. Photo Richard Haughton, courtesy of the Royal College of Art

United Kingdom

London

1 RCA
2 Serpentine Gallery
3 Victoria and Albert Musuem
4 The Southbank Centre
5 The Nordic Bakery

Park

Water

Railway

Main road

Course
Interior Design

School
Royal College of Art

City Facts

See more London City Facts on p.286

Serpentine Gallery ②
Located in the middle of Kensington Gardens, the Serpentine is as well-known for its exterior artworks as its interior ones. Each year, a different architect is commissioned to create an outdoor pavilion for visitors to enjoy. Past pavilions were created by the likes of Zaha Hadid and Frank Gehry.
serpentinegalleries.org

Victoria and Albert Museum ③
With a collection that spans 2000 years, the V&A really has something for every taste. In the great halls of the building, visitors can find art and design from nearly every medium, from most parts of the world. Its current exhibitions are huge productions that are, more often than not, incredibly timely.
vam.ac.uk

Tate Modern
Billed as one of the UK's top three tourist attractions, the Tate Modern has become an icon in its own right. Located in the former Bankside Power Station, the gallery encapsulates over 100 years of modern and contemporary art across seven floors.
tate.org.uk

Shakespeare's Globe
The modern reconstruction of the round theatre where Shakespeare staged his plays is one of many around the world, but this is the only one that is built – very nearly – on the original site. The first priority of the theatre may be to explore the playwright's endeavours, but a variety of other events can also be enjoyed.
shakespearesglobe.com

The Southbank Centre ④
Located on the banks of the Thames, the Southbank Centre offers a huge variety of cultural events, with many free activities. Built on the belief that the arts should be available to everyone, the centre hosts dance performances, concerts, and much more.
southbankcentre.co.uk

Columbia Road Flower Market
On Sundays between 8am and 3pm this East-London street turns into a leafy refuge for weary Londoners. As well as an abundance of potted plants, trees, and bouquets, the street is filled with a range of independent shops.
columbiaroad.info

Brick Lane
The former stomping ground of Jack the Ripper is now a hip area filled with vintage clothes stands, organic food stalls and, let's not forget, a whole street of London's 'best' curry houses.
visitbricklane.org

Notting Hill Carnival
What began as a local festival set up by Notting Hill's West Indian community has morphed into a Caribbean extravaganza. Taking place over the August Bank Holiday weekend every year, more than a million visit to enjoy parades, stalls and impromptu after-parties.
thenottinghillcarnival.com

The Barbican
The world-class arts centre boasts a theatre, cinemas, galleries, a library, conference facilities, three restaurants and public spaces. An impressive amenity situated in the heart of London, the centre has something for everyone, even if it is just a quiet seat on the lakeside terrace.
barbican.org.uk

The Nordic Bakery ⑤
Visitors to this Scandinavian-style bakery can expect to be immediately hit by the sweet smell of cinnamon. A quiet space for some Nordic-inspired treats, the closest outlet to the RCA is tucked in behind Piccadilly Circus.
nordicbakery.com

How to get around
Getting around London is very easy. London has an extensive tube, bus and train network and a cycle hire scheme. Many students choose to cycle. While it is the quickest, cheapest and most environmentally friendly way to travel, London has a reputation for its busy and dangerous roads that are not entirely bicycle-friendly. The nearest tube stations to the RCA's Kensington campus are High Street Kensington and South Kensington. Buses 9, 10, 52, 70, 360 and 452 all stop right outside the RCA. There is also a cycle-hire docking station directly outside the college.

Arranging housing
Difficult

Housing support by school
The RCA doesn't have any housing provision for students but it does provide advice through the Student Support Office.

Cost of room in the city
Between GBP 450 and GBP 550 per month (approx. EUR 570 to EUR 700)

Cost of campus housing
n/a

City
London

Country
United Kingdom

Sandberg Institute

The Sandberg, whose current director is Jurgen Bey, is the postgraduate department of the Gerriet Rietveld Academy, a highly regarded art and design school where 45% of undergraduate come from outside the Netherlands. Photo Branko Collin

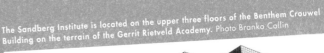

The Sandberg Institute is located on the upper three floors of the Benthem Crouwel Building on the terrain of the Gerrit Rietveld Academy. Photo Branko Collin

Sandberg Institute
Frederik Roeskestraat 98
1076 ED Amsterdam
The Netherlands

T +31 (0)20 5882 400
contact@sandberg.nl
immediatespaces.nl,
sandberg.nl

Course
Studio for Immediate Spaces

School
Sandberg Institute

ntroduction

'We are exploring a field where we believe discoveries are still to be made and potentials are to be found'

Anne Holtrop, head of the Studio
for Immediate Spaces

What is studying at this school all about?
The programme aims to develop new ways of looking at the immediate spaces around us. By selecting students with different backgrounds like fine art, graphic design, interior architecture or textile design, and inviting tutors from diverse backgrounds, we hope to open up new ways of seeing space and to train innovators in the interior architecture discipline.

Why is the most important thing for students to learn on this course?
The programme is based on supporting the development of each individual practice related to space. First of all we can say we follow our intuitions and our personal interests with an open mind. We do not know yet what immediate spaces are and what our work is precisely about, but we know we are exploring a field where we believe discoveries are still to be made and potentials are to be found. A field defined in between buildings and objects, a field full of spaces that are everywhere around us.

What kind of teaching method is applied here?
The studio work forms the backbone of the course. Here you develop your own practice, working as you wish individually or in collaboration. In the studio we seek for a development of every participant's practice, as we seek for a dialogue amongst the different practices and a dialogue in relation to the Studio for Immediate Spaces. Emphasis is placed on the physical work and on reflection and questioning through the work.

The theory programme provides a space for theoretical reflection on the practice, while experimenting with theory as a practice in its own right: one that encompasses writing, critical thinking and the fabrication of concepts.

What is expected from the students?
Basic criteria for admission include general suitability; quality, expressiveness and authenticity of your work; an independent and enterprising attitude; and the demonstrable usefulness of an advanced course of study for the candidate. We expect that participants already have enough background in drawing software and building techniques or are willing to learn these subjects through self-study, as this is not part of the education. The educational programme is completely in English and takes 2 years.

What kind of jobs do your former students mostly go on to do?
Some of the first alumni of this programme started their own practices and others went to work in small offices in the areas of architecture, interior architecture, design and art. As the programme attracts a very international public, after studying here some go back to their home country and start teaching there.

City
Amsterdam

Country
The Netherlands

247

Programme

The Studio for Immediate Spaces is a place for understanding and defining the specific spaces where people live, work, eat, socialise, discuss, or perform.

This 2-year master's degree course is set up around four practice-based studios, each led by a practitioner in the field of architecture, design or fine arts. A studio revolves around a topic. Current topics are: Autobiographical Construction, Let's Dance – from Studio to Situation, Material Gesture and the graduation studio. Through them, participants develop and understand their own intuitions, the tangible aspects of their work, the context they relate to and the environments they make.

Next to the studios, a theory programme provides a space for reflection on the practice while experimenting with theory as a practice in its own right. Besides regular seminars and individual tutorials, the theory programme comprises a series of talks by invited speakers, the Monday evening talks, as well as the 2 day-long roundtable discussions, both of which are open to the public.

Additionally guests from different disciplines and nationalities are invited for up to a week during the weekly programme. The general rule for these visits is that there is no rule. The guests can organise a lecture, a discussion, a walk, create work, or build a space.

The course embraces a rather philosophical attitude towards its subject, space. Photo Max Royakkers

Students can use the wide range of facilities at the Rietveld Academy. Photo Max Royakkers

Students have the opportunity to invite whoever they want for a workshop of their choosing. Photo Max Royakkers

Programme
   Studio for Immediate Spaces

Leads to
   Master Interior Architecture

Structure
   The programme is a full-time course. Its duration is based on 4 semesters of 16 weeks each and it accounts for 120 ECTS.

Head of programme
   Anne Holtrop

Mentors and lecturers
   Pascal Flammer, Hanne Hagenaars, Laure Jaffuel, Elise van Mourik, Tom Vandeputte, plus guest tutors including (2012-2014), Petra Blaisse, Alice Foxley and Kersten Geers, Krijn de Koning, Lex Pott, Jerszy Seymour and Melle Smets.

School Facts

Duration of study
2 years

Full time
Yes

Part time
No

Female students
50%

Male
50%

Local students
25%

Students from abroad
75%

Yearly enrolment
10

Tuition fee
- EUR 2106 per year for EU citizens
- EUR 5016 per year for EU citizens who have spent over 3 years studying for a master's degree in the Netherlands
- EUR 5016 per year for non-EU citizens

Funding/scholarships
No

Minimum requirements for entry
Bachelor's degree in relevant field and proof of English proficiency. Your work must show spatial qualities and an interest in research.

Language
English

Application procedure
Submit your application online and include the following:
a portfolio
your curriculum vitae
a motivational letter.
The admission exam involves assessing a participant's portfolio, CV and motivation letter. The second round consists of individual meetings of selected candidates with the admissions committee.

Application details
sandberg.nl/apply

Application date
Before 1 April

Graduation rate
80%

Job placement rate
80%

Memberships/affiliations
None

Collaborations with
Stroom Den Haag, The One Minutes Foundation, Z33, Momart and the National Institute Of Design (India).

Facilities for students
Rietveld Academy's workshops (metal, wood, CAD-CAM, ceramics, glass, printing and binding), media centre with sound and video workshop and library.

Student Work

Untitled (2013)
By Alicja Nowicz

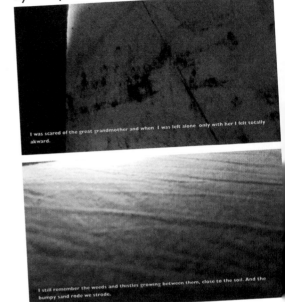

I was scared of the great grandmother and when I was left alone only with her I felt totally akward.

I still remember the weeds and thistles growing between them, close to the soil. And the bumpy sand rode we strode.

Models of remembered places are filmed and a video composed, adding a narrative to them and obtaining a new level of meaning

Swimming Pool (2013)
By Luuc Sonke

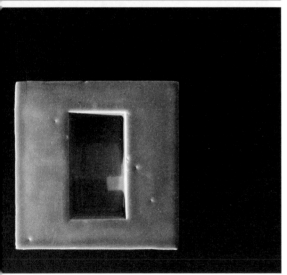

Objects around the idea of a swimming pool, and the representation of a swimming pool through objects.

Experiene of Colour of Light (2013)
By Juri Suzuki

An installation that explores the 'now' through space, objects and lig

Course
Studio for Immediate Spaces

School
Sandberg Institute

Writing a Landscape (2013)
By Esther Bentvelsen

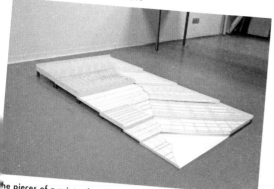

The pieces of a printer found outside the Rietveld Academy are used to create an installation of 'machines' that suggest the Dutch landscape. Films record ink and water running through the 'machines'.

Mining Ritual (2013)
By Ewelina Niedziella

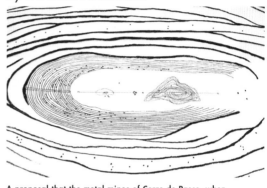

A proposal that the metal mines of Cerro de Pasco, when exhausted, be handed over to the residents of the city, transforming them into a place of mining ritual to memorialise the industry and link it to the future.

Study for Construction (2013)
By Roeland Otten

One-minute video performance in collaboration with Alonso Vazquez, documented by Nicolo Scatola. Photo Nicolò Scatola

Alumna

Name Laura Holzberg
Residence Berlin, Germany
Year of birth 1985
Year of graduation 2013
Current job Assistant manager exhibition design and projects for the BDA and German Architecture Centre DAZ

Why did you choose this school?
I was looking for a school that would offer an open and experimental approach towards architecture and space. The Sandberg Institute is informal and collaborative. Courses are small (10–12 students) which enables intense supervision.

What was the most important thing you learned here?
To trust in the work and myself, and especially in the process of creating. This process is an uncertain path with a lot of struggles. I learned to follow my intuition and do things without knowing or predicting what the outcome will be.

What was your graduation project?
It was called Aligning, Unfolding, Building, Digging, Grouping, Pulling. As an architect, I look for new ways and tools to deal with space. In my master thesis I took elements from performance art and applied them to spatial practice. I intervened in various empty lots and vacant construction sites. The work shows the outcome and residues of myself physically altering present elements with the actions and movements listed in the work's title. This is documented by photographs and a video that shows the performance of the movements on site.

Any words of advice for future students?
Be open to the unexpected and unusual. There will be a lot of new, inspiring, challenging and fun experiences to come. From modelling in the workshop of Rem Koolhaas' OMA to performances in The Hague for the Stroom Festival, to public investigations in Singapore – I conceived and worked with space in many different ways, experiencing the immediacy of it.

What was your favourite place to hang out?
I spent every day in the studio of the Sandberg Institute, even the weekends. This was my favourite place to develop and swap ideas with fellow students. My favourite place to hang out and relax was the canteen of the Rietveld Academy – where I also worked 2 days a week – which is a lively place of interaction and meeting.

Are you still in contact with your fellow students?
Since we were a very multicultural group, a lot of my fellow students moved back to their home countries: Iran, Japan, Taiwan, Brazil. But we are still in contact. As far as we can, we also help each other by giving advice or communicating job offers or projects that might be interesting.

If you were to do the course again, what would you do differently?
I think that I would try to focus on one theme, research and explore it in depth and set up a network of people to continue working within that field. This could help to individually create projects after studying and stay connected.

In her graduation project, Holzberg explored the application of elements of performance to spatial practise.

Course
Studio for Immediate Spaces

School
Sandberg Institute

'Future students should not expect to learn architecture, or interior architecture here. We study everything that is "spatially related" in a more philosophical way. We don't learn how to design a house or how to build a wall. It is really about *you*, exploring and developing your skills.'
Esther Bentvelsen

nything is allowed. This
n mean writing, making
ulptures, models, drawings,
deo works, audio works.
nything can be your topic
interest, but you need to
ke it seriously and then
mething amazing can
velop. I learned that the
ost seemingly unimportant
ing can become a great
ork, if you are able to
llow up on it and hold on
your own motivation for
veloping the idea.'
Elejan van der Velde

'I chose this school because of the freedom you get as a student to experiment and explore. For me it was about defining what I want to do in the realm of architecture by exploring the boundaries of the discourse while gaining a more critical attitude towards practice by acquiring theoretical knowledge.'
Luuc Sonke

City Life

Amsterdam is the largest city and the capital of the Netherlands. It has a population of over 790,000 within the city limits, an urban population of over 1,200,000 and a metropolitan population of over 2,250,000. The city comprises the northern part of the Randstad, one of the larger conurbations in Europe, with a population of approx. 7 million.

As the Netherlands' commercial capital and one of the top financial centres in Europe, Amsterdam is considered an Alpha World City by the Globalization and World Cities Study Group and Network. Many large Dutch institutions have their headquarters here, and seven of the world's top 500 companies are based in the city, as well as the Amsterdam Stock Exchange, the oldest stock exchange in the world.

Amsterdam is intensely urbanised, as is the Amsterdam metropolitan area surrounding the city. Comprising 219 km² of land, the city proper has 4457 inhabitants per km² and 2275 houses per km².

Amsterdam is situated 2 m above sea level. The surrounding land is flat as it is formed of large polders. Amsterdam is connected to the North Sea through the long North Sea Canal.

Dam Square, the town square in the heart of Amsterdam with the grand Royal Palace in the background. Photo Sandeep Pawar

The Netherlands

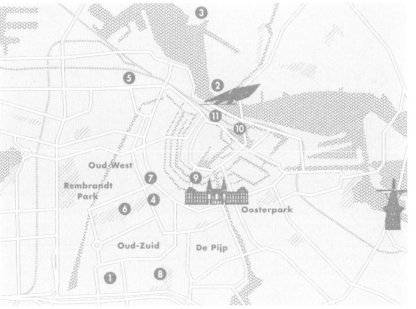

Amsterdam

1 Sandberg Instituut
2 Eye
3 IJhallen
4 Museumkwartier
5 Westergasfabriek
6 Vondelpark
7 Friday Next
8 Restaurant As
9 Foam
10 Chinatown
11 Central Station

Park

Water

Railway

Main road

Course
Studio for Immediate Spaces

School
Sandberg Institute

City Facts

nal Ring
Recently elected as an UNESCO
World Heritage Site, the Canal Ring
was dug in the 17th century to attract
wealthy home owners. It is still a posh
neighbourhood with many Dutch
celebrities owning property.

e ②
Situated on the northern bank of
Amsterdam's waterfront and designed
by Delugan Meissl Associated
Architects, Eye became Amsterdam's
latest hotspot. It hosts a cinema and a
film museum, plus a cafe with the best
terrace ever.
eyefilm.nl

allen ③
It might be a bike ride of more than
an hour from the Sandberg Institute,
but it's worth it. Every first weekend of
the month the flea market at the
IJhallen offers truckloads full of
vintage treasures.
ijhallen.nl

Premsela Institute
The Premsela institute, named after
the late Dutch designer of exhibitions,
shop windows, interiors, innovative
carpets and lamps Benno Premsela,
organises lectures, debates and
exhibitions and publishes *Morf*
magazine and the international web
portal design.nl.
premsela.org

Museumkwartier ④
The museum quarter in the south of
Amsterdam is home to the three most
popular museums of the city:
Rijksmuseum, Van Gogh Museum and
Stedelijk Museum.
amsterdam.info/museumquarter

Westergasfabriek ⑤
A former industrial complex,
Westergasfabriek is now a creative
centre, with an arthouse cinema,
cafes, events and creative start-ups
adjoining one of the city's pleasantest
parks.
westergasfabriek.nl/en/westergasfabriek-
en/park

Inside Design Amsterdam
An inspiring design event, organised by
the Dutch branch of international
magazine *Elle Decoration* featuring
installations, shops and showrooms by
designers, architects and artists.
elle.nl/insidedesign

Vondelpark ⑥
There are many parks in the city, but
the Vondelpark in Amsterdam South
stands out because of its size and the
crowds it attracts on a sunny day. As
soon as the weather allows it, the
locals light their barbecues and stay
till the sun goes down.
hetvondelpark.net

Friday Next ⑦
Next to the Vondelpark, concept store,
cafe and interior design agency
Friday Next sells beautiful stuff and
delicious food.
fridaynext.com

Restaurant As ⑧
This restaurant combines pure food that
changes every season with a stunning
interior by studio Muller & Van Tol.
restaurantas.nl

w to get around
Amsterdam Schiphol Airport is less
than 20 minutes by train from the city
centre. It is the tenth largest airport in
the world, handles about 48 million
passengers a year and is home base
to KLM (Royal Dutch Airlines). From
Central Station ⑪ there are regular
train services with destinations in
Belgium, France, Germany and
Switzerland.
Navigating by car through the city
centre is discouraged, with the
government sponsoring initiatives to
reduce car usage. Large motorways
only exist around the city.

The Sandberg Instituut can be
reached from several stations. From
Central Station you take bus lines 170
or 172 or tramlines 16 or 24. The stop
is called IJsbaanpad. From Sloterdijk
Station or Zuid WTC Station you take
metro line 50 and get off at
Amstelveenseweg. By car you should
take highway exit S108 on the A10.
But of course the best way to reach
the institute is by bike, like all the
locals do.

Arranging housing
Very difficult

Housing support by school
Yes (limited possibilities)

Cost of room in the city
Between EUR 300 and
EUR 600 per month

Cost of campus housing
n/a

Scuola Politecnica di Design

**Scuola Politecnica
di Design (SPD)**
Via Carlo Bo 7
20143 Milan
Italy

T + 39 02 2159 7590
info@scuoladesign.com
scuoladesign.com

The open, transparent building design reflects the philosophy of the school. Photo Delfino Sisto Leg

Course
Interior Design

School
Scuola Politecnica di Design

'As with any creative profession, an open mind and solid cultural background are extremely important'

Rita Preatoni, head of the Academic Programme

Why should students choose SPD?
At SPD, every student is followed individually by a faculty made up of designers, tutors, researchers and professionals in the specific professional discipline. The project works are carried out in association with companies such as Heineken, Artemide, Planetaria Hotels and Poltrona Frau Group. The final internship is a crucial experience at SPD: students join an interior architecture firm in Milan to round off their skills in a professional setting.

What is studying here all about?
Interior design today is a complex cultural system and requires a broad set of skills to respond to multiple demands for identity, performance, emotional and physical comfort of individuals and groups. Our mission is to offer studio practice plus cultural and technical training to postgraduate students wanting to enhance their design thinking and professional skills. The programme has an architectural orientation and places a great emphasis on the conceptual approach. Besides the ever-changing challenges of this profession, designing for our living environment implies blending functions with a meaning.

What is expected from the students?
Participants are expected to engage in an open and collaborative dialogue with tutors and colleagues for the continual progression of their projects. A high motivation for learning and personal growth, a constant spur toward innovation and an openness to explore cross-disciplinary themes are critical factors for this professionally oriented empowerment process.

What is the most important thing students learn during this course?
First of all, they learn to be aware of the people that will share the spaces they created. A conscious and responsible attitude in the broader sense is needed as designer sare a fundamental part of society. Secondly, they need to play with intangible aspects well beyond the physical experience of a place, learning how to reinforce a sense of identity and trigger emotional engagement.

What is the most important skill to master when one wants to become an interior designer?
Beside the technical aspects and those abilities related to space planning, designers must master the language of lighting, materials, colours and surface finishing in order to craft rich sensory experiences. For any creative profession, an open mind and solid cultural background is extremely important. Curiosity, an experimental approach and design sensitivity complete the profile.

What sort of careers do your students tend to move on to do?
Some graduates continue their growth inside large companies acquiring solid managerial skills, whereas others choose to start an independent studio to gain complete control of the creative process.

Programme

The course, organised in association with IULM University, is a career-driven specialisation path in interior design with an architectural orientation. The programme lasts 14 months and is aimed at graduates in relevant design disciplines. Course contents deal with concept design, space planning, interior layout, display and furniture design, branding and communication. The programme provides discerning insights into the language of materials, lighting, colour and the integration of technical components.

All these aspects meet in the studio classes le by renowned professionals who support the creation of a working knowledge base. As a result of this education, on the one hand students are encouraged to develop a conceptual approach in design practice, gaining a strategic understanding of elemen and processes involved. On the other hand, sound design abilities, detailing and advanced visualisation techniques enable th participants to complete their professional skill set. The projects developed every year and the young professionals that SPD offers to the market are a testimony to the quality of this education pathway and to the rewarding dialogue of the school with companies, manufacturers and the various actors along the design chain.

Students attend a combined lecture and workshop. Photo Delfino Sisto Legnani

Programme
Interior Design

Leads to
Master of Arts

Structure
The master programme lasts for a little over 1 year; from October to December of the following year, with a summer break in August. Attendance is compulsory and full time. Students start the programme with several studio projects and practical classes. Followed by a 3-month internship at a Milan-based interior architectural firm to complete the programme.

Head of programme
Rita Preatoni

Mentors and lecturers
Armando Bruno, Fernando and Humberto Campana, Giulio Cappellini, Mauricio Cardenas, Pac Cesaretti, Matali Crasset, Stefano Giovannoni, Diego Grandi, Piero Lissoni, Guendalina di Lorenzo, Ros Lovegrove, Denis Santachiara, Patricia Urquiola, Francesca Valan and Alessandro Villa.

Notable alumnus
Aldo Cibic, Lorenzo Damiani, Martí Guixé, Ferruccio Laviani and Cino Zucchi.

Course
Interior Design

School
Scuola Politecnica di Design

School Facts

...ration of study
1 year (14 months)

...ll time
Yes

...rt time
No

Female students
65%

Male
35%

Local students
22%

Students from abroad
78%

Yearly enrolment
20

Tuition fee
- EUR 14,200 for EU citizens
- EUR 15,200 for non-EU citizens

Funding/scholarships
No

...nimum requirements for entry
Bachelor degree in architecture,
interior design or another degree with
significant experience in the field.

...nguage
English

...plication procedure
The following documents must be
submitted:
your motivational letter
your complete portfolio of projects
your degree certificate with original
transcripts
your curriculum vitae.
A motivational interview is required
for admission to the programme

...plication details
info@scuoladesign.com

...plication date
Before 1 September

Graduation rate
95%

Job placement rate
100%

Memberships/affiliations
Cumulus/ADI

Collaborations with
Alfa Romeo, Alias, Audi, Beiersdorf,
Casamania, Ceramiche Flaminia,
Feltrinelli, Gebrüder Thonet Vienna,
Gruppo Miroglio, Heineken,
La Murrina, La Triennale di Milano,
Lamborghini, Maison Martin
Margiela, Microsoft, Museo Nazionale
della Scienza e Tecnologia Milano,
Pepsi, Planetaria Hotels, Poltrona Frau
Group, Rapsel, Serralunga, Silhouette,
Stone Island, Volkswagen and WMF.
Academic collaborations with
IULM Libera Università di Lingue
e Comunicazione in Milan
and Politecnico di Milano.

Facilities for students
Studios, IT labs, modelling
workshops, libraries and a cafeteria.

Student Work

NovantaNoveAngoli (2013)
By Giulia Ferrari, Martine Hanff and Elena Moliotsias

A restaurant and hotel for business and leisure tourism that changes according to time and to the clientele. A structural frame organises the dining area into separate booths to allow privacy and comfort without physically dividing the space. For each module lighting, colour and material vary throughout the day, taking inspirations from Rothko's emotional palette.

Rue de la Maison Hotel (2013)
By Alicja Miszczuk, Sara Syvähuoko and Alberto Jose Trevino

Rue de la Maison is a piece of old Paris transformed into an unconventional budget hotel with an atmosphere. The project plays with contrasts: an old Parisian neighbourhood is reconstructed inside a huge warehouse. Fake vs. real is the key theme behind the choices of textures, materials and furniture.

Collapse Collection For Rapsel (2013)
By Gustavo Branco Nosralla, Dario Costa and Burak Kocak

A bathroom based on simple, clean and geometric shapes. The collection has a strong architectural presence and adapts to different layouts. Neat but not minimalistic volumes are juxtaposed to suggest the sense of a movement breaking the rigidity of the composition. Functional details are integrated in the broken geometry of each piece.

Course
Interior Design

School
Scuola Politecnica di Design

Urban Bike Club (2013)
By Maria José Albuja, Meric Akay and Adriana Maass

A space dedicated to bicycle lovers, urban trendsetters identified with an alternative lifestyle and an ecological consciousness. The concept came up in response to a brief launched by Pepsi asking for an experiential retail store environment merging the local feel with the global perspective of the brand. The bike club represents a communication bridge between the brand and the emerging urban lyfestyle.

Origami (2013)
By Jacopo Arcangeli

This design was born from the study of the Japanese paper-folding technique as a construction principle to make the most of a minimal space. Despite its compact dimension, the cabin manages to offer many solutions for the comfort of the occupant, with concealed storage areas which can flip open and close keeping the surfaces clean. The functional elements are also adjustable to accommodate different users' positions and can fold down to create extra space when not in use.

Concept Store For Maison Martin Margiela (2013)
By Mihai Denes, Mathilde Massiet du Biest and Ali Zalzali

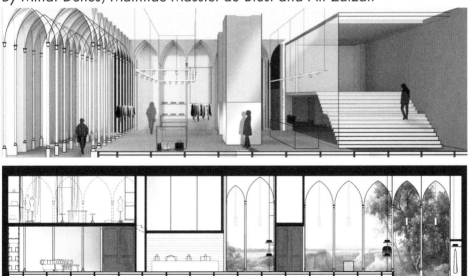

In this world where architectural deconstruction and complexity are the new modern classic, the project follows a counter-movement, going back to the times of gothic cathedrals and their sense of control and geometric orderliness. Cut-out arches form a flatly vaulted ceiling.

Alumnus

Name Stefano Giussani
Residence Milan, Italy
Year of birth 1976
Year of graduation 2004
Current job Project manager and partner at Lissoni Architettura
Clients Private, hotels, food companies
Website lissoniassociati.com

Stefano Giussani's graduation project was based on the process of working at Piero Lissoni's studio, where he participated on the first phases of an actual project.

Why did you choose this school?
After graduating in architecture I was looking for a school which could satisfy my interest in the field of interiors. I immediately recognised that SPD was able to provide me with everything I wanted to learn, thanks to its wide range of courses and its teaching staff drawn from world-famous architects.

What was the most important thing you learned here?
To fully appreciate the complexity and excitement of the design process. Thanks to the real case studies brought in by the lecturing professionals, we were provided with a direct link to the real world of interior design.

Were there any classes you found particularly difficult?
To be honest, I was just very excited at having the opportunity to attend all the classes and, partly because I was highly motivated, I found the courses both well within my scope and also intensely stimulating.

What was your favourite place to hang out?
An iconic Scandinavian design furniture store in Milan where I wanted to breath real design by touching the furniture I was studying. It was like being in a 1:1 scale design book.

Are you still in contact with the school?
Yes, I am. Indeed, a few years after graduation I became the assistant for the Piero Lissoni workshops. This lasted for 3 years and I now give lectures there in the interior or visual design classes.

Are you still in contact with your fellow students?
Yes, but due to the lack of time, we mainly use social networks as a way of exchanging thoughts and ideas, or sometimes we might meet on our travels around the world. The experience we had together during the SPD year was very intense and positive and I am sure it will remain forever in our memory.

Was the transformation from graduation to working life a smooth one?
I was contacted by Piero Lissoni's studio just before graduation and was given the opportunity to spend 2 months as a trainee there. One thing led to another and I have no been in the studio for 10 years. Last year I became a partner at Lissoni Architettura wher I coordinate the interior design team. Nothin(was easy, as work in the real world makes no allowances for delays or second chances. It is extremely competitive and requires lots of passion and dedication.

Any words of advice for future students?
Listen to your passions. Live the experience li a sponge, soaking up every single detail the teachers give you. Never stop asking questio in order to catch every little secret of this incredible profession.

'SPD offers its students a grasp of the outside business world. For instance, project briefs were focused on finding architectural solutions for companies such as LaFeltrinelli, Maison Martin Margiela and the universal EXPO happening in Milan in 2015, and we interacted with them throughout the project phase.'

Roya Semaan

'SPD is one of the most important design schools in Europe and its complex, design-oriented educational programme is very well structured. It offers an intensive and creative environment that simulates the real-life work experience, from facing the clients to building up a project on specific requirements and later delivering the final product.'

Mihai Dénes

Milan is a very versatile city with something for everyone. Besides the numerous aperitivo bars and shopping areas, I like going to the Parco Sempione on sunny days and to the Colonne di an Lorenzo, where you can find a very international environment.'

Martine Hanff

'The mandatory internship was an amazing learning experience for me. Seeing and being included in big international projects has helped me to manage my current work.'

Sara Syvähuoko

City Life

Studying in Milan means a year of total immersion in design that sets the tone on an international scale. You can live design and fashion 24/7 in the city. The annual Salone del Mobile furniture fair provides updates on the most advanced trends in the furnishing industry and interior design. All year round, the showrooms of the major Italian furniture brands, and independent design galleries, provide further interiors inspiration: Milan's centre is full of important design and fashion flagship stores, including Cappellini, Driade, Kartell and Versace, as well as Armani and Valentino. Now, the EXPO event in 2015 will also set new standards in architectural and interior design projects.

The city is a magnet for innovative and creative people and emerging labels. Milan is the engine of the Italian economy too, but what really sets the city apart is the work of the world's leading designers. In addition, the rich historical background of Milan provides multifaceted inspiration for design students – the city contains some of the greatest example of Italian Renaissance art.

People relaxing on a warm summer evening by the Colonne di San Lorenzo, one of the few remains of the Roman Mediolanum dating from the 3rd century AD. Photo Alex Roe

Italy

Milan

1 SPD
2 Museo Del Novecento
3 Triennale Design Museum
4 Studio Museum Achille Castiglioni
5 Franco Albini Foundation
6 Pinacoteca di Brera
7 Santa Maria Delle Grazi
8 Teatro La Scala
9 Castello Sforzesco

Park

Water

Railway

Main road

Course
Interior Design

School
Scuola Politecnica di Design

City Facts

See more Milan City Facts on p.56 and p.166

Salone del Mobile (Milan Design Week)
The largest trade fair of its kind in the world, Salone showcases the latest in furniture and design from countries around the world.
cosmit.it

Museo Del Novecento 2
This museum dedicated to the 20th century has sections devoted to Futurism, Spatialism and Arte Povera, and works by Modigliani, De Chirico, Pellizza Da Volpedo, Boccioni, Balla, Carrà, Fontana, Morandi, Sironi and many international artists.
museodelnovecento.org

Triennale Design Museum 3
Lushly located in Parco Sempione, the museum hosts exhibitions and events which highlight contemporary Italian design, urban planning, architecture, music, and media arts. Also has a good permanent collection.
triennaledesignmuseum.it

Studio Museum Achille Castiglioni 4
The studio of the important industrial designer Achille Castiglioni offers plenty of insight into his work.
achillecastiglioni.it

Franco Albini Foundation 5
The original studio of industrial designers Franco Albini and Franca Helg houses a fascinating archive of their oeuvres.
fondazionefrancoalbini.com

Pinacoteca di Brera 6
The Brera art gallery features a major collection of Italian art, including stunning Renaissance masterpieces by Piero della Francesca, Andrea Mantegna, Giovanni Bellini and Raphael.
brera.beniculturali.it

Santa Maria Delle Grazie 7
The big draw here is *The Last Supper* by Leonardo da Vinci, which is in the refectory of this medieval convent.
grazieop.it

Teatro La Scala 8
La Scala, Milan's famous and fabulous opera house, first raised its curtain in 1778. Practically destroyed during WWII, it was rebuilt and reopened in 1946 under the baton of Arturo Toscanini.
teatroallascala.org

Navigli Area
The history of Milan is closely connected with the system of canals which pass through the whole city – nowhere more picturesquely than in the lovely Navigli area.
navigli.milano.it

Castello Sforzesco 9
Originally a military fortress, the Castello Sforzesco was completely remodelled by the more comfort-minded Francesco Sforza. The new and improved defences were designed by uber-engineer Leonardo da Vinci.
milanocastello.it

How to get around
Milan is easy to get around by bus, tram, metro, foot or bike. Car sharing is another option. Buses, trams, metro (underground) and trains are run by the same company, ATM (Azienda Trasporti Milanese). With more than 50 urban bus routes, the bus system sometimes offers a more direct route than the underground.

The fare costs EUR 1.50 and you can get on and off as many times as you want for 90 minutes. The metro system consists of three lines: M1 (red), M2 (green), M3 (yellow). There is also a blue line, the *passante ferroviario*, which is a railway but can be used with the same ticket as the urban tracks.

Arranging housing
Quite easy

Housing support by school
Yes

Cost of room in the city
Between EUR 300 and EUR 600 per month

Cost of campus housing
n/a

SUPSI

Located in a beautiful natural setting, SUPSI sits on top of a hill and offers a great view of the town and Lake Lugano.
Photo Renato Quadroni

Outside the school's Department of Construction and Design. Photo Renato Quad

**Scuola Universitaria Professionale
della Svizzera Italiana (SUPSI)**
Campus Trevano
6952 Lugano (Canobbio)
Switzerland

T +41 (0)58 666 6300
info-ai@supsi.ch
supsi.ch

Course
Interior Architectural Design

School
SUPSI

'Studies focus on real and effective tasks which allow students to develop professional competences'

Pietro Vitali, head of the IMIAD programme

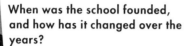

When was the school founded, and how has it changed over the years?
It was founded in 1997, with the integration of various specialised schools in southern Switzerland. The interior architecture faculty was part of the former applied arts school, which dates from early last century. Since 1997, SUPSI has considerably increased the number of students and staff, by creating new study programmes, research activities and partnerships with professional companies and institutions. Today, the school offers more than 30 bachelor's and master's courses of study.

What is studying at this school all about?
Our university is strongly oriented towards the competences and skills expected for a professional career. On the one hand, studies focus on real and effective tasks which allow students to develop professional competences; on the other hand, they are based on theoretical and scientific knowledge from the research institutes of the school.

What kind of teaching method is applied here?
The teaching method is based on first-hand experience. The empirical approach is cultivated and practiced within our design studios, understood not only as a common physical space, but also as a group of co-working students and teachers, enhancing their competences through the exchange and sharing of processes and experiences. All teachers are designers operating both in the school and in the professional world. Every teacher coaches a small number of students and so can meet each of them regularly for effective individual tutoring.

What is the strength of this school?
The connection between creativity and techniques in key sectors of interior architecture prepares our graduates to enter and operate successfully in the working environment.

What is expected from the students?
We start from the principle that the school and its standards are a reflection of the engagement of both students and lecturers. We therefore expect a high level of commitment, geared towards a productive environment. We encourage initiative and openness.

When did you start offering the master's degree course in interior architecture?
We started in 2006 with the IMIAD international master programme.

What is the most important thing for students to learn during this course?
To be ambitious. And to target this ambition towards the quality of the projects. This requires a lot of work.

What is the most important skill to master for an interior architect?
A critical awareness of the designer's role and responsibility to clients, society, the environment and the profession.

Programme

The programme focuses on the transformation and renovation of existing spaces. The highly professional approach entails the full integration of technique, as well as function and aesthetics. Theoretical knowledge is developed by single-themed seminars in four different domains: techniques, culture, professional skills and knowledge, and innovation. Design skills are mainly oriented to the transformation and reuse of existing buildings and focuses on four key sectors of the interior architecture: health and education, tourism and leisure, work and retail, and housing.

Having completed the programme, the student is ready to work as an independent designer or in multidisciplinary teams, with strong skills concerning space, light, construction, material, technology and communication. The course stands out for the immediate relationship of every project with real needs and real spaces. Most of the activities take place in the studio, where every student has his or her own working space, which is accessible 24 hours a day. The studio is both a working space and a creative factory, which promotes the exchange of ideas, the debate, the comparison of solutions. Working in a common space allows for sharing procedures and experiences.

The atelier is a laboratory for the production of work and ideas, like these models of working spaces. Photo Sara Daepp

A final review of the project Shared Ground Floor, guided by Virginia Moretti with Yolanda Castillo. Photo Sara Daepp

Programme
Interior Architectural Design

Leads to
International Master of Interior Architectural Design (IMIAD)

Structure
The programme consists of 4 semesters of 19 weeks each, in collaboration with the IMIAD partners, and accounts for 120 ECTS (30 per semester). It is organised in different format of teaching modules (workshops, supervised projects, lessons, seminars) focusing on design skills, integrating theory, technology and operational competences. The course is strongly oriented towards the mobility of students, as one semester has to be followed in one of the partner universities abroad. Throughout the study programme, the student prepares the subject of the master's thesis. The thesis itself is undertaken and completed during the last semester.

Head of programme
Pietro Vitali

Mentors and lecturers
Peter Brack, Yolanda Castillo, Veruska Gennari, Lukas Meyer, Virginia Moretti, Joao Machado, Chiara Napolitano, Alessandro Scandurra and Pietro Vitali

Course
Interior Architectural Design

School
SUPSI

Duration of study
2 years

Full time
Yes (45 hours a week)

Part time
Yes (30 hours a week over 3 years)

Female students
80%

Male
20%

Local students
80%

Students from abroad
20%

Yearly enrolment
6–10

Tuition fee
Between CHF 800 and CHF 1000
per semester (approx. EUR 660 to
EUR 820)

Funding/scholarships
Yes

Minimum requirements for entry
Bachelor's degree in interior
architecture or similar. Admission
is also possible for those with
exceptional professional skills.
Proficiency in English.

Language
English

Application procedure
Every application starts with a
pre-enrolment request containing
study degrees and work certificates.
If the pre-enrolment is satisfactory,
an application file is requested
containing the following:
your curriculum vitae
your portfolio with three recent and
meaningful works
a statement
your motivation letter.

Application details
info-ai@supsi.ch

Application date
Before 1 April

Graduation rate
95%

Job placement rate
92%

Memberships/affiliations
IMIAD, GIDE, VSI.ASAI

Collaborations with
HFT Stuttgart, Stuttgart, Germany;
ITU Istanbul Technical University,
Istanbul, Turkey; CEPT University,
Centre for Environmental Planning
and Technology, Ahmedabad,
India; and ECA, Edinburgh College
of Art, Edinburgh, UK.
In 2015, a Swiss master's in interior
architecture will be launched,
involving the four interior
architecture schools in the country.

Facilities for students
Centre for language and
international relations, research
service, library, sports, counselling
service, day nursery, student advisory
and accommodation facilities.

Student Work

New Life in the Quartiere Soldini in Chiasso (2014)
By Jasmin Hirt

From Public to Private (2013)
By Sonja Schröcker

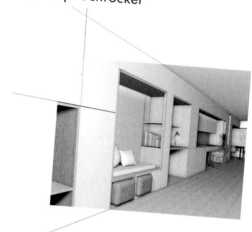

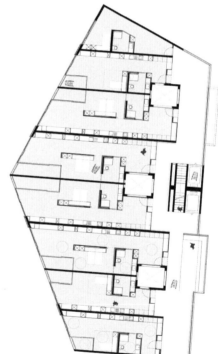

Via Guisan 19, opposite a new park, becomes a place for various community activities thanks to the introduction of new facilities organised in a welcoming, barrier-free way. Facilities include a cafe, co-working offices a kitchen, laundry, playroom, sport and communication spaces and more.

In a residence for elderly people, reorienting the units from the street to the garden solves the issue of noise and creates community space.

Course
Interior Architectural Design

School
SUPSI

ace B (2012)
Julia Fehrl

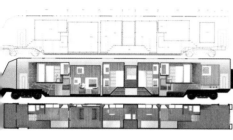

space in between is experienced from the inside and
phasises the approach to private areas reached by the stairs.
ferent levels enable a variety of perspectives, atmospheres
d views, with each level containing a different task.

Let's Have a Look... (2013)
By Isabel Vogel

 view to garden

 view to pizzo di claro

 view to 3 castles

Elderly people who are housebound enjoy looking outside and
observing their environment. So a design for the elderly in
Bellinzona reflects the outdoor environment and brings the outside
inside.

eep Up: Rethink | Reuse | Reinvent (2014)
Carina Illy

project to apply the theme of ecological thinking to the Quartiere Soldini in Chiasso. The conversion of a social housing project shows how even
omparatively small interventions can cause a rethink on a large scale.

Alumnus

Name Jan Eckert
Residence Lucerne, Switzerland
Year of birth 1981
Year of graduation 2007
Current job Senior researcher at CCTP and head of thesis committee MA design at Lucerne University of Applied Sciences and Arts
Website janeckert.ch

Why did you choose this school?
The international master's programme seemed like the perfect choice for me.

What was the most important thing you learned here?
Mainly I learned how to critically approach projects of a larger complexity, and how to feed a good part of my preliminary research into my work.

What was the most interesting project you did?
During my stay at Edinburgh College of Art we were asked to develop a solution for turning Edinburgh's former Royal High School into a National Museum for Photography. Working in a historical context and with a constantly evolving subject like photography was an interesting challenge.

Was there any class you found particularly difficult?
For one of the projects we had to design and build a piece of furniture. I started off with the idea of designing a lounge chair which would be made from a single folded sheet of aluminium. I got into real trouble while building it! One of the reasons was that, back in 2007, 3D printers and other hi-tech machines weren't yet as available as they are today.

What was your graduation project?
I dedicated the main part of my master's thesis to the question of whether there is something we can call the identity of a specific location or place. As a case study I chose the so-called 'roccoli' towers, formerly used to hunt migrant birds. My project finally became a proposal to transform one of these towers and adopt it for future use as a meeting point and open-air cinema during summertime.

Any words of advice for future students?
A master's in an international context is a huge opportunity, especially as it allows students to visit more than one university.

What was your favourite place to hang out?
The studio lab was probably the best place to meet up with other students, discuss our projects and have a nice drink in the afternoon.

How are you in contact with your fellow students?
One of them happens to be a colleague of mine now. I keep in contact with others via social media or we meet up from time to time.

Was the transformation from graduation to working life a smooth one?
As a PhD candidate and now as a researcher and teacher I've remained in an academic context. Therefore the transition into my current work position was rather a sequential path. At the same time I worked as a freelancer for a couple of years which fed into my theoretical work quite well. Still it was a big challenge to pursuit both an academic career and a practice-oriented one as well. Now I'm happy to concentrate on one thing.

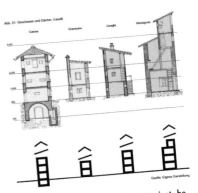

As a case study of Eckert's thesis project, he transformed one of the 'roccoli' towers into a meeting point and open-air cinema.

Course
Interior Architectural Design

School
SUPSI

'Lugano is great small city with an incredible environment. The lake is beautiful and the people very friendly. The spring begins really early and the climate makes it very pleasant to live there.'
Felix Bischoff

found that SUPSI has motivated teachers, while e schedule is well balanced d planned precisely, yet is adapted to the respective eds of the students at the me time.'
Carina Illy

'The university offers an interesting and diversified spectrum of courses and I simply love Swiss architecture. Moreover, the fact that I could improve my English and Italian language skills had a certain attraction.'
Julia Federhofer

'The most interesting class was definitely the Architecture and Design class. We spent 4 days traveling in Italy to visit various buildings and sites by Carlo Scarpa and Palladio. Discovering a culture through its architecture is one of the most satisfying experiences in life for me.'
Sandrine Sardi

'The main project was really interesting because it was about a design in the cultural context, which meant getting in touch with the locality, the mentality and the history of the place.'
Jasmin Hirt

City Life

Lugano is a great place to live, study and work. Its cultural variety, beautiful landscape and innovative environment offer first-class surroundings for personal wellbeing and career advancement. Located in a bay on the northern side of Lake Lugano, the town is surrounded by mountains and alpine scenery, while its centre has Mediterranean-style squares and numerous sub-tropical parks such as the Parco Ciani. The city is an important crossroads of cultural and artistic influences and relationships. In particular, the Canton Ticino is now a major centre of contemporary architecture thanks to the heritage of famous Swiss architects like Le Corbusier, Rino Tami, Mario Botta, Aurelio Galfetti, Luigi Snozzi, Livio Vacchini, Mario Campi, Fabio Reinhart and Flora Ruchat.

Switzerland is one of the most competitive countries in the world and is widely recognised internationally as a centre of excellence in education, research, and innovation. SUPSI, USI and the Mendrisio Academy of Architecture are the main educational centres in Ticino. Cultural vibrancy is provided by numerous museums, art galleries, cultural foundations and major international events such as the Locarno film festival, music festivals, exhibitions and conferences.

Switzerland

The view from Parco Ciani across Lake Lugano with Monte San Salvatore in the distance. Photo Jasmin Hirt

Lugano

1 SUPSI
2 Museo d'Arte Lugano
3 Spazio -1
4 LAC (Lugano Art and Culture)
5 Cantonal Art Museum
6 Villa Ciani
7 Lugano Canton Library
8 Il Tra
9 Museo delle Culture

Park

Water

Railway

Main road

Course
Interior Architectural Design

School
SUPSI

City Facts

useo d'Arte Lugano ②
Located in the 18ᵗʰ-century Villa Malpensata, this museum hosts exhibitions of mainly 20ᵗʰ-century art.
mda.lugano.ch

azio -1 ③
A space devoted to the collection of Giancarlo and Danna Olgiati and featuring nearly 150 works ranging from Arte Povera, futurism and Nouveau Réalisme to contemporary art.
collezioneolgiati.ch

C (Lugano Art and Culture) ④
LAC is a cultural centre devoted to promoting the visual and performance arts, music and architecture. It comprises a theatre, concert hall, exhibition and studio spaces, and more.
luganolac.ch

Cantonal Art Museum ⑤
The collection includes works by old masters from Ticino, Lombardy and Veneto, ranging from medieval to early modern. There are also exhibitions of contemporary (local and international) art and photography.
museo-cantonale-arte.ch

Villa Ciani ⑥
The magnificent, rose-coloured 1840s villa in the park of the same name is open to the public for exhibitions and special events.

Lugano Canton Library ⑦
An early example of the work of the founding father of contemporary architecture in Ticino, Rino Tami (1908-1994).

Il Tra ⑧
The library-café Il Tra hosts various events and exhibitions as well as providing organic vegetarian food and books.
bibliocafetra.blogspot.ch

Museo delle Culture ⑨
Cultural artefacts from the peoples of the Americas, Africa, Asia and Oceania. Based on the Brignoni Collection, an important collections of Oceanic art.

Lugano Longlake Festival
With over 300,000 visitors, this is one of the biggest open-air events in Switzerland. Every July, music of all kinds plus theatre, dance, art, film and more transform the city into a meeting of artists, public, entertainment and culture seekers.
longlake.ch

Locarno Film Festival
For 67-years, this festival has occupied a unique position on the cultural calendar. Every August, for 11 days, Locarno, right in the heart of Europe, becomes the world capital of auteur cinema.
pardolive.ch

w to get around
Lugano has a wide range of public transport, with a dense network of buses. The school is served by bus 3 and 4 (TPL line) and 441 (ARL line). Although it is possible to cycle, the streets tend to be quite steep, so many students opt to take the bus. Switzerland boasts a very efficient train system, the Swiss Federal Rail, which connects Lugano to the rest of the country. Direct connections to most major cities operate every 30 minutes. There are also high-speed train connections to Paris and Milan several times a day. Trains take passengers to Lugano airport and Milano-Malpensa airport, from where there are daily flights departing to every corner of the world.

Arranging housing
Average

Housing support by school
Yes

Cost of room in the city
CHF 600 per month
(approx. EUR 500)

Cost of campus housing
n/a

City
Lugano

Country
Switzerland

The academy building was built between 1882 and 1885.

The Academy of Arts, Architecture and Design

The Academy of Arts, Architecture and Design in Prague (AAAD)
nám. Jana Palacha 80
11693 Prague
Czech Republic

T +420 251 098 111
umprum.cz

The Academy of Arts, Architecture and Design occupies a stately and monumental bu

'The studio is a special environment where personal tuition is combined with cooperation with more experienced peers right from day one'

Jiří Pelcl, head of the Studio of Furniture and Interior Design

What is studying at this school all about?

The mission of the department of Interior and Furniture Design at AAAD is to provide a platform where talents can grow, develop, broaden their knowledge, gain experience and create. The school aims to be a melting pot of ideas, a place where opinions can clash, where it is possible to make mistakes on the way to perfection. Rather than being taught a specific methodology, students are confronted with a series of challenging projects and guided to eventually create their own method of problem solving. We strive to have graduates with an educated opinion but one that is their own.

What kind of teaching method is applied here?

The course consists of studio work. Students are given between one and three design projects per semester, and guided by the head of studio in combination with theory classes with various professors. The studio projects are as diverse as possible so it's not uncommon for students in the interior design studio to be working on an industrial design project or a strictly architectural task. While some projects are more conceptual, some are very real-world, often in collaboration with leading companies and manufacturers.

Why should students choose this school?

With its long history, the academy is one of the most important institutions in the country. All studios at AAAD average around 20 students in total. This number includes everyone from first year students to those working on their diploma projects and this gives us a unique student:tutor ratio. The studio is a special environment where personal tuition is combined with cooperation with more experienced peers right from day one. Every semester we also have at least a couple of exchange students joining us from abroad. Most graduates agree that the biggest asset of AAAD are the people you meet here.

What is expected from the students?

You could summarise it as the will to work hard, think hard, to experiment and stay open-minded.

What is the most important thing for students to learn during this course?

Probably creative critical thinking so that they can apply their factual knowledge in any situation.

What is the most important skill to master when one wants to become an interior designer?

To be creative and communicative, to think outside the box, to notice and question the things that most people take for granted.

Where do your former students mostly end up?

While many of our graduates find jobs in either architectural or design firms, almost half work as freelance designers or set up their own studios. It is also quite common for companies collaborating with AAAD on academic projects to later employ our graduates. Currently we have former students working worldwide.

Programme

Students apply to the Visual Arts programme and selecting the studio of their interest. The programme emphasises theoretical and practical knowledge of creative processes of design work. It reflects design in the context of the current debate on the future development of global post-industrial society. Students are taught to understand design in a wider perspective, with a critical view of the possible social and environmental consequences.

The Furniture and Interior studio's thematic task covers a wide range of products influencing our everyday lives. The studio respects each student's individuality, and their projects reflect their personality and his or her relationship to the present. The created designs could be reproduced in serial industrial production, or could be conceived as conceptual art works. Students are invited to search for new issues that should be addressed and learn to provide reasoning for their solutions. Working with and understanding materials is also a vital part of the learning process and there is a range of workshops for everything from old traditional crafts to CAD prototyping.

Student work is evaluated according to the following criteria: introduction of the given issue; analysis; proposal of a concept; possible solutions; preparation of a model; graphic presentation; and description of the process.

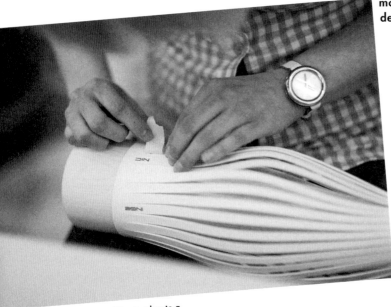

A student puts the finishing touches to a piece for the end-of-semester presentation of the Studio of Ceramics and Porcelain.
Photo Peter Fabo

Programme
Furniture and Interior Design

Leads to
Master of Arts

Structure
The 2-year programme consist of 4 semesters.

Head of programme
Jiří Pelcl

Mentors and lecturers
Ondřej Tobola

Notable alumni
Jan Plecháč, Henry Wielgus, Zbyně Krulich and Libor Motyčka.

Course
Furniture and Interior Design

School
The Academy of Arts, Architecture and Desi

School Facts

Duration of study
2 years

Full time
Yes (20 hours a week)

Part time
Possible, not recommended

Female students
52%

Male
48%

Local students
70%

Students from abroad
30%

Yearly enrolment
4

Tuition fee
- CZK 95,000 per semester (approx. EUR 3600)
- Free for all students with a basic level of the Czech language

Funding/scholarships
Accommodation Scholarship, Social Scholarship and Merit Scholarship available.

Minimum requirements for entry
Bachelor's degree

Language
English and Czech

Application procedure
The following documents must be submitted in order to complete the application:
a filled in application form
your CV with relevant information about your professional history
a letter of motivation – at least two pages in English
a portfolio containing your own pieces of work related to the area of studies (at least ten examples)
two recommendation letters
proof of completed BA studies
proof of your capability of studying in English.
Applicants have to pass the talent entrance examination. The two-rounds examinations take place in January and last for 1 week (1 and 3 days). Two to four applicants are accepted at the studio.

Application details
umprum.cz/en/study/application-process

Application date
Before 30 November

Graduation rate
56%

Job placement rate
High

Memberships/affiliations
Cumulus, NICA, ČKR, RVŠ

Collaborations with
Ajeto, Cotto – Lysice, Czech Porcelain a.s., Inge, Lasvit, Meva a.s., mminterier, Osram, Sapho and TON.

Facilities for students
Specialised wood workshop, metal fabrication and jewellery workshops, plaster and ceramics workshop, model-making workshop, CAD prototyping, glass workshop, printing letterpress and binding workshop and a student canteen.

Student Work

Stick Lights (2013)
By Libor Motyčka

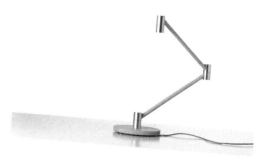

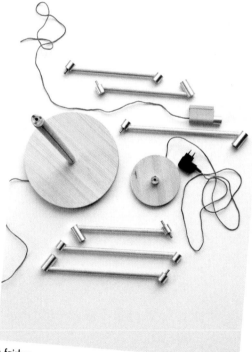

A fairly uncommon combination of materials is chosen for hi-tech lighting: using wood and aluminium together gives an atmosphere more suited to private interiors. This cooperation with Osram uses LED technology along with hidden touch sensor switches, allowing for minimalist detailing. Several versions were produced, from table and floor lamps to wall-mounted lights.

Mikado Furniture (2013)
By Zbyněk Krulich

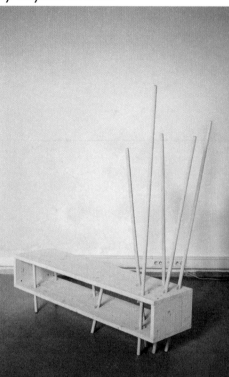

The Mikado collection was Krulich's diploma project. The foc was on utilising parametric modelling and generative design vital part of this project was the design of a an interactive software application coupled with a CAD/CAM production process allowing customer customisation of each furniture ite
Photos Tomáš Brabec

ol Box for Fablab (2013)
y Michael Tomalík

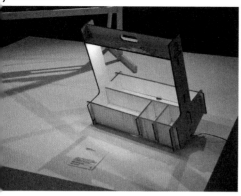

entry for the Domus FabLab competition, this tool box can be
t as data and then manufactured by fablabs all over the
rld. This plywood design was one of the competition winners
d was exhibited at the Salone del Mobile.

ons (2010)
y Jan Plecháč

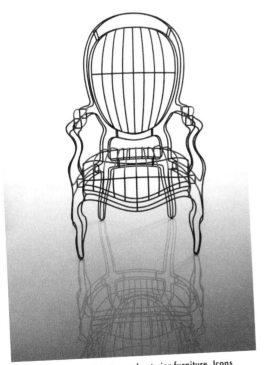

Somewhere between interior and exterior furniture, Icons
revive old iconic forms by putting them into a new context.
Delicately hand-soldered structures on steel poles allow the
designs to float in space like a thought between fantasy and
reality. Although Icons look fragile, they are durable enough to
be used in public spaces.

Foam Seats (2013)
By Barbora Přibylová

The brief for this semester project was entitled 'form follows
material'. The aim was to first create a production process with
materials and then apply that to a specific product. Using a
combination of fabric volumes and construction foam, the
approximately 30-minute window before the foam sets resulting
in the spontaneous shaping of each piece.

Family House (2013)
By Kristýna Fránková

In response to a sloping plot and floor space limits, this ad hoc
approach concentrates all the living areas into a box, wrapped in
a transparent staircase which winds towards each level. Inside, the
house is designed to be as open as possible with views of Prague.

Alumnus

Name Henry Wielgus
Residence Prague, Czech Republic
Year of birth 1982
Year of graduation 2009
Current job Co-owner Jan Plecháč &
Henry Wielgus design office
Clients Cappellini, Lasvit, Menu, Gispen
Website janandhenry.com

The sofa Wielgus designed as his thesis project is called Laur

Why did you choose this school?
Honestly, I never wanted to go anywhere else.
The studios are led by professors who are experts
in their respective fields, and the school has a
view of Prague Castle – it was an obvious choice.

What was the most important thing you learned here?
In our studio we mainly focused on the draft
process itself. We always tried to take the
selected topic apart to find its true nature. Then
we reflected that in a final draft, so the thing
will be as it should be and it won't be
pretending to be anything else. Also, I learned
that everything has to be clear and
understandable at first sight.

What was the most interesting project you did?
I tried to approach everything without
restraint but some topics are simply
more attractive. I loved creating a
small pocket light. Light is a beautiful
and unlimited topic and it doesn't
matter that it's only a small pocket one.
I tried to find something personal in it,
light as a guide.

What subject do you wish you paid more attention to?
If I studied again, I would pay more
attention to everything. But on the
other hand during my studies I had to
earn my living and skimp on school a
little bit because of that.

Was there any class you found particularly difficult?
It always depends on whether you like
something or not. But it's true that the subject
called civil engineering was really difficult for

me, even though I liked it. I am a haptic kind o
person so I have to touch everything and all th
pure theory was sometimes simply too much fo
me.

What was your graduation project?
As my dissertation thesis, I chose upholstered
furniture. I divided a sofa into two necessary
components – the load-bearing construction
and the soft seating part. The wire constructio
was made from 75cm-wide segments which
were connected to each other using a simple
lock. For upholstery I used old clothes but I ha
to figure out how to attach them. The result wc
a simple wire construction without any
unnecessary details.

Any words of advice for future students?
Don't focus on others but only on yourself.

Are you still in contact with the school?
I'm still in contact with Jiří Pelc who was my stud
leader. I have a great relationship with him.

Are you still in contact with your fellow students?
My life partner and my studio partner are
fellow students – it's pretty intense! I meet
others occasionally.

If you were to do the course again, what would you do differently?
I would try to enjoy it more in general. Your
student years are great – but people usually
realise it later.

Course
Furniture and Interior Design

School
The Academy of Arts, Architecture and Desi

Current Students

'You spend your time in one studio, with one tutor and a small number of students – the attention of the tutor is very personal, which deepens the discussion of the projects.'
Michael Tomalík

'For me, the most valuable aspect of the course was working in the studio with other students. The atmosphere inspired me and I made a lot of good friends.'
Kristýna Fránková

'If you do this course, you can expect a lot of hard work, a lot of learning, but also great fun and some moments that you'll never forget.'
Libor Motyčka

'I loved the mix of the theoretical and practical sides of design, also all the discussions about what design is, its meaning and the context of society and the environment. The complexity of the course was great – we worked on a wide range of projects, from designing a glass to designing a house.'
Zbyněk Krulich

City Life

Prague, the capital of the Czech Republic, is one of Europe's oldest and best-preserved cities. The academy is situated right in the centre of the historic Old Town, in front of the Galerie Rudolfinum and next to the oldest university in Eastern Europe. You can see the Moldau river and Prague Castle from the studios.

Prague is an attractive mix of must-see sights, easy-going atmosphere, reasonable prices, cultural hotspots and a lively art scene. It is also very safe, with a perfect infrastructure. Every year, millions of tourists visit Prague, but the city absorbs them easily, and there are still quiet, unspoiled areas such as Vinohrady, Dejvice and Vršovice. The city is unique for its well-preserved old centre, which has been beautifully restored. There are a lot of green spaces too, which add to the relaxing atmosphere. Although Prague is a capital, it is compact and not over-crowed. The city offers several design events and shops, including student design shops, and the art, design and architecture student sector is broa yet tightly interconnected thanks to the relatively small size of the city.

Czech Republic

Prague's atmospheric Old Town has a fairy-tale quality.

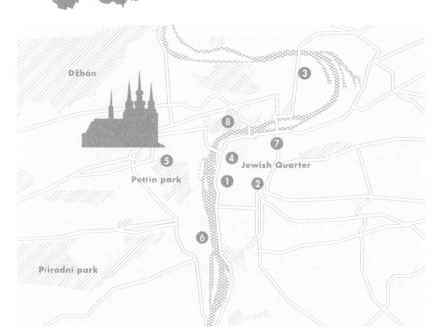

Prague

1 AAAD
2 Old Town Square
3 DOX Centre for Contemporary Art
4 Galerie Rudolfinum
5 Prague Castle
6 Meet Factory
7 Roxy Music Club
8 Letná Beer Garden

Park

Water

Main road

Course
Furniture and Interior Design

School
The Academy of Arts, Architecture and Desig

d Town Square
Prague's Old Town Square is a patchwork of architecture – from the Rococo Kinsky Palace to the Gothic Tyn Cathedral and the Baroque St. Nicholas Church. Street performers add a further touch of colour.

wish Quarter
The best preserved complex of Jewish historical monuments in Europe, with six synagogues plus the Jewish Town Hall and the Old Jewish Cemetery, which is the most remarkable of its kind in Europe.

)X Centre for Contemporary Art ③
Avant-garde contemporary art is on show here, with frequently changing exhibitions that often feature local artists – plus room for reflection with its cafe and roof terrace.
dox.cz

Galerie Rudolfinum ④
A contemporary art gallery and classical music venue combine in this spectacular building, which also boasts a spatially magnificent cafe.
galerierudolfinum.cz/en

Prague Castle ⑤
The largest ancient fortress in the world, Prague Castle has been built and renovated over 13 centuries and includes churches, gardens, alleyways and royal residences. A highlight is St. Vitus Cathedral.
hrad.cz/en

Baba
This area was selected by the Union of Czechoslovak Arts in 1928 as the place to build a modern garden villa settlement, which would become model of modernist living. Today, it remains the world's largest Functionalist housing development.

Villa Müller
An epochal early modernist house designed in 1930 by architect Adolf Loos.
mullerovavila.cz

Meet Factory ⑥
A non-profit cultural centre combining a huge gallery with ateliers and housing for artists, a concert hall, sound studios, cafe and bookshop – plus some enormously varied programming.
meetfactory.cz

Roxy Music Club ⑦
A popular venue in the Old Town, attracting big-name DJs.
roxy.cz

Letná Beer Garden ⑧
This green, leafy oasis is perfect for enjoying a beer – plus an amazing view of the city. Located in Letná Park, which runs along the bank of the Vltava.

w to get around
The public transport infrastructure in Prague consists of an intensely used system of the underground (its length is 59 km with 57 stations in total) and tram, but you can also get around the city by bus, bicycle, ferry or by foot. In Prague there are also three cable cars. The first is the on Petrin Hill and the other is on the hill Mrázovka and the third is at the zoo in Troja.

The nearest stop to the academy is Starom stská, which is served by tram 17 and 18 stop, underground line A and bus 207. The city forms the hub of the Czech railway system, with services to all parts of the Czech Republic and abroad. The nearest airport is 15 km away from the city centre.

Arranging housing
Quite easy

Housing support by school
Yes. The academy offers a limited number of places in low-cost student halls of residence.

Cost of room in the city
CZK 7500 per month on average (approx. EUR 280)

Cost of campus housing
Between CZK 5000 and CZK 9000 per month (approx. EUR 180 to EUR 325)

The Cass

The Sir John Cass Faculty of Art,
Architecture and Design (The Cass)
London Metropolitan University
41 Commercial Road
London E1 1LA
United Kingdom

T +44 (0)20 7423 0000
thecass.com

The Cass boasts a great London location on Commercial Road, just minutes from Aldgate and Aldgate East tube stations.

Course
Interior Design

School
The Cass

'The studio approach ensures a stimulating student experience, providing excellent preparation for professional practice'

Andrew Stone, deputy dean

What is studying at this school all about?
There are several themes which run through The Cass. These include a focus on socially engaged forms of practice at every scale; a focus on London as case study and context for many of our projects and collaborations; and a faculty-wide interest in making as well as designing.

What kind of teaching method is applied here?
The studio approach is at the heart of our delivery. Studios are smaller study groups, launched at the beginning of each academic year and focusing on a specific theme. Practice-based learning, field trips, research and critical studies are delivered in an integrated way within these groups. Students vote to join the studio that interests them – at present there are 66 studios in The Cass. Our studios bring together students, academic staff, practitioners, industry leaders and clients nurturing a sense of ownership and competitiveness which enhances a high quality of student experience and work to be produced.

Why should students choose this particular school?
We have many strengths. The studio approach ensures a stimulating student experience, providing excellent preparation for professional practice. Students are taught by and engage with a wide range of successful practitioners, many with links to the city's creative practices, agencies and organisations. There are four unique cross-faculty areas which greatly benefit the students. Cass Works is a

service providing excellent workshops, technologies – and the technicians to support them – from traditional workshops through to contemporary manufacturing technologies to digital media production. Our Cass Projects Office bridges study and real world engagement ensuring The Cass has an excellent reputation for live projects locally and globally. The recently launched Cass Cities supports a growing interest in urbanism, and Cass Culture delivers critical and contextual studies in an innovative way, using London and its galleries and collections as a library.

What is expected from the students?
Students are required to be inquisitive, innovative, critical and ambitious about the interior. They are expected to challenge their subject, their practice and the interior's capacity to choreograph human activity.

What is the most important thing for students to learn during this course?
We encourage students to develop a reflective and critical approach to practice. We want students to engage with, and understand contemporary design but also to develop their own framework and language.

Where or in what kind of jobs do your former students mostly end up?
We have alumni all over the world working in architectural and interior design studios or in their own design practices.

Programme

The overall theme and content of the course is intended to encourage independent design thinking in the field of the interior. In this respect, the curriculum begins to focus in a more advanced and systematic way on aspects of the profession and practice. Design occupies a large proportion of the course and the process of design is rehearsed through the vehicle of project work, which is carried out within an optional thematic studio. This year's studio 'City, Country, Coast' has three projects with real clients: the City Project, with The Royal Academy of Arts, London; the Country Project with the National Trust at Knole House in Kent; and the Coast Project in collaboration with the Fisherman's Preservation Society in Hastings, Sussex.

The studio platform situates the student in a more real, complex and ambiguous context for project work, with many more parameters that cover social, political and economic contexts as well as the physical context. In addition to studio study there are thematic modules that expand and deepen knowledge of a chosen area of cultural context or professional expertise particular to the student. The programme is designed to set out the breadth of the field of interior design and help students to secure a sufficient depth of understanding to ground their own work.

A student takes a short course in woodworking at the Commercial Road Woodmill facility.

Programme
Interior Design

Leads to
Master of Arts

Structure
This 1-year full-time, or 2-year part-time, study programme covers 2 semesters and the summer. Students should expect 12 hours of teachings a week plus the time spent on studio study.

Head of programme
Susan Ginsburgh

Mentors and lecturers
Janette Harris, Suzanne Smeeth-Poaros and Andy Stone.

Notable alumnus
Xenia Gyftaki

Course
Interior Design

School
The Cass

ration of study
1 year

l time
Yes

rt time
Yes (2 years)

Female students
62%

Male
38%

Local students
25%

Students from abroad
75%

Yearly enrolment
12

Tuition fee
- GBP 7,650 (approx. EUR 9512)
  for EU citizens (full time; part time
  GBP 850 / approx. EUR 1056
  per 20 credit module)
- GBP 10,800 for non-EU citizens
  (approx. EUR 13,428)
  Fees stated are for September 2014.

Funding/scholarships
Yes, many scholarschips including
The Cass Alumni School of Design
Postgraduate Scholarship.

nimum requirements for entry
Bachelor's degree

nguage
English

plication procedure
Apply online and submit the following
materials:
a written piece of work outlining your
design approach
a project idea
a portfolio that demonstrates
academic and creative potential.
Admission depends on a portfolio
interview in the form of a discussion
around the applicant's range of
interests and portfolio of work.

plication details
thecass.com/apply/overview

plication date
While there is no formal deadline,
application by March in the year
of intended study is strongly advised.

Graduation rate
100%

Job placement rate
Depends on the economy

Memberships/affiliations
Interior Educators

Collaborations with
The Royal Academy of Arts, The
National Trust, London Jewellery
Week, Orange and London Transport.

Facilities for students
Cass Works provides workshops for
wood, metal, plastic, print, ceramics,
textiles, photography, film making
and more. Services at Metropolitan
Works Digital Manufacturing Centre
include CAD, Rapid Prototyping,
Laser Cutting, Waterjet Cutting and
CNC Routing.

City
London

Country
United Kingdom

Student Work

Light Lounge (2013)
By Xenia Gytaki

A responsive night club in the Old Truman Brewery creative hub, Brick Lane.

Reynolds Room Knole House (2013)
By Anna Jane Derbyshire

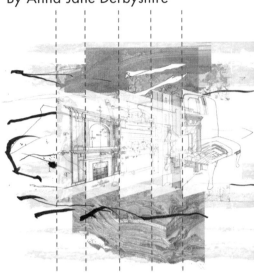

The Reynolds room is situated in a 500-year-old stately home call Knole House in Sevenoaks, Kent. The custodian of the house, the National Trust, asked for an interior in response to the painting a artefacts housed there. The resulting design schemes were display in an exhibition at the Orangery at Knole.

Floating Casino on the River Thames (2013)
By Aslan Karosh

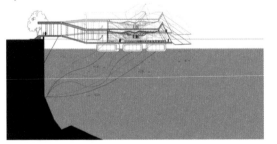

This self-generated student project was the result of spatial experiments exploring illusion and transformation.

The Orangery at Knole House (2014)
By the class of 2014

The students designed and built this exhibition to display their projects inspired by the Reynolds Room at Knole House. Photo Susan Ginsburgh

Course
Interior Design

School
The Cass

he Net Hut, Hastings (2013)
y Sophie-Louise Bynam

The net hut has been designed as a fisherman's living archive and social club to preserve the memory of the fishermen of Hastings.

nole House (2013)
y Edoardo Verbigrazia

s reflective installation gave a detailed narrative about the nting hung in the Reynolds Room.

A Community Dance Centre at Building 100, Woolwich Arsenal (2013)
By Anna Terebinski

Woolwich Arsenal, a redundant armoury in South East London, has gone under a huge transformation over the last 15 years. This project develops a new use for the site, one would be more inclusive for the community as a whole.

Alumna

Name Yan Guo
Residence London, United Kingdom
Year of birth 1981
Year of graduation 2010
Current job Design director at ZedFactory
Clients Local government of Zhangwu, local government of Shanchuan, Jeffery. H, Sogal China
Website zedfactory.com

Why did you choose this school?
The Cass is well known for multiple majors like jewellery design, painting and fine art. I believe that the vision here is not just created by tutors, but also by the international students around the school, and it affects your levels of thinking on design through interactions with them. Plus, financially the tuition fee is affordable, for international students especially.

What was the most important thing you learned here?
The most essential thing I was learned that to be able to join parametric design onto
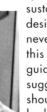
sustainable high-end retail interior design. My tutor, Sue Ginsburgh, never limited my personal interest in this special area. I felt she was guiding me with her practical suggestions, rather than tell me what I should do. Surprisingly, we students had to provide our own topic and direction for the final graduation project of the MA course.

What subject do you wish you paid more attention to?
Sustainable parametric interior design!

What was the most interesting or fun project you did?
That was the London pavilion for Shanghai exports at ZedFactory in 2010. ZedFactory is a specialist in zero carbon, zero waster building projects. All the furniture I picked up for the project, which was called ZedHouse, was made from recycled materials – for example, cafe tables were made using the wheels of construction trolleys with glass on top. The ceiling light was created using 2236 recycled beer bottles.

What was your graduation project?
It was called Cardboard Fashion Boutique. In it, I used paper to create a high-end retail store design.

Any words of advice for future students?
You really need to have a serious think about what you actually want to achieve in the course, otherwise you will probably be lost up until the final project. The MA course is just 1 year long, and the course sections pass by very quickly. You need to be as active as possible with the programme, and even if you fail to find your personal direction initially, you can receive lots of suggestions, support and inspiration. You should never be afraid to share your thoughts and feelings.

Are you still in contact with your fellow students?
Yes – we are all on Facebook.

Was the transformation from graduation to working life a smooth one?
I was working before I started studying at The Cass. And I have been continually working part time in an office to support my study in both practical and financial ways. I realised that the more working experience I got, the quicker I would be able to fit into a job.

Current Students

'The most important elements for me were the exposure and direct access to real clients, live projects and other designers working in the industry. This interaction is key for young professionals, who must shortly leave the safety of being students to dive into the professional world.'
Ana Maria Dumitru

'I choose this school because it has a conceptually focused master's programme. It is more tailored towards research and conceptual development than the technical aspect of interior design which I studied for 3 years for my first degree.'
Ana Caetano Alves

'My favourite places to hang outs were the live music venues and the art, architecture and design galleries. London offers a wide range of all these – it is really hard to get bored in this city!'
Edoardo Verbigrazia

his is a very much self-driven arning experience that allenges you to push your ilities.'
Anna Jane Derbyshire

'I really enjoyed the studio work because it teaches you new skills and begins to hone your own personal style and talents.'
Sophie-Louise Bynam

'I came here after hearing positive feedback about the school from a friend. The most valuable part of the course for me was the tutorial class about the dissertation.'
Mostafa Ghazian

City Life

London is a wonderful city for a student of any subject, offering an incomparable wealth of social, cultural, entertainment, educational and life experiences. A design student based in the capital has access to a huge number of world-renowned galleries, museums, collections and specialists. London is also home to the main UK, European or global offices of many design, architectural, technology and media organisations that help with live projects, work experience during study and future employment after graduation.

The Cass is in Aldgate, at the point where city's main financial district meet the East End. It's about a 10-minute walk to the Tower of London and the River Thames, and the West End – celebrated for its shopping and theatres is about a 15-minute journey by underground.

The school's Central House building is close to Aldgate East underground station and opposite the world-famous Whitechapel Gallery. This exciting part of London – which includes areas such as Spitalfields, Shoreditch and Hoxton – boasts a vibrant social scene.

There are also about 3500 creative companies, from galleries and design agencies to jewellers and digital innovators, in this immediate locale so it is a great place to see work, network and interact.

United Kingdom

The Old Truman Brewery off Brick Lane, a casebook example of London's contemporary creativity at work.

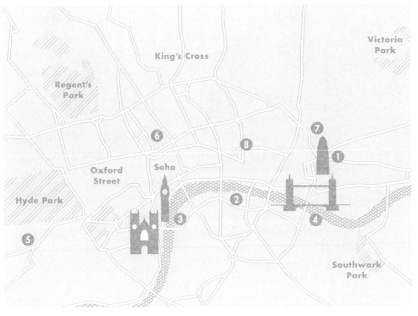

London

1 The Cass
2 Tate Modern
3 The Millennium Wheel
4 Design Museum
5 The Victoria and Albert Museum
6 The British Museum
7 Brick Lane and the Old Truman Brewery
8 Museum of London

Park

Water

Main road

Course
Interior Design

School
The Cass

City Facts

ee more London City Facts on p.236

te Modern 2
Located in Herzog and Demeurons iconic former Bankside Power Station, the Tate Modern displays over 100 years of modern and contemporary art over seven floors.
tate.org.uk

e Millennium Wheel 3
Also known as the London Eye, a ride on the wheel offers spectacular views and is a great way to get your city bearings.
londoneye.com

esign Museum 4
Design in all its manifestations in contemporary culture is the subject here, both of the interesting permanent collection and excellent exhibition programme.
designmuseum.org

Victoria and Albert Museum 5
Over 2000 years of art and design, with a wealth of exhibits and information on changing fashions in interior design.
vam.ac.uk

London Design Festival
The annual September shindig celebrates and promotes London as the design capital of the world.
londondesignfestival.com

The British Museum 6
A vast collection of world artefacts numbering 8 million works plus temporary blockbuster exhibitions, all sheltering underneath the spectacular glass roof of Norman Foster's Great Court.
britishmuseum.org

Brick Lane and the Old Truman Brewery 7
This once neglected street is now a hip area filled with vintage clothes stands, organic food stalls, curry houses and the cutting-edge arts and media quarter, the Old Truman Brewery.
visitbricklane.org
trumanbrewery.com

London Festival of Architecture
This month-long, city-wide celebration of architectural experimentation, thinking, learning and practice is held in June.
londonfestivalofarchitecture.org

The Queen Elizabeth II Olympic Park
Stroll through the park, get fit in the original 2012 Olympic venues and take in some cutting-edge architecture and art in one of London's newest quarters.
queenelizabetholympicpark.co.uk

Museum of London 8
From Boudicca to Shakespeare to Sherlock Holmes, a fascinating look back at the long and eventful history of one of the world's great cities.
museumoflondon.org.uk

ow to get around
Getting around London is easy thanks to its extensive tube, bus and train network and a cycle hire scheme. The Cass is located on Commercial Road, which is located just a few minutes from Aldgate and Aldgate East tube stations, which are served by the Circle, Metropolitan, District and Hammersmith & City lines. Liverpool Street and Fenchurch Street stations are also a short walk away.

London's airports are easily accessible from the school, with London City being the closest at just 8 km away. Many students choose to cycle, as it is the quickest, cheapest and most environmentally friendly way to travel.

Arranging housing
Average

Housing support by school
Yes, the university has an ccomodation Bureau

Cost of room in the city
Between GBP 90 and GBP 140 per week (approx. EUR 112 to EUR 174)

Cost of campus housing
n/a

Brighton University is spread over several campuses, including the city centre Grand Parade complex.

University of Brighton

School of Arts, Design and Media
University of Brighton
College of Arts and Humanities
Moulsecoomb Campus
Lewes Road
Brighton BN2 4AT
United Kingdom

T +44 (0)12 7364 2361
fo@brighton.ac.uk
arts.brighton.ac.uk

Students' creative efforts take over the university campus during the annual Art Show.

Course
Interior Design

School
University of Brighton

'Students are encouraged to challenge, re-think, collaborate and innovate'

Professor Anne Boddington, dean of the College of Arts and Humanities

What is the story behind this school and course?

The Faculty of Arts (formerly Brighton School of Art) was founded in 1859 in rooms adjacent to the kitchens of the Brighton Pavilion. The school was founded to enhance industry skills and knowledge and to develop the quality and competitiveness of the English workforce. Throughout its history the school has sustained a focus on developing the design skills and quality of its graduates and to ensure that their work is of the highest calibre. Since the late 1990s, when the MA Interior Design course was founded as a research-led progression from the successful undergraduate programme, it has developed a significant international reputation for the creative examination of interior spaces and how these are theoretically conceived and developed.

Why should students choose this particular school?

The strengths of the school include a dual emphasis on creative and critical enquiry in the broad context of the visual and performing arts, design and humanities.

What is studying at this school all about?

The school is committed to developing high-quality undergraduate disciplinary education and to shaping and interdisciplinary understanding through creative, theoretical and technical studies that support students to become professional leaders in the field of interior design.

What kind of teaching method is applied?

Teaching is undertaken in the design studio, in lectures and in small seminar groups. The course also supports the development of a series of interdisciplinary workshops that encourage postgraduate students to work across a wide range of design fields including architecture, urban design, fashion and textiles.

What is the most important thing for students to learn during this course?

Collectively, our MA Interior Design students and tutors aspire to a level of understanding of the boundaries of their respective design methodologies, in order that they will know, intuitively, when and how to transcend them.

What is the most important skill to master when one wants to become an interior designer?

Our aim is to provide an environment where students are encouraged to challenge, re-think, collaborate and innovate. To do this we believe that we must be prepared to learn from the design practices of related disciplines and at the same time be prepared to re-think what it is we do in the light of the changes in perspective that come from international discourse and the sharing of culturally diverse research.

Programme

The MA Interior Design programme, part of the School of Art, Design and Media, is designed to promote interdisciplinary research and practice: the school is looking to develop creative collaborations between fine artists, designers, architects and thinkers. The starting point for all student is to acknowledge the complexities and paradoxes inherent in orthodox architectural documentation in order to unearth the dubious simplifications and missed opportunities that result from the tendency to privilege the visual at the expense of our other senses. In anticipation of 'The Creative User' all of the students proposals originate from a close focus on the existing condition, paying particular attention to local take-overs, autonomous occupations and the blurring of boundaries of ownership and programme. In considering issues of technology, students are concerned as much with intuition, desire and chance as with precedent, economy and established practice

A range of student work is displayed at Brighton University Art Show.

Thinking space: the school emphasises critical enquiry, as well as creative originality.

Programme
Interior Design

Leads to
Master of Arts

Structure
The MA Interior Design course is a 3-semester full-time programme. The first 2 semesters, both 6 months long, are followed in the studio. The whole of semester three is taken up by a self-directed research project, the Masterwork. The first semester contains the modules preliminary design and research methods. The second semester has two modules; main design and critical readings and technology. Students can also choose to the part-time route which typically takes 30 months.

Head of programme
Frank O'Sullivan

Mentors and lecturers
Dr Mary Anne Francis, Ersi Ioannidc Frank O'Sullivan and Susan Roberts

School Facts

Duration of study
18 months

Full time
Yes

Part time
Yes (30 months)

Female students
70%

Male students
30%

Local students
11%

Students from abroad
89%

Yearly enrolment
20

Tuition fee
- GBP 4635 per year for EU citizens (approx. EUR 5835)
- GBP 11,845 per year for non-EU citizens (approx. EUR 14,914)

Funding/scholarships
In 2014, there are 40 University of Brighton international scholarships available to new, full-time international undergraduate and postgraduate taught-degree students.

Minimum requirements for entry
An undergraduate degree in a design subject. All overseas students have to meet the university's MA level English language requirements.

Language
English

Application procedure
All applicants must fill out the application form and send it to the University of Brighton, on line or by post, together with a printed or digital portfolio.

Application details
arts.brighton.ac.uk/study/postgrad/pgdipma-interior-design

Application date
Before 1 September

Graduation rate
90%

Job placement rate
High

Memberships/affiliations
None

Collaborations with
Tsinghua Academy of Art & Design, Beijing, China and the Politecnico di Milano, Milan, Italy.

Facilities for students
All of MA students are allocated individual studio space and have access to workshops, laser cutter technology, computer hardware and print facilities.

Student Work

In Place of the Museum (2013)
By Heng Tan

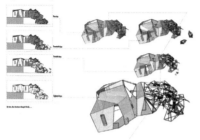

A partially 'dissolving' structure of paper combines with exhibitions presented on high-tech opaque glass.

In Place of the Museum (2013)
By Annalisa Meli

A re-think of the concept of the exhibition, using a lightweight, aluminium 'tree' hung with boxes that conceal the exhibits which visitors must actively discover. Screens project the process for those too busy to explore.

In Place of the Museum (2013)
By Vicky Willis

A transparent riverside canopy acts as a viewing platform, shelter and an exhibition space.

Course
Interior Design

School
University of Brighton

In Place of the Museum (2013)
By Tanaporn Sukkasem

A concept of a 'museum' in which visitors see not objects, but projections of objects, which are created by using the principle of a pinhole camera.

Artist in Residence (2011)
By Alexandra Kharakoz

Myriad of Mirrors (2012)
By Karin Artmann

An installation on the North Bank of the River Thames, London, uses mirrors to playfully disrupt sightlines of St Paul's Cathedral.

A proposal for a combined live/work space for the artist Gerhard Richter, with a spectacular view overlooking the City of London.

Alumna

Name Karin Artmann
Residence London, United Kingdom
Year of birth 1967
Year of graduation 2012
Current job Spatial consultant
Website studioartmann.com

Some of Artmann's work during her studies.

Why did you choose this school?
Brighton has a reputation of excellence for its academic rigour and provides a taught, structured MA, in contrast to MA degrees by project or those with a looser curriculum offered by some of the other universities. Both of these aspects were an important part of my decision in the light of my less than conventional background. Brighton's selection process also took account of the potential of a candidate beyond portfolio and academic considerations: the university accepted me, a lawyer onto the MA course and successfully turned me into an interior designer!

What was the most important thing you learned here?
That the unexpected is often the most obvious choice to open the door to new ideas.

What was the most interesting project you did?
I enjoyed every project of the course, since together they form a logical and gradual progression which interlink at all critical points with relevant theory: disparate pieces began to form an interrelated set of information, ideas and meanings. Things started to fall into place along the way and brought that sometimes elusive insight.

Were there any classes you found particularly difficult?
I saw challenges not difficulties: each hurdle pushed the envelope and gave an impetus to further exploration. I had an obvious advantage with respect to the theoretical aspects of the course, though my familiar routine required modification in the new context.

What was your graduation project?
My graduation project proposed the notion of void between the Millennium Bridge and Tate Modern, London resulting from the final, truncated design of the Millennium Bridge: the late Sir Anthony Caro's original ideas had created a link between the architecture of the bridge and the art at Tate Modern. Spaces for supposed artist in residence at Tate Modern filled the void by creating tangible and intangible links between the Millennium Bridge and Tate Modern.

Are you still in contact with the school?
Yes, with the course leader of the MA. Also, I keep updated via the Alumni Society, which has been a great source of information and practical support. And I keep in touch with my fellow students virtually too.

Was the transformation from graduation to working life a smooth one?
Fairly smooth, since I had a clear idea of the type of work I wanted to focus on.

If you were to do the course again, what would you do differently?
A little more collaboration with the 'research teams' that undertook to discover Brighton's 'cultural' aspects of which there are plenty at all times of the night.

'I think that this course is really valuable if you want to become a designer, but it is important to be aware that it is really hard work. There are lots of deadlines and presentations – but these are useful, because they help you to be productive and to develop your projects.'

Annalisa Meli

'My favourite hang outs? For food Kanok Thai, Black Bird, Cocoa, The Bali Brasserie. For entertainment, Komedia is great for gigs and movies. The Lanes for Brighton's best vintage goods. Seven Sisters and Devil's Dyke for calming the mind with breath-taking nature.'

Raja Imran Raja Azhar

'Future students can expect to learn research methods and critical thinking from this school, as well as practical skills obtained via the design process. Critical readings and cross-border materials, such as movies, 3D architecture, cities and music, are important here.'

Heng Tan

think the most important aspect of e course is the emphasis on f-learning. What I mean here is t studying without tutors, but being le to choose and build your own ics. The tutors respect your ideas d guide you in improving them.'

Bowen Li

'Our studio-based design module with Frank O'Sullivan and Ersi Ioannidou was inspirational. Challenging us to the maximum in every tutorial, we were encouraged to think for ourselves and push our ideas to their limits.'

Victoria Willis

'This course is not only taught in interior design terms, but across the boundaries of interior design so as to blur with landscape and architectural design.'

Tanaporn Sukkasem

City Life

Brighton, one of the UK's most diverse, energetic and popular cities, has a relaxed and forward-thinking attitude that makes it a compelling place to be. Brighton provides an ideal setting in which to study interior design. The city has a magnificent heritage of Regency and Victorian buildings, set in one of Europe's most celebrated cityscapes centred on the Royal Pavilion. The University of Brighton exploits its location as a gateway for Britain to continental Europe, with a strong international programme. Brighton's clubs and bars offer some of the best nightlife in the country, and the beach adds an aspect of the great outdoors. All this, and this friendly and engaging seaside town is only an hour from central London by train, bringing all the resources of the capital within easy reach.

Since its beginnings, about 150 years ago, the University of Brighton has developed into one of the most popular universities in the UK. Today, it has 22,000 students and forms a diverse academic community from over 15 countries. The university is spread across the city from the seafront to the South Downs.

Iconic Brighton Pier is one of this vibrant seaside town's most popular landmarks.

United Kingdom

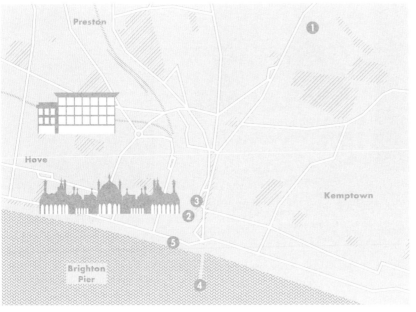

Brighton

1 University of Brighton
2 Royal Pavilion
3 Brighton Museum and Art Gallery
4 Brighton Pier
5 Brighton Beaches

Park

Water

Railway

Main road

Course
Interior Design

School
University of Brighton

City Facts

oyal Pavilion ②
The Prince Regent's pleasure palace is a wonderful example of Regency interior design. Built between 1787-1823, this exotic extravaganza features flying dragons, a mega-gilded Banqueting Room, nodding mechanical Mandarin figurines and exquisite hand-painted Chinese wallpaper.

ighton Museum and Art Gallery ③
Located in part of the Prince Regent's old stable complex, the museum features a significant collection of world art, a dazzling 20th-century decorative art and design gallery, and much more.

ighton Pier ④
The place to go for seaside fun – complete with dodgem rides and candyfloss, as well as superb sea views.
brightonpier.co.uk

Brighton Beaches ⑤
A bustling promenade fronts the large expanses of pebble beach. To the west of the pier, an arty enclave occupies the old fishing huts and boat builders' sheds known as the King's Road Arches.

Kemptown
Kemptown is Brighton's boho alter ego – a mix of gay bars, design shops, seaside cottages and Regency crescents. Blue plaques indicate the former homes of Laurence Olivier and Joan Plowright, Terence Rattigan, Flora Robson and other theatre greats.

Lewes
Six miles east of Brighton, Lewes is a charming mix of cobbled lanes, medieval cottages and antique shops. You can tour the Norman castle and visit the house of Anne of Cleves – one of Henry VIII's luckier wives.

Devil's Dyke
Take the open-top bus to Devil's Dyke for a taste of the South Downs National Park – a beautiful and ancient landscape.

Brighton Festival
Brighton Festival is the largest arts and culture festival in England. This annual celebration of music, theatre, dance, circus, art, film, literature, debate, outdoor and family events takes place in venues both familiar and unusual across Brighton and Hove for 3 weeks every May.
brightonfestival.org

Burning the Clocks – Winter Solstice Parade
On 21st December Brighton celebrates the winter solstice, and thousands gather on the streets with paper and willow lanterns, before burning them on the beach in honour of the ancient festival.

Brighton Comedy Festival
Big names in British stand-up like Dave Gorman, Jimmy Carr, Russell Kane and Alexi Sayle perform at the festival. Each year the city really will be awash with laughter for 16 days.
brightoncomedyfestival.com

w to get around
Brighton is 30 minutes by train from Gatwick Airport. Getting around the city is easy, as it's so compact, many people find it easiest to explore the city on foot. But also the public transport within the city is arranged well. Bus 24, 25, 25A, 25C, 28 and 49 all provide a frequent service from central Brighton. The 24 links the Moulsecoomb campus with Varley Park and the 25, 25A and 25C go on to the Falmer campus. By train, Moulsecoomb station is situated behind the Watts and Cockcroft buildings and is two stops from the main Brighton station.

Arranging housing
Never a problem.

Housing support by school
Yes, there are 1500 places in halls of residence in Brighton.

Cost of room in the city
Between GBP 390 and GBP 690 per month (approx. EUR 490 to EUR 870)

Cost of campus housing
Between GBP 350 and GBP 600 per month (approx. EUR 440 to EUR 750)

<u>Map</u>

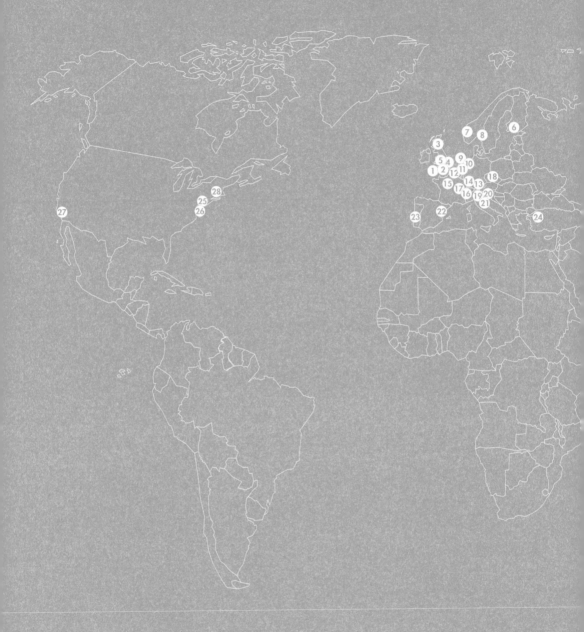

School Summary

School	Location	Leads to	Duration of study
Aalto University	Helsinki, Finland	Master of Arts	2 years
Art Center College of Design	Pasadena, United States	Master of Science	2–3 years
ArtEZ Institute of the Arts	Arnhem/Zwolle, the Netherlands	Master of Arts	2 years
Arts University Bournemouth	Bournemouth, United Kingdom	Master of Arts	1 year
Bergen Academy of Art and Design	Bergen, Norway	Master of Arts	2 years
Domus Academy	Milan, Italy	Master in Interior and Living Design	1 year
École nationale supérieure des Arts Décoratifs	Paris, France	Master of Arts	2 years
ELISAVA Barcelona School of Design and Engineering	Barcelona, Spain	Master of Arts	1 year
Escola Superior de Artes e Design	Porto, Portugal	Master of Arts	2 years
Glasgow School of Art	Glasgow, United Kingdom	Master of Design	1 year
HEAD - Genéve	Geneva, Switzerland	Master of Arts	2 years
Hochschule für Technik Stuttgart	Stuttgart, Germany	IM Interior Architectural Design	2 years
Hochschule Mainz University of Applied Sciences	Mainz, Germany	Master of Arts	1.5 years
Istanbul Technical University	Istanbul, Turkey	IM Interior Architectural Design	2 years
Kuwasawa Design School	Tokyo, Japan	Specialist Diploma	3 years
Kyoto Institute of Technology	Kyoto, Japan	Master of Design	2 years
NABA – Nuova Accademia di Belle Arti Milano	Milan, Italy	Master of Arts	2 years
Oslo National Academy of the Arts	Oslo, Norway	Master of Design	2 years
Parsons The New School for Design	New York, United States	Master of Fine Arts	2 years
Piet Zwart Institute	Rotterdam, the Netherlands	Master in Interior Architecture	2 years
Pratt Institute	New York, United States	Master of Fine Arts	2–3 years
Rhode Island School of Design	Providence, United States	Master of Arts/Master of Design	1 year (MA) 2 years (MDes)
Royal Academy of Art	The Hague, the Netherlands	Master of Arts	2 years
Royal College of Art	London, United Kingdom	Master of Arts	2 years
Sandberg Institute	Amsterdam, the Netherlands	Master Interior Architecture	2 years
Scuola Politecnica di Design	Milan, Italy	Master of Arts	1 year
SUPSI	Lugano, Switzerland	IM Interior Architectural Design	2 years
The Academy of Arts, Architecture and Design in Prague	Prague, Czech Republic	Master of Arts	2 years
The Cass	London, United Kingdom	Master of Arts	1 year
University of Brighton	Brighton, United Kingdom	Master of Arts	1.5 years

Full time	Part time	Language	Tuition fee	Funding/scholarships	Yearly enrolment	Female students	Male students	Local students	Students from abroad	Arranging housing	Housing support by school
es	No	English	No	No	14	65%	35%	55%	45%	Average	No
es	No	English	Yes	Yes	20	49.5%	50.5%	74%	26%	Average	Yes
es	No	Dutch	Yes	Yes	20	75%	25%	90%	10%	Average	Yes
es	Yes	English	Yes	Yes	3–10	66%	34%	34%	66%	Never a problem	Yes
es	No	English and Norwegian	No	Yes	40	65%	35%	79%	21%	Average	Yes
es	No	English	Yes	Yes	58	85%	15%	5%	95%	Quite easy	Yes
es	No	French	Yes	Yes	15	60%	40%	90%	10%	Difficult	No
es	No	English or Spanish	Yes	Yes	25	90%	10%	20%	80%	Never a problem	Yes
es	No	English and Portoguese	Yes	Yes	24	85%	15%	90%	10%	Never a problem	No
es	Yes	English	Yes	Yes	18–20	90%	10%	5%	95%	Quite easy	Yes
s	No	English and French	Yes	No	18	50%	50%	50%	50%	Difficult	No
s	No	English and German	No	Yes	25	–	–	70%	30%	Varies per area	Yes
s	No	English and German	Yes	Yes	16	90%	10%	80%	20%	Average	Yes
s	No	English and Turkish	No (Turkey) Yes (rest of world)	Yes	12	77%	23%	80%	20%	Average	No
s	No	Japanese	Yes	Yes	60	60%	40%	98%	2%	Difficult	No
s	No	English and Japanese	Yes	Yes	25	50%	50%	90%	10%	Average	Yes
s	No	English	Yes	Yes	23	81%	19%	38%	62%	Quite easy	Yes
s	No	English and Norwegian	No	Yes	8–10	60%	40%	61%	39%	Average	No
s	No	English	Yes	Yes	45	82%	18%	48%	52%	Average	Yes
s	No	English	Yes	No	15	75%	25%	5%	95%	Average	No
s	No	English	Yes	Yes	140	85%	15%	60%	40%	Average	Yes
s	No	English	Yes	Yes	65–70	80%	20%	40%	60%	Never a problem	Yes
s	No	English	Yes	Yes	15	80%	20%	0%	100%	Average	No
s	No	English	Yes	Yes	18	69%	31%	11%	89%	Difficult	Yes
s	No	English	Yes	No	10	50%	50%	25%	75%	Very difficult	Yes
es	No	English	Yes	No	20	65%	35%	22%	78%	Quite easy	Yes
s	Yes	English	Yes	Yes	6–10	80%	20%	80%	20%	Average	Yes
s	Yes	English and Czech	No (Czech speaking) Yes (non-Czech speaking)	Yes	4	52%	48%	70%	30%	Quite easy	Yes
s	Yes	English	Yes	Yes	12	62%	38%	25%	75%	Average	Yes
s	Yes	English	Yes	Yes	20	70%	30%	11%	89%	Never a problem	Yes

Credits

Masterclass: Interior Design
Guide to the World's Leading Graduate Schools

Publisher
Frame Publishers

Production
Marlous van Rossum-Willems
Sarah de Boer-Schultz

Authors
Jane Szita
Kanae Hasegawa
Enya Moore

Graphic Design Concept
Cathelijn Kruunenberg

Graphic Design
Federica Ricci

Prepress
Edward de Nijs

Trade distribution USA and Canada
Consortium Book Sales & Distribution, LLC.
Thirteenth Avenue NE, Suite 101,
Minneapolis, MN 55413-1007
United States
T 612 746 2600
T 800 283 3572 (orders)
F 612 746 2606

Trade distribution Benelux
Frame Publishers
Van der Hesperiden 68
1076 DX Amsterdam
The Netherlands
distribution@frameweb.com
frameweb.com

Trade distribution rest of world
Thames & Hudson Ltd
181A High Holborn
London WC1V 7QX
United Kingdom
T 44 20 7845 5000
F 44 20 7845 5050

ISBN: 978-94-91727-25-2

© 2014 Frame Publishers, Amsterdam, 2014

Whilst every effort has been made to ensure
accuracy, Frame Publishers does not under any
circumstances accept responsibility for errors
or omissions. Any mistakes or inaccuracies will
be corrected in case of subsequent editions upon
notification to the publisher.

The Koninklijke Bibliotheek lists this publication
in the Nederlandse Bibliografie: detailed
bibliographic information is available on the
internet at http://picarta.pica.nl

Printed on acid-free paper produced from
chlorine-free pulp. TCF ∞
Printed in Turkey

987654321